D0082742

# The
# Right to Die
# Debate

# THE
# RIGHT TO DIE
# DEBATE

*A Documentary History*

Edited by MARJORIE B. ZUCKER

Primary Documents in American History and Contemporary Issues

GREENWOOD PRESS
Westport, Connecticut • London

**Library of Congress Cataloging-in-Publication Data**

The right to die debate : a documentary history / edited by Marjorie
  B. Zucker.
       p.     cm.—(Primary documents in American history and
  contemporary issues, ISSN 1069–5605)
    Includes bibliographical references and index.
    ISBN 0–313–30522–6 (alk. paper)
    1. Right to die—Moral and ethical aspects—History.
  2. Euthanasia—Moral and ethical aspects—History.   3. Death—Social
  aspects—History.   4. Terminal care—Moral and ethical aspects—
  History.   I. Zucker, Marjorie B. (Marjorie Bass), 1919–   .
  II. Series.
  R726.R498   1999
  174'.24—dc21            99–11266

British Library Cataloguing in Publication Data is available.

Library of Congress Catalog Card Number: 99–11266
ISBN: 0–313–30522–6
ISSN: 1069–5605

First published in 1999

Greenwood Press, 88 Post Road West, Westport, CT 06881
An imprint of Greenwood Publishing Group, Inc.
www.greenwood.com

Printed in the United States of America

The paper used in this book complies with the
Permanent Paper Standard issued by the National
Information Standards Organization (Z39.48–1984).

10 9 8 7 6 5 4 3 2 1

Document 96 is taken from Marcia Angell, "The Right to Die in Dignity." *Newsweek,* July 23 (1990): 9. Used by permission of the author.

Excerpts from Document 104 and Document 105: From *The Least Worst Death: Essays in Bioethics on the End of Life* by Margaret Pabst Battin. Copyright © 1994 by Oxford University Press, Inc. Used by permission of Oxford University Press, Inc.

Excerpts from Document 108 are taken from Derek Humphry with Ann Wickett, *Jean's Way.* Quartet Books: London and New York, 1978.

Excerpts from Document 109 are taken from Betty Rollin, *Last Wish.* New York: Linden Press/Simon & Schuster, Warner Books edition, 1985.

Document 110 is taken from "Death's Dissident." *Economist*, November 13 (1993): 34. © 1993 The Economist Newspaper Group, Inc. Reprinted with permission. Further reproduction prohibited.

Document 112 is taken from Geoffrey Nels Fieger, "Kevorkians' Crusade." *The New York Times* (Jan. 1, 1994). Copyright © 1994 by the New York Times Co. Reprinted by permission.

Excerpts from Document 116 are taken from "It's Over, Debbie" (Name Withheld by Request), *Journal of the American Medical Association* 259, no. 2 (January 8, 1988): 272. Copyright 1968–97, American Medical Association.

Excerpts from Document 118 are taken from Timothy E. Quill, *Death and Dignity: Making Choices and Taking Charge.* New York and London: W. W. Norton, 1993.

Document 120 is taken from Diane E. Meier, M.D., "A Change of Heart on Assisted Suicide." *The New York Times* (April 24, 1998). Copyright © 1998 by the New York Times Co. Reprinted by permission.

Graphs in Document 123 are taken from Robert J. Blendon, Ulrike S. Szalay, and Richard A. Knox, "Should Physicians Aid Their Patients in Dying?" *Journal of the American Medical Association* 267 (1992): 2658–2662.

Excerpts from Document 126 are taken from Paul Longmore and Andrew Batavia, "Death Do Us Part," *New Mobility* (April 1997): 48–51.

Excerpts from Document 127 are taken from Daniel Callahan, "Self-Extinction: The Morality of the Helping Hand." In *Physician-assisted Suicide* Robert F. Weir, ed. Bloomington and Indianapolis: Indiana University Press, 1997, p. 71.

Every reasonable effort has been made to trace the owners of copyright materials in this book, but in some instances this has proven impossible. The editor and publisher will be glad to receive information leading to more complete acknowledgments in subsequent printings of the book and in the meantime extend their apologies for any omissions.

# Contents

# Series Foreword

This series is designed to meet the research needs of high school and college students by making available in one volume the key primary documents on a given historical event or contemporary issue. Documents include speeches and letters, congressional testimony, Supreme Court and lower court decisions, government reports, biographical accounts, position papers, statutes, and news stories.

The purpose of the series is twofold: (1) to provide substantive and background material on an event or issue through the texts of pivotal primary documents that shaped policy or law, raised controversy, or influenced the course of events, and (2) to trace the controversial aspects of the event or issue through documents that represent a variety of viewpoints. Documents for each volume have been selected by a recognized specialist in that subject with the advice of a board of other subject specialists, school librarians, and teachers.

To place the subject in historical perspective, the volume editor has prepared an introductory overview and a chronology of events. Documents are organized either chronologically or topically. The documents are full text or, if unusually long, have been excerpted by the volume editor. To facilitate understanding, each document is accompanied by an explanatory introduction. Suggestions for further reading follow the document or the chapter.

It is the hope of Greenwood Press that this series will enable students and other readers to use primary documents more easily in their research, to exercise critical thinking skills by examining the key documents in American history and public policy, and to critique the variety of viewpoints represented by this selection of documents.

# Acknowledgments

This volume could not have been written without the help of Choice In Dying, Inc., a national nonprofit organization dedicated to fostering communication about complex end-of-life decisions and well known for pioneering living wills and providing the only national hotline to respond to patients and their loved ones during end-of-life crises. This organization is a direct descendant of the Euthanasia Society, founded in 1938 and described in Part II of this volume. In 1967, the Euthanasia Society spun off the tax-exempt Euthanasia Educational Fund (later the Euthanasia Educational Council) and limited its work to influencing legislation. Concerned about the negative connotations of the term "euthanasia," in 1974, the Euthanasia Society became the Society for the Right to Die, and, in 1979, the Euthanasia Educational Society became Concern for Dying. In 1991, the organizations amalgamated as Choice In Dying. Despite its origin as the Euthanasia Society, Choice In Dying neither advocates for or against physician-assisted suicide. Rather, the organization devotes considerable resources to making sure that unbiased information is easily available about the full range of end-of-life treatment choices.

Choice In Dying owns the archives and bulletins of the Euthanasia Society, a trove of historical information. Anthony Doyle, then a budding librarian, was most helpful in searching through and organizing them. Karen Orloff Kaplan, executive director of Choice In Dying since 1993, wrote the Introduction; I admire her creative energy and keen mind. Choice In Dying's former Director of Program Mary Meyer was enormously helpful in amplifying and correcting the text, and Choice in Dying's Staff Attorney Carol Sieger was indispensable in advising me about the laws and court decisions that have shaped the way deaths occur in America. Although I am responsible for any errors or misinterpretations, their help was invaluable.

Margaret Battin, professor of philosophy at the University of Utah, helped to guide me through the complex literature on suicide and assisted suicide, areas in which she is expert. My acquisitions editor, Emily Birch, was always patient and helpful.

Rapid changes in medical care and in society's attitudes about death and assisted suicide have made the right-to-die debate a timely topic. Its evolution will, I hope, be clarified by this documentary history.

# Introduction

## Karen Orloff Kaplan

As the twentieth century draws to a close, we can look with pride and satisfaction at the abundant wonders brought about by the technological revolution. In no area of endeavor have there been greater strides than in medicine. We are surrounded daily by the medical miracles that have improved the quality of millions of lives and saved millions more. Antibiotics, transplant technology, cardiopulmonary resuscitation, and life-support systems such as ventilators and kidney dialysis are just a few of the spectacular gifts of modern medicine.

However, in recent decades, we have learned that the great technical strides in medicine have another, quite different aspect. In addition to embracing modern medicine to save and improve life, physicians can and frequently do use this technology to prolong the dying process. As physicians became increasingly adept at using developing technology and justifiably dependent upon it, they began to be uncomfortable with the notion that some patients ultimately could not be saved. Medical professionals received a great deal of positive reinforcement for refusing to "give up," and many looked upon the death of a patient as a failure of their own.

Physicians are not the only ones who encourage the use of technology to postpone the moment of death. The public also puts a great deal of pressure on the health care system to do everything possible for every patient. Thus, well beyond a point where cure or even improvement in quality of life is possible, our health care system utilizes technology to defer the inevitable moment of death, and many patients and their families strongly approve.

By condoning the use of technological means to prolong dying, society has brought about many changes in the way Americans view death. In the early part of this century, people customarily died in their own homes, surrounded by their families and, when possible, comforted by their physicians. Death was very much a family life-cycle event. However, the birth of more rigorous and effective medical interventions meant moving people into hospitals where they could be close to the requisite machinery and the health care professionals skilled at using it. Death began to occur not at home among loved ones, but in the hospital among machines and away from the eyes of most of us. Americans became unfamiliar and profoundly uncomfortable with death and the dying process. As much as Americans applaud modern technology and look continually for new ways to apply it, many are aware that it also has its downsides.

In response to the way death in America has changed, many health care professionals, lawyers, ethicists, educators, and members of the public began raising significant ethical and public policy questions. When, they ask, does the use of technology become overuse or abuse? When in the course of an individual's illness should technology be focused on providing comfort rather than prolonging dying? When is enough enough? And how much say does any individual have over the circumstances of his or her death—when and where and how it will occur? These are complex, multifaceted questions that require us to contemplate not just available technology, but also the spiritual and ethical values upon which we base our lives and our national policies. These questions defy quick, simple answers. They have led to considerable controversy and a national conversation known as the right-to-die debate.

The purpose of this volume is to explore this controversy in depth. Using primary source materials, the text helps us understand the positions taken by the various stakeholders participating in the right-to-die debate, the ways the debate has developed, and what new laws, public policies, and societal conduct might emerge from it. From great ancient and modern literature, state and federal laws and related legal documents, newspapers and academic journals, and religious and scientific organizations' publications, this text explores the impact of technology on death in America.

The materials in this volume examine how the health care system and the public's understanding and approach to death have changed as medical technology has blossomed. They provide a picture of the range of frequently conflicting perspectives and approaches that various groups bring to answering basic questions about the extent of influence any individual should have over the circumstances of his or her death. The opinions and rationales of multiple groups are represented, including, among others, religious organizations, organized medicine, and consumer groups. Further, and vitally important, this volume delineates the issues that remain still far from resolved. There are many.

This volume serves as both a history of a vital part of American culture and a road map into evolving public policy. As with most other crucial issues, public policy centering on how Americans deal with death and dying is not evolving rapidly in a straightforward, unemotional fashion. Rather, the right-to-die debate is often heated, heads in seemingly disparate directions, and moves painfully slowly. The answers are not yet at our fingertips. The conversation—the debate—is not over.

By examining the many voices in the debate about the choices people should or should not have with regard to death, the reader can establish a clear understanding of how difficult it can be to develop policies that satisfy the needs of the majority. *The Right to Die Debate: A Documentary History* provides an opportunity for the reader to participate in the debate by clarifying his or her own thinking about this challenging subject and preparing to share that thinking in private and public conversations. As each new issue is raised in the text, the reader is encouraged to ask, "Where am I on this issue?" and "Where do we go from here?"

The debate about life-and-death choices is not one likely to be resolved in the near future, as is reflected by the myriad points of view presented here. Readers will be challenged and encouraged to consider these many different viewpoints when they are drawing their own conclusions and helping society redefine its relationship to the end of life.

# Timeline

1906    The first euthanasia bill in the United States is drafted in Ohio.

1937    A bill to legalize active euthanasia is introduced in Nebraska.

1938    The Euthanasia Society of America is founded, with many eminent members.

1938–
1953    A number of so-called "mercy killers" fail to be convicted or receive light sentences.

1967    A document called the living will is proposed, in which an individual can express his or her wishes for treatment at the end of life. The Euthanasia Educational Fund (later Council) is formed as the tax-exempt arm of the Euthanasia Society.

1973    Over 250,000 living wills have been distributed.

1973    The American Hospital Association creates the Patient's Bill of Rights, including the right to informed consent and the right to refuse treatment.

1974    The Euthanasia Society is renamed the Society for the Right to Die.

1976    The New Jersey Supreme Court articulates a constitutional basis for Joseph Quinlan's request to discontinue the "extraordinary procedures" that have maintained his daughter Karen in a persistent vegetative state.

1976    Governor Edmund G. Brown, Jr., of California signs into law the nation's first Natural Death Act.

1979    The Euthanasia Educational Council is renamed Concern for Dying.

1980    Pope John Paul II issues the Declaration on Euthanasia, opposing mercy killing but permitting increased use of painkillers and a patient's refusal of extraordinary means for sustaining life.

         The Hemlock Society is founded.

1983    Nancy Cruzan is left in a persistent vegetative state in a car accident. Her parents go to court to implement their request to stop artificially supplied nutrition and hydration.

1986    The American Medical Association approves withdrawing tubal nutrition and hydration from dying patients who request it and from irreversibly comatose patients.

1990    Dr. Jack Kevorkian uses a suicide machine to enable Janet Adkins to kill herself. A judge dismisses a charge of first-degree murder, saying that Adkins caused her own death.

1990    In the *Cruzan* decision, the U.S. Supreme Court recognizes that the right to refuse treatment is guaranteed by the liberty clause of the U.S. Constitution and also upholds the Missouri Supreme Court's decision that a state has the right to require extensive evidence that the patient would have refused life support.

1990    The federal Patient Self-Determination Act is passed, requiring all hospitals and other health care facilities to inform patients of their right to make end-of-life treatment decisions.

1991    The Society for the Right to Die and Concern for Dying unite to become Choice In Dying, Inc.

1992    All fifty states and the District of Columbia now have laws recognizing advance directives, that is, living wills and/or appointment of an agent to carry out one's wishes.

1993    Kevorkian is charged under a new Michigan law criminalizing assisting in a suicide; a judge strikes down the law.

Compassion In Dying is founded.

1994    Oregon becomes the first state to pass a referendum legalizing physician-assisted suicide; it is challenged in court.

1996    Kevorkian is acquitted for the third time.

1997    The U.S. Supreme Court upholds Washington and New York state laws banning assisted suicide, asserting that such bans are reasonable and that terminally ill patients do not have a fundamental right to physician-assisted suicide. Thus the decision to ban or to legalize physician-assisted suicide is left to the states. In November, Oregon voters vote to sustain the law permitting physician-assisted suicide.

1998    The Oregon Health Division reported that twenty-three persons received prescriptions for lethal medications in 1998. Of these, fifteen died after taking the medication, six died of their underlying illness, and two were alive on January 1, 1999.

# Part I

# Death and How We Face It

## SOME LITERATURE ABOUT DEATH

The finality and sense of loss related to death have inspired authors of every age, using every sort of literary expression, to create a bountiful and timeless literature. A few examples from different eras follow.

## DOCUMENT 1: *Hamlet*, William Shakespeare (1564–1616)

> To die,—to sleep,—
> To sleep! perchance to dream: ay, there's the rub;
> For in that sleep of death what dreams may come,
> When we have shuffled off this mortal coil,
> Must give us pause: there's the respect
> That makes calamity of so long life;
> For who would bear the whips and scorns of time,
> The oppressor's wrong, the proud man's contumely,
> The pangs of despised love, the law's delay,
> The insolence of office, and the spurns
> That patient merit of the unworthy takes,
> When he himself might his quietus make
> With a bare bodkin? who would fardels bear,
> To grunt and sweat under a weary life,
> But that the dread of something after death,—
> The undiscover'd country, from whose bourn
> No traveller returns,—puzzles the will,
> And makes us rather bear those ills we have
> Than fly to others that we know not of?

*Source*: William Shakespeare, *Hamlet*, Act III, Scene 1.

## DOCUMENT 2: "Death Be Not Proud," John Donne (1572–1631)

Death be not proud, though some have called thee
Mighty and dreadful, for, thou art not so,
For, those, whom thou think'st, thou dost overthrow,
Die not, poor death, nor yet canst thou kill me;
From rest and sleep, which but thy pictures be,
Much pleasure, then from thee, much more must flow,
And soonest our best men with thee do go,
Rest of their bones, and soul's delivery.
Thou art slave to fate, chance, kings, and desperate men,
And dost with poison, war, and sickness dwell,
And poppy, or charms can make us sleep as well,
And better than thy stroke; why swell'st thou then?
One short sleep past, we wake eternally,
And death shall be no more, Death thou shalt die.

*Source*: John Donne, "Death Be Not Proud." See *On Doctoring*, ed. Richard Reynolds and John Stone (New York: Simon and Schuster, 1991), 24.

\* \* \*

### DEFINITIONS OF DEATH

At first glance, death would seem easy to define. A dictionary defines death simply as "a permanent cessation of all vital functions: the end of life." A physician provided a more tentative definition in 1967; it illustrates the complexity of defining death.

## DOCUMENT 3: Definition, Dr. Pierre H. Muller (1967)

Death is a process and not a moment in time, as the law believes. During the process there are a series of physical and chemical changes, starting before the medico-legal time of death and continuing afterwards.

*Source*: Dr. Pierre H. Muller, "Legal Medicine and the Delimitation of Death," *World Medical Journal* 14 (1967): 140–142. Cited by Howard P. Lewis, "Machine Medicine and Its Relation to the Fatally Ill," *Journal of the American Medical Association* 206 (1968): 387.

* * *

The President's Commission for the Study of Ethical Problems in Medicine and Biomedical and Behavioral Research devoted an entire volume to defining death. Here is its comment.

---

## DOCUMENT 4: *Defining Death*, President's Commission for the Study of Ethical Problems in Medicine and Biomedical and Behavioral Research (1981)

Death is the one great certainty. The subject of powerful social and religious rituals and moving literature, it is contemplated by philosophers, probed by biologists, and combatted by physicians. Death, taboo in some cultures, preoccupies others.

*Source*: President's Commission for the Study of Ethical Problems in Medicine and Biomedical and Behavioral Research, *Defining Death* (Washington, DC: U.S. Government Printing Office, July 1981), 3.

* * *

In earlier days, persons were pronounced dead when their hearts ceased beating or when they stopped breathing. Persons with severe brain damage or certain other serious incapacities could not survive very long until methods such as cardiopulmonary resuscitation, artificial ventilation, and artificial nutrition and hydration made it possible to sustain life nearly indefinitely, even when the person was totally unaware of life or of his or her surroundings. Thus the line between life and death was blurred, and it became difficult to define death rigorously. Uncertainty about the moment of death led to macabre tales such as "The Premature Burial," which opens with the following paragraph.

---

## DOCUMENT 5: "The Premature Burial," Edgar Allan Poe (1844)

To be buried while alive is, beyond question, the most terrific of these extremes which has ever fallen to the lot of mere mortality. That it has frequently, very frequently, so fallen will scarcely be denied by those who think. The boundaries which divide life from death are at best shadowy and vague. Who shall say where the one ends and where the other begins? We know that there are diseases in which occur total cessations of all the apparent functions of vitality, and yet in which these cessations are merely suspensions, properly so called. They are only temporary pauses in the incomprehensible mechanism. A certain period elapses, and some unseen, mysterious principle again sets in motion the magic pinions and the wizard wheels. The silver cord was not for ever loosed, nor the golden bowl irreparably broken. But where, meantime, was the soul?

*Source*: Edgar Allan Poe, *The Premature Burial*. See *The Complete Tales and Poems of Edgar Allan Poe* (New York: Barnes and Noble, 1992).

* * *

A complicating factor in the definition of death was the development of organ transplantation. A beating heart was essential to maintain the viability of the organs to be transplanted, but artificial respiration and, if necessary, artificial nutrition and hydration could accomplish this for several days without a functioning brain. The dilemma this posed to physicians is portrayed in the following anecdote.

## DOCUMENT 6: *Death, Dying, and the Biological Revolution,* Robert M. Veatch (1976)

Late one evening a thirty-three-year-old man was deposited at the door of the emergency room of a metropolitan hospital by three anonymous friends who made a swift departure. He showed no sign of life. A nurse initiated mouth-to-mouth resuscitation until the respirator team could attach the appropriate mechanical devices. Laboratory analysis confirmed the visual diagnosis of the resident on duty: heroin overdose. Lack of oxygen to the brain left the patient in a deep coma, but by morning the heart was functioning normally while respiration was being maintained by machinery.

After an extensive examination, the neurologist announced that the patient showed no signs of brain activity; he met the criteria of irreversible coma proposed by the Harvard Medical School Ad Hoc Committee to Examine the Definition of Brain Death. The tests were repeated after the heroin had clearly been metabolized and again twenty-four hours later as called for by the Harvard committee.

At this point there was complete agreement among the medical staff about the patient's medical condition. All the evidence indicated that the patient would never recover consciousness, although the respirator, combined with intravenous feeding and careful monitoring, might keep his cells and organs functioning for an indefinite period, perhaps years. The neurologist claimed that the patient was dead; the Harvard criteria were met. He suggested that they go ahead and remove the kidneys, which were urgently needed by a young girl on the nephrology service. The sooner they operated the better if she were to get the organs in good condition.

At this point dispute broke out among the medical staff, and three camps emerged. The first, representing about 40 percent of the staff, agreed with the neurologist that the patient could be considered dead. A second group, perhaps another 40 percent, argued that the patient's heart was still beating. "How," one of them asked, "can you possibly call the patient dead when he has a functioning heart?" This group conceded that he was in irreversible coma. In fact, he had reached a point where he should be allowed to die with dignity, but he was still living. The third and smaller group took one of the traditional positions of physician ethics that the medical professional's duty is to preserve life when it can be preserved. They agreed with the second group that a patient with a beating heart is still alive, but they differed in saying that treatment, by whatever means, should be continued.

This debate took place even though all of the medical staff involved were agreed about the medical facts of the patient's condition. It took place because the issues dividing the groups are ethical issues. Recent advances in the biomedical revolution have made possible intervention into the once irreversible and simple process of dying, permitting ever greater prolongation of dying or, if not dying, of the functioning of body organs and tissues. This has raised ethical and social issues so fundamental and controversial that the debate can no longer be contained within hospital walls. The public as well as professionals—physicians and philosophers and lawyers—must confront these issues raised by our partially successful biological revolution.

*Source*: Robert M. Veatch, *Death, Dying, and the Biological Revolution* (New Haven: Yale University Press, 1976), 1–2.

\* \* \*

A committee at the Harvard Medical School, chaired by anesthesiologist Henry K. Beecher, published a classic article in 1968 that defined irreversible coma rather than death.

**DOCUMENT 7: "A Definition of Irreversible Coma," Ad Hoc Committee of the Harvard Medical School to Examine the Definition of Brain Death (1968)**

Characteristics of Irreversible Coma

An organ, brain or other, that no longer functions and has no possibility of functioning again is for all practical purposes dead. Our first problem is to determine the characteristics of a *permanently* nonfunctioning brain.

A patient in this state appears to be in deep coma. The condition can be satisfactorily diagnosed by points 1, 2, and 3 to follow. The electroencephalogram (point 4) provides confirmatory data, and when available it should be utilized. In situations where for one reason or another electroencephalographic montioring [*sic*] is not available, the absence of cerebral function has to be determined by purely clinical signs, to be described, or by absence of circulation as judged by standstill of blood in the retinal vessels, or by absence of cardiac activity.

1. *Unreceptivity and Unresponsitivity.*—There is a total unawareness to externally applied stimuli and inner need and complete unresponsiveness—our definition of irreversible coma. Even the most intensely painful stimuli evoke no vocal or other response, not even a groan, withdrawal of a limb, or quickening of respiration.

2. *No Movements or Breathing.*—Observations covering a period of at least one hour by physicians is adequate to satisfy the criteria of no spontaneous muscular movements or spontaneous respiration or response to stimuli such as pain, touch, sound, or light. After the patient is on a mechanical respirator, the total absence of spontaneous breathing may be established by turning off the respirator for three minutes and observing whether there is any effort on the part of the subject to breathe spontaneously. (The respirator may be turned off for this time provided that at the start of the trial period the patient's carbon dioxide tension is within the normal range, and provided also that the patient had been breathing room air for at least 10 minutes prior to the trial.)

3. *No reflexes.*—Irreversible coma with abolition of central nervous system activity is evidenced in part by the absence of elicitable reflexes. The pupil will be fixed and dilated and will not respond to a direct source of bright light. Since the establishment of a fixed, dilated pupil is clear-cut in clinical practice, there should be no uncertainty as to its presence. Ocular movement (to head turning and to irrigation of the ears with ice water) and blinking are absent. There is no evidence of postural activity

(decerebrate or other). Swallowing, yawning, vocalization are in abeyance. Corneal and pharyngeal reflexes are absent.

As a rule the stretch of tendon reflexes cannot be elicited: ie, tapping the tendons of the biceps, triceps, and pronator muscles, quadriceps and gastrocnemius muscles with the reflex hammer elicits no contraction of the respective muscles. Plantar or noxious stimulation gives no response.

4. *Flat Electroencephalogram.*—Of great confirmatory value is the flat or isoelectric EEG. We must assume that the electrodes have been properly applied, that the apparatus is functioning normally, and that the personnel in charge is competent. We consider it prudent to have one channel of the apparatus used for an electrocardiogram. This channel will monitor the ECG so that, if it appears in the electroencephalographic leads because of high resistance, it can be readily identified. It also establishes the presence of the active heart in the absence of the EEG. We recommend that another channel be used for a noncephalic lead. This will pick up space-borne or vibration-borne artifacts and identify them. The simplest form of such a monitoring noncephalic electrode has two leads over the dorsum of the hand, preferably the right hand, so the ECG will be minimal or absent. Since one of the requirements of this state is that there be no muscle activity, these two dorsal hand electrodes will not be bothered by muscle artifact. The apparatus should be run at standard gains 10 μv/mm, 50 μv/5 mm. Also it should be isoelectric at double this standard gain which is 5 μv/mm or 25 μv/5 mm. At least ten full minutes of recording are desirable, but twice that would be better.

It is also suggested that the gains at some point be opened to their full amplitude for a brief period (5 to 100 seconds) to see what is going on. Usually in an intensive care unit artifacts will dominate the picture, but these are readily identifiable. There shall be no electroencephalographic response to noise or to pinch.

All of the above tests shall be repeated at least 24 hours later with no change.

The validity of such data as indications of irreversible cerebral damage depends on the exclusion of two conditions: hypothermia (temperature below 90 F [32.2 C] or central nervous system depressants, such as barbiturates.

## Other Procedures

The patient's condition can be determined only by a physician. When the patient is hopelessly damaged as defined above, the family and all colleagues who have participated in major decisions concerning the patient, and all nurses involved, should be so informed. Death is to be declared and *then* the respirator turned off. The decision to do this and the responsibility for it are to be taken by the physician-in-charge, in consultation with one or more physicians who have been directly involved in the case. It is unsound and undesirable to force the family to make the decision.

*Source*: Ad Hoc Committee of the Harvard Medical School to Examine the Definition of Brain Death, "A Definition of Irreversible Coma," *Journal of the American Medical Association* 205 (1968): 337–338.

\* \* \*

In 1978, increasing numbers of complex bioethical problems led the U.S. Congress to authorize the creation of the President's Commission for the Study of Ethical Problems in Medicine and Biomedical and Behavioral Research, with continuing responsibility to study and report on the ethical and legal implications of a number of issues in medicine and research. Members of the commission were named by President Jimmy Carter, with Morris B. Abram, J.D., L.D.D., as chairman, and Alexander Morgan Capron, L.L.B., as executive director. In the succeeding five years, the commission published five reports and a *Summing Up* on topics related to the provision of health care. Two of the reports relevant to this volume are *Defining Death* (July 1981) and *Deciding to Forego Life-sustaining Treatment* (March 1983).

The commission's brief discussion of the physiology of death will be helpful in understanding the physiopathology of some of the patients who are the subjects of the landmark court decisions that will be described in Part V.

---

## DOCUMENT 8: *Defining Death*, President's Commission for the Study of Ethical Problems in Medicine and Biomedical and Behavioral Research (1981)

---

### Conclusion: The Need for Reliable Policy

Medical interventions can often provide great benefit in avoiding *irreversible* harm to a patient's injured heart, lungs, or brain by carrying a patient through a period of acute need. These techniques have, however, thrown new light on the interrelationship of these crucial organ systems. This has created complex issues for public policy as well.

For medical and legal purposes, partial brain impairment must be distinguished from complete and irreversible loss of brain functions or "whole brain death." The President's Commission, as subsequent chapters explain more fully, regards the cessation of the vital functions of the entire brain—and not merely portions thereof, such as those responsible for cognitive functions—as the only proper neurologic basis for declaring death. This conclusion accords with the overwhelming consensus of medical and legal experts and the public.

Present attention to the "definition" of death is part of a process of development in social attitudes and legal rules stimulated by the unfolding of biomedical knowledge. In the nineteenth century increasing knowledge and practical skill made the public confident that death could be diagnosed reliably using cardiopulmonary criteria. The question now is whether, when medical intervention may be responsible for a patient's respiration and circulation, there are other equally reliable ways to diagnose death.

The Commission recognizes that it is often difficult to determine the severity of a patient's injuries, especially in the first few days of intensive care following a cardiac arrest, head trauma, or other similar event. Responsible public policy in this area requires that physicians be able to distinguish reliably those patients who have died from those whose injuries are less severe or are reversible.

*Source*: President's Commission for the Study of Ethical Problems in Medicine and Biomedical and Behavioral Research, *Defining Death* (Washington, DC: U.S. Government Printing Office, July 1981), 15–16, 18–19 (notes omitted).

\* \* \*

The President's Commission concluded that "the 'Harvard Criteria' [see Document 7] have been found to be quite reliable. Indeed, no patient has yet been found that met these criteria and regained any brain functions despite continuation of respirator support" (*Defining Death*, 25). In 1983, the commission proposed a new statute.

## DOCUMENT 9: *Summing Up*, President's Commission for the Study of Ethical Problems in Medicine and Biomedical and Behavioral Research (1983)

. . . the Commission worked with the major professional bodies in medicine, law, and legislative reform to develop a new proposed statute. The American Bar Association, the American Medical Association, and the National Conference of Commissioners on Uniform State Laws joined the Commission in endorsing the Uniform Determination of Death Act, to replace their previous, separate proposals:

An individual who has sustained either (1) irreversible cessation of circulatory and respiratory functions, or (2) irreversible cessation of all functions of the entire brain, including the brain stem, is dead. A determination of death must be made in accordance with accepted medical standards.

The Commission recommended the adoption of this statute in all jurisdictions in the United States. The proposal recognizes that the traditional means to determine death will continue to be applied in the overwhelming majority of cases. In those instances in which artificial means of support require direct evaluation of the functions of the brain, the statute would recognize the use of accepted medical procedures.

*Source*: President's Commission for the Study of Ethical Problems in Medicine and Biomedical and Behavioral Research, *Summing Up* (Washington, DC: U.S. Government Printing Office, March 1983), 15–16.

* * *

A National Mortality Followback Survey of deaths that occurred in 1993 was released by the National Center for Health Statistics of the Centers for Disease Control and Prevention. Most deaths, 56 percent, occurred in a hospital, clinic, or medical center; 19 percent occurred in a nursing home; and 21 percent occurred at home.

## RESPONSES TO THE REALITY OF DEATH

Responses to the reality of death have varied in different cultures, both ancient and contemporary. Some of these cultures are described by Benjamin Boshes.

## DOCUMENT 10: "Death: Historical Evolution and Implication of the Concept," Benjamin Boshes (1978)

For primitive man death was a mystery, an absence of life that he looked upon with a mixture of fear, fascination and superstition all the while he sought to alter it by ritual dances and incantations. . . . The paleolithic people not only interred their dead but also provided them with food and other equipment, implying the belief that the dead have needs in the next life.

These early customs would suggest that man refused to accept death as the definitive end of life and insisted that something of the individual continued to survive the dying experience. The concept of a personal extinction through death was unknown until the sixth century B.C., when it appeared in the metaphysical thinking of Indian Buddhism. This did not find expression in the Western world until the time of the Greek philosopher, Epicurus, in the third century B.C.

The mortuary rituals and funeral customs reflected the culture from which they were derived. Some provided tools, ornaments and food; others covered the corpse with red ochre, the color of blood, to revitalize the dead one. The corpse was sometimes placed in the fetal crouch, interpreted by some as evidence of the belief in rebirth. Yet other cultures bound the limbs tightly in this position, implying a fear that the dead might return to do harm. The Greeks and the Romans believed that the dead must cross a barrier dividing the world of the living from that of the dead, the river Styx, across which the boatman, Charon, carried the corpse in whose mouth a coin was placed to pay for the trip. Many groups describe bridges of death, a crossing, and the nineteenth-century poem "Crossing the Bar" by Lord Tennyson continues the idea.

The concept of resurrection of the dead is found in the eschatologies of the various ancient cultures, but nowhere is the preparation more clearly demonstrated than in the practices in ancient Egypt. Here the body was put through an elaborate mortuary ritual which included mummification to preserve the corpse from disintegration. . . .

The Egyptians were not alone. In Peru and in China tombs were found with life-prolonging substances such as jade placed in the orifices of the corpse, substances alleged to have life-prolonging properties. . . .

Inhumation or burial was the most general method of disposal throughout the ages. To some it symbolized a return to the womb of Mother Earth; to others it served to remind: "For dust thou art and unto dust thou shall return." Sometimes the body was laid directly on the earth with or without clothes. The use of coffins dates back to 3000 B.C. in Egypt. Later, in the Christian era, these sculptured containers gave much information about the attitude toward death. . . .

The ritual of burial required that the deceased be brought to a place of burial or cremation. The ancient Egyptians carried the embalmed body on a sledge, accompanied by mourners and priests. The Mohammedans ported their corpse on an open bier, followed by women relatives with dishevelled hair and by hired mourners as well. This body was interred with its right side towards Mecca. In Hinduism the funeral procession moves to the place of cremation and it is a great honor to be a carrier. All relatives come to the funeral, and even enemies attend, because death transcends interpersonal animosities during life. To view the dead body is a good omen, for death has dignity. The body is burned to free the soul and the cremation is the ultimate purifying act. Sometimes a hollow tube, a holy straw, is used to guide this soul in its route outward where it may enter into another living being, be it man or animal. The soul remains immortal here, and death anniversaries are a time for celebration, not for grief.

In Bali, Indonesia, the Hindu ceremony of cremation is altered in that the body is carried inside a gilded papier-mâché animal or a tower which is set afire. It is never made clear exactly where the body is placed so as to confuse the evil spirit and ensure the soul freedom as it leaves. . . .

Christian funerary rituals were developed in medieval Catholicism and were closely related to the doctrinal belief concerning purgatory. The entire ceremony was marked by black clothes, unbleached wax candles, solemn tolling of church bells. The coffin was carried to the church, trailed by a sad cortege and accompanied by sounds of mourning and the smells of incense.

In some cultures, the body was dismembered for burial. Thus, the Egyptians removed the viscera, which were preserved in four canopic jars. The Romans buried one finger joint that was disconnected from the hand. In medieval Europe the heart and sometimes the intestines of important persons were interred in separate places, for example, William the Conqueror, whose body was buried at St. Étienne at Caen, his heart in Rouen Cathedral, and his intestines in the Church of Chalus.

Post-funerary ceremonies were held in various cultures, not only to mourn the dead, but also to purify the mourners. These included the wearing of old or colorless clothes, shaving of the hair, or letting it grow long and unkempt. Avoidance of amusement, denial of emotional gratification, and other forms of mortification were common practices. . . .

Following the burial it was customary to place a tombstone or a marker on the grave with an accompanying inscription. Sometimes a picture or sculpture of the person buried was included. . . .

In some cultures provisions were made for communication with the dead. The earliest Romans buried their deceased next to the hearth in their houses, and when laws prohibited this custom, they interred the body just outside the city walls. They believed that the dead continued to live in intimacy with their family and from this concept sprang up a "cult of the dead." It was the custom to gather periodically near the dead body to tighten the bonds that tied him to the living. Tombs were constructed with seats in a semicircle to accommodate the visitors.

Other customs provided for continued expiation to God in hopes of alleviating the sufferings of the departed soul. Wealthy Christians facing purgatory endowed monasteries, and chapels were established by a family where masses could be said regularly for the repose of the soul of the dead and those of his relatives. To this day the Jewish believer awaits anxiously the birth of a son or grandson who will "be" his Kaddish. This paean of benediction written in Aramaic expresses the highest and noblest aspiration of the Jewish faith and is used in every religious ceremony, even in daily prayers. It speaks nothing of grief, but only of the praise of God, and phrases from the Kaddish become part of the Lord's Prayer. It also became a mourner's prayer and the living Jew uses it as a means of assuring his future. When the time comes he must have a loved one, a son or a grandson, to say "Kaddish" for him after he is gone, he hopes, to his heavenly paradise.

All of the foregoing draws only lightly on the treasury of record, the customs and practices of human beings, as separate from other animals, as they have faced the question of death. The mystery of death constituted a fearful problem, and in order to cope with it man developed an ideology and a ritual to handle its emotional challenge. This was built into his religious life. All religions are concerned with post-death security, the linking of mortal man to an eternal realm, whether it be achieved by ritual magic, divine assistance, or mystic enlightenment.

As human societies become more sophisticated, particularly in recent times, the traditionalistic eschatologies begin to lose their import. Medieval concepts of death and judgment are not as meaningful, and beliefs that inspired some of these images and traditions have been forgotten or abandoned. The elaborate funeral processions are gone, except for a dignitary of state. . . . Modern society has a longer expectancy of life and a higher standard of living, but the mystery of death and its impact on the emotions has not lessened. Instead man now faces death less equipped and more hopelessly than at any other time in his history. Let us examine what is happening.

Today's man no longer finds a deep resource in religion. His educated mind does not let him accept the mystical philosophies of earlier periods. The priest, the rabbi, or the minister is not seen as endowed with magical powers, and current religious ritual does not fulfill his need. The devout Catholic misses his Latin Mass, the Jew his ritual incantation. With the industrialization of society, generalized education and rapid growth of mass communication, modern man finds himself in a world where he must deal with ecology, civil rights, overpopulation, violence, international crises and the threat of war. His scientists have conquered infection and improved medical care, but no insight has been provided about the termination of life—death. Furthermore, all about him is a social revolution. The rise of democracy provides egalitarian status for everyone, and each man is free, an individual with rights; he expects equal justice. Therefore, he has the right to resist implied and vested authority and to challenge abuse. Inherent in this is the question of right to decision of life or death by medical authority. "Is the individual subject to the decision of the doctor or does he belong to himself?" Thus is man seeking, even in death, to determine his own destiny. Some are frightened by what is happening about them and are dismayed by the experimentation and accomplishments of the "technological priesthood." Powers once attributed to God, such as massive destruction by earthquakes and floods, can be matched by man. The atomic scientist with his nuclear bomb can readily destroy civilization. Man even has some control over death-producing processes. The modern physician can neutralize the effect of previously fatal bacteria; he can start a heart that has stopped; and he can substitute a machine for a failing lung-heart system to maintain a patient indefinitely. The ethicist queries, "Does the person so managed have a choice as to whether he wishes to be saved?" Do the people about him, his family, those who love him, have a voice in the decision or is this exclusively the prerogative of the physician?

*Source*: Benjamin Boshes, "Death: Historical Evolution and Implication of the Concept," in "Brain Death: Interrelated Medical and Social Issues," ed. Julius Korein, *Annals of the New York Academy of Sciences* 315 (1978): 11–14.

* * *

Dr. Elisabeth Kübler-Ross is a psychiatrist who has focused the attention of the medical community and society in general on facts and contemporary views about death. She distinguished five stages of dying: (1) denial and isolation; (2) anger; (3) bargaining; (4) depression; and (5) acceptance. Of course, not all dying persons experience all of these stages, but many do.

## DOCUMENT 11: *On Death and Dying*, Elisabeth Kübler-Ross (1969)

When we look back in time and study old cultures and people, we are impressed that death has always been distasteful to man and will probably always be. From a psychiatrist's point of view this is very understandable and can perhaps best be explained by our basic knowledge that, in our unconscious, death is never possible in regard to ourselves. It is inconceivable for our unconscious to imagine an actual ending of our own life here on earth, and if this life of ours has to end, the ending is always attributed to a malicious intervention from the outside by someone else. In simple terms, in our unconscious mind we can only be killed; it is inconceivable to die of a natural cause or of old age. Therefore death in itself is associated with a bad act, a frightening happening, something that in itself calls for retribution and punishment.

*Source*: Elisabeth Kübler-Ross, *On Death and Dying* (New York: Macmillan Publishing Co., 1969), 2.

* * *

A physician who has written about death thinks that the dying turn to God much less commonly than in earlier times.

## DOCUMENT 12: *How We Die*: *Reflections on Life's Final Chapter*, Sherwin B. Nuland (1994)

In ages past, the hour of death was, insofar as circumstances permitted, seen as a time of spiritual sanctity, and of a last communion with those being left behind. The dying expected this to be so, and it was not easily denied them. It was their consolation and the consolation of their loved ones for the parting and especially for the miseries that had very likely preceded it. For many, this last communion was the focus not only of the sense that a good death was being granted them but of the hope they saw in the existence of God and an afterlife.

It is ironic that in redefining hope, I should find it necessary to call attention to what was until recently the very precinct in which most people would seek it. Much less commonly than at any other time in this millennium do the dying nowadays turn to God and the promise of an afterlife when the present life is fading. It is not for medical personnel or skeptics to question the faith of another, particularly when that other is facing eternity. Agnostics and even atheists have been known to find solace in religion at such times, and their drastic changes of heart are to be respected.

*Source*: Sherwin B. Nuland, *How We Die: Reflections on Life's Final Chapter* (New York, Alfred A. Knopf, 1994), 256.

* * *

The results of a national survey taken by the Gallup Organization about spiritual beliefs and the dying process were summarized in a publication of the National Conference of Catholic Bishops.

## DOCUMENT 13: "Survey Probes Spiritual Concerns about Dying," *Life at Risk*, Richard Doerflinger, National Conference of Catholic Bishops (December 1997)

When asked about the kinds of support that would be most important if they were dying, at least half the respondents ranked the following as "very important": Having someone with whom you can share your fears or concerns (55%), having someone with you (54%), having the opportunity to pray alone (50%), and having someone pray for you (50%). Yet when asked about people who would be comforting during the dying process, 81% said a member of their family would be comforting in "many" ways and 61% said this of "a close friend," while only 36% said this of "a member of the clergy." Commenting on the poll, George Gallup says this is "a wake up call for the clergy," because "not many see the clergy in providing broad spiritual support in their own dying days." Even fewer thought they would receive comfort in many ways from a doctor (30%) or a nurse (21%).

Emotional concerns about death that worry the respondents "somewhat" or "a great deal" include: not having the chance to say goodbye to someone (with 70% saying they worry about this), and thinking that your death will be the cause of inconvenience and stress for those who love you (64%). The most widely shared practical concern was how family or loved ones will be cared for (shared by 65%). Spiritual concerns included: not being forgiven by God (57%), and not reconciling with others (56%). Out of six medical concerns, the only two that worried more respondents were: the possibility of being vegetable-like for some period of time (73%), and the possibility of great physical pain before you die (67%). While 32% worried "a great deal" about physical pain, more respondents worried a great deal about loved ones being cared for (44%), God's forgiveness (42%), and not having the chance to say goodbye (39%). Generally, 38% rated spiritual concerns as worrying them the most about their death, with medical concerns rated fourth (14%) after practical concerns (21%) and emotional concerns (19%).

Respondents were also asked what kind of care they would choose if they had a serious illness with only a 25% chance of survival. The option of "relieving pain and discomfort as much as possible, even if that meant not living as long" was chosen by 70%, while "extending life as much as possible even if it meant more pain and discomfort" was chosen by 23%. Over two-thirds of the latter group still chose aggressive treatment if the chance of survival was 10%. Somewhat to the surprise of the researchers, more deeply religious respondents were not more willing to let go of life but were more likely to want aggressive treatment at the cost of more pain and discomfort.

Overall, 67% said they believe they will exist in some form after death, 72% believe in Heaven, and 56% in Hell, and most said that religious faith is "the most important influence" (21%) or "a very important influence" (39%) in their life. When asked about ownership of human life, only 18% agreed with the statement that "your life belongs to you," while 56% agreed that "your life belongs to God or a higher power" and 20% said that "your life belongs to your family."

Asked to choose among three options on legalization of physician-assisted suicide, 33% said they support making it legal "under a wide variety of specific circumstances": 32% support making it legal "in a few cases" but "oppose it in most circumstances"; and 31% oppose making it legal "for any reason." Half the respondents could imagine a situation in which they themselves might want a doctor to end their life by some painless means. Opposition to physician-assisted suicide was highest among those who are deeply religious, those who are age 55 or over, and those who are black or members of another racial minority.

*Source*: Richard Doerflinger, "Survey Probes Spiritual Concerns about Dying," *Life at Risk*, National Conference of Catholic Bishops (Washington, DC: December 1997), 3.

* * *

A medical student has written about her first encounter with death. It is a moving description of what occurs when the technological imperatives of modern medicine collide with the human dimensions of death.

## DOCUMENT 14: "Shreds of a Flowered Shirt," Emily R. Transue (1995)

I watched someone die today.

It's the first week of Medicine, my first rotation. We're in the middle of morning rounds when a code blue blasts suddenly over the pager. The patient is coming in by ambulance in 10 minutes, time enough for a carefully unhurried walk to the ED.

The team stands in readiness in the resuscitation room. I linger by the ambulance entrance, watching the still-quiet drive, the softly falling rain.

Finally the ambulance pulls up, lights whirling. The stretcher emerges with the patient (we know it's a woman, about 60 years old), feet first, legs slightly apart, thin, deathly white, and naked.

The EMTs wheel her in. A swarm of medical personnel descends instantly: intubating, inserting IVs, sticking on leads, attaching monitors, calling for shock: "Charging, everybody clear? One, two, three—" The body lurches on the table; all eyes fix on the ECG screen.

"Some epi . . ." A flutter (if you can have a flutter, superimposed on chaos), needles, vials, tubes. A vial drops on the floor, the sound of breaking glass. Someone kicks it under the cart.

Words fly across the table responding to blips on the screen: V-tach, V-fib, asystole; others I don't catch. Periodically CPR is halted for a few seconds and everyone reaches to feel for a pulse, hope outweighing the evidence of the ECG. "I have something . . ." someone cries occasionally; then a moment later, "Gone . . ." "Agonal rhythm," Steve, my resident, says matter-of-factly.

Shreds of a flowered shirt dangle from the table (I'd heard they cut your clothes off when you had a cardiac arrest, but never really knew): pitiful remnants of personhood.

She is naked. After a while someone drapes a towel over her exposed genitals, but it quickly falls off again and no one bothers to replace it. I am too frightened to—frightened of what? Of the body, of being seen as "soft"?

Steve (we, the students, love Steve, we want to become Steve) officiates, under the watchful eye of the ED attending. He is calm and competent, a walking manual of proper code blue protocol.

At first they don't even know who she is: "No ID," reports the ambulance team. "No ID? Anything? A purse?" The word "purse," emanating from the lips of these sterile scrubs-clad ED personnel in this bleak white room full of sharp metallic instruments, is oddly out of place, a lay object evinced in this utterly medicalized world. What kind of a purse did she have, this woman, back when she was a woman, before she became only a body? A tight black leather clutch with a folding flap and gold metal buckle? A bright basket-weave bag?

But later—oddly soon, in fact, after the cry of "No ID"—they have not only a name but a chart: this body has CAD, CHF, a history of lymphoma. Her daughters are here—Ah, at last, a confirmation of those shreds of flowered cloth, this WAS a person after all. Daughters. Somewhere in a hallway are daughters waiting to hear that their mother is dead, maybe not knowing yet what all but the greenest of us (meaning me—but even I knew) have known from the beginning, that this exercise in resuscitation is a futile one. Daughters who will weep and grieve and someday heal.

Someone, mercifully, closes the door.

When the CPR team is tired, Steve says, "Med students, you want to do compressions?" I nod, put on gloves (one tears, as I pull it on), step in. From above I can see for the first time her face, albeit deformed by the tape holding the intubation tube in place, her curly graying hair. Her eyes are open. What is she feeling? I wonder. Anything? I find myself hoping fervently that her brain is dead already from lack of oxygen. Dear God, when I die, don't let them do all this to me—Meanwhile I am thrusting on her chest, firm and fast, over and over. "Faster," someone says, and I speed the pulses. Her rib cage is resilient, neither rigid nor relaxed, but moves satisfyingly under my pressure. I am irrationally concerned with not breaking her ribs. "Good compressions," they say approvingly. "You can feel the pulse." They will repeat this later, as if to console me, as if it made any difference; what matter good compressions or no, she was dead anyway.

The new intern does compressions until he is clearly exhausted, but he will not complain—later I will be the same way, refusing relief even when a nurse suggests it, holding out to the bitter end: "I'm calling it," says Steve. "Anyone object to my calling it?" Silence. Everyone steps away from the body. There is no moment of last respect, only a rush for the sink as gloves are tossed into the wastebasket. The body is forgotten. It lies on the stretcher, only an obstacle now to be pushed aside on the way to the sink, the new center of attention, cleanliness, departure, sanity.

Others come to cover the corpse—officially a corpse, at last, no longer that strange, pale, intermediate object, neither alive nor dead—with a cloth.

Somewhere daughters are being told that their mother is dead, the final shreds of hope being torn away. A harrowing day for them, the daughters; the dread call from the hospital ("We're sorry, something has happened—"), the breathless over-the-speed-limit drive, double-parking in the ED lot. Waiting helplessly, clinging together, in sterile foreign hallways, trying to be strong, "for her." "We're doing our best," they're told. "But we have to be honest with you, it doesn't look good." And now the doctor comes to confirm their worst fears. I don't know who tells them; so many doctors rushing in and out, no one leaps out at me as being the One. I would like to ask, even to go with him, to meet the daughters; to grasp with something more than torn flowered cloth the humanity of this body, this person who is the first I have seen die. But my team is going, and I need them, Steve, my intern, the other medical student, some semblance of security. And I don't realize until too late that what I want is to go and offer my sorrow to the daughters, in so doing to get back perhaps a little of my own humanity.

And the code has made me late. I have to run to get to conference by noon.

*Source*: Emily R. Transue, "Shreds of a Flowered Shirt," *Journal of the American Medical Association* 273, no. 8 (1995): 623.

## FURTHER READING

Bertman, Sandra L. *Facing Death: Images, Insights, and Interventions.* Washington, DC: Hemisphere Publishing Corporation, 1991.

DeSpelder, Lynne Ann, and Albert Lee Strickland. *The Last Dance: Encountering Death and Dying.* Palo Alto, CA: Mayfield Publishing Company, 1983.

Lewis, C. S. *A Grief Observed.* New York: Bantam Books, 1979.

Nuland, Sherwin B. *How We Die: Reflections on Life's Final Chapter.* New York: Alfred A. Knopf, 1994.

Quill, Timothy E. *A Midwife through the Dying Process.* Baltimore: Johns Hopkins University Press, 1996.

Spiro, Howard M., Mary G. McCrea Curnen and Lee Palmer Wandel, eds. *Facing Death: Where Culture, Religion, and Medicine Meet.* New Haven: Yale University Press, 1996.

Webb, Marilyn. *The Good Death: The New American Search to Reshape the End of Life.* New York: Bantam Books, 1997.

# Part II

## Medical Advances, Care of the Dying, and the Euthanasia Movement before 1952

### DEATH IN THE NINETEENTH CENTURY

Death came early to most people not only in prehistoric times, but also for most of recorded history. The tombstones in old cemeteries from the eighteenth and nineteenth centuries provide stark evidence of the frequency of death during childbirth as well as high mortality among infants and children. Nutrition and hygiene were poor, and effective treatments for diseases and injuries were virtually nonexistent.

Surgery was horrifying because there was neither anesthesia nor an understanding of the cause of infections. Death usually occurred at home unless it took place on the battlefield. Hospitals as we know them did not exist, and very little could be done to help the dying person.

#### The Crimean War

The Crimean War, between Russia on one side and Turkey, England, France, and Sardinia on the other, was one of several struggles that followed the slow disintegration of the Ottoman Empire and was related to Russia's ambition to obtain an outlet to the Mediterranean through the straits that were held by Turkey. The charge of the Light Brigade, immortalized in Tennyson's poem, took place during the battle of Balaklava.

The death rate among the troops was horrendous, not only because of the primitive state of medical care, but also because of the lack of sanitation. Conditions were enormously improved by the nursing care instituted by Florence Nightingale (1820–1910). In 1854 she was asked to organize thirty-eight nurses to serve in the Crimean War. The conditions that she found are described in the following letter. It was fortunate that she had known Sidney Herbert and his wife socially, and that he had been appointed secretary of war in 1852.

She and her fellow nurses cared for the soldiers day and night; her evening rounds gave her the name of "The Lady with the Lamp." As a result of the greatly improved hygiene and personal care that they instituted, the death rate among the troops plummeted. By the end of the war, Florence Nightingale was a legend. She received $150,000, an enormous sum at the time, and founded the Nightingale School and Home for Training Nurses at St. Thomas' Hospital in London. She was the first woman given the British Order of Merit. The U.S. government sought her advice early in the Civil War.

## DOCUMENT 15: Letter of Florence Nightingale to Sidney Herbert (November 25, 1854)

To Sidney Herbert　　　　　　　　　　Barrack Hospital, Scutari
　　　　　　　　　　　　　　　　　　　　　　25 Nov 1854
*Private*　　　　　　　　　　　　　　British Sisters Quarters

Dear Mr. Herbert

(1) It appears that in these Hospitals, the Purveyor considers washing both of linen & of the men a minor 'detail'—& during the three weeks we have been here, though our remonstrances have been treated with perfect civility, yet no washing whatever has been performed for the men either of body linen or of bed-linen except by ourselves, & a few wives of the Wounded, & a story of a Contractor, with which we have been amused, turns out to be a myth. The dirty shirts were collected yesterday for the first time, & on Monday *it is said* that they are to be washed,— & we are organizing a little Washing Establishment of our own—for the bandages &c. When we came here, there was neither basin, towel nor soap in the Wards, nor any means of personal cleanliness for the Wounded except the following.

Thirty were bathed every night by Dr. MacGrigor's orders in slipper-baths, but this does not do more than include a washing once in eighty days for 2300 men.

The consequences of all this are Fever, Cholera, Gangrene, Lice, Bugs,

Fleas—& may be Erysipelas—from the using of one sponge among many wounds.

And even this slipper-bathing does not apply to the General Hospital.

(2) The fault here is, *not* with the Medical Officers, but in the separation of the department which affords every necessary supply, except medicines, to them—& in the insufficient supply of minor officers in the Purveying Department under Mr. Wreford, the Purv'r Gen'l, as well as in the inevitable delay in obtaining supplies, occasioned by the existence of one single Interpreter only, who is generally seen booted.

(3) Your name is also continually used as a bug-bear, they make a deity of cheapness, & the Secretary at War stands as synonymous here with Jupiter Tonans whose shafts end only in 'brutum flumen.' The cheese-paring system which sounds unmusical in British ears is here identified with you by the Officers who carry it out. It is in vain to tell the Purveyors that they will get no 'kudos' by this at home. See Note A

(4) The requirements are, unity of action & personal responsibility.

It is a sad joke here that a large reward has been offered for any one who is personally responsible, barring the Commandant.

(5) Another cause is, the imperfection of distinct order in England as to *packing*. The unfortunate 'Prince' who was lost at Balaklava had on board a quantity of medical comforts for us which were so packed under shot & shell as that it was found impossible to disembark them here & they went on to Balaklava & were lost at the same time as your Commissioner Dr. Spence.

(6) In consequence of the Duke of Newcastle's letter to Mr. Cumming, the latter has not taken the command here, & in consequence of Dr. Spence being lost on board the 'Prince', the Commission of Enquiry has not yet begun its labours. Mr. Maxwell visits us *en amateur*.

(7) Two or three hundred Stump Pillows, ditto Arm Slings, ditto *Paddings* for Splints—besides other Medical Appliances are being weekly manufactured & given out by us—& no provision appeared to have been made for these things before.

All the above is written in obedience to your *private* instructions. Do not let me appear as a Gov't spy here which would destroy all my usefulness & believe me, in greatest haste,

Yours ever truly

F. Nightingale

P.S. Lord Napier & the Visitors generally remark that the Hospital is improved since we came.

Note A—

The habits & the honor of the Purveying Department, as inferior officers, fix their attention upon the correctness of their book-keeping as the primary object of life.

Note B—

Mr. Osborne & Mr. Macdonald have been profuse of offers. We have accepted wine, shirts, flannel, calico, sago, &c—delay being as fatal to us as denial in our requisitions.

*Entre nous*, will you let me state that Lady Stratford, with the utmost kindness & benevolent intentions, is, in consequence of want of practical habits of business, nothing but good & bustling, & a time waster & impediment. As the Commission is not yet doing anything, the Ambassador should send us a *man* who, with prompt efficiency, can also defend us from the difficulties & delays of mediating between conflicting orders in the various departments—to which I ascribe most of the signal failures, such as those in washing &c, which have occurred.

F.N.

P.S. Mrs. Herbert gave me a fright by telling Mrs. Bracebridge that your private letter to me had been published. That letter was shewn to no one but my own people & it appears to me impossible that it can have found its way into any other hands.

P.P.S We are greatly in want of Hair Mattrasses [*sic*] or even Flock, as cheaper. There are but 44 Hair Mattresses in store. Our very bad cases suffer terribly from bed-sores on the Paillasse, which is all we have—while the French Hospital is furnished throughout with mattrasses having an elastic couche of Hair between two of Flock & a Paillasse underneath.

*Source*: Florence Nightingale, letter to Sidney Herbert, November 25, 1854, in *Ever Yours, Florence Nightingale: Selected Letters*, Martha Vicinus and Bea Nergaard (Cambridge, MA: Harvard University Press, 1990), 88–90 (notes omitted).

* * *

### The Civil War

Medical care was hardly better during the early days of the U.S. Civil War, in part because of disorder in the field and in part because of inadequate training of doctors.

## DOCUMENT 16: *Doctors in Blue*, George Worthington Adams (1952)

The Army Medical Department entered the war unprepared. . . .

Almost incredible anarchy characterized the field relief work at this battle [the Second Battle of Bull Run, August 29 to September 1, 1862].

There was no organized ambulance system except in the two corps from the Army of the Potomac; there were not enough ambulances. The best-equipped of the three corps in the original Army of Virginia had a total of 45 ambulances and carts instead of the scheduled 170. In the maneuvering many had broken down and had been abandoned before the battle opened. The reinforcements from the Army of the Potomac were even worse off. They had been embarked at Harrison's Landing in such haste and with such limited ship-space that the majority of the ambulances were left behind. Whole divisions were without ambulances.

McParlin, the medical director in charge, made poor use of what he had. Instead of setting up division or corps hospitals, he established one large field hospital, leaving the regimental hospitals to act as dressing stations. Located some miles from the nearest railroad point, this hospital was unsuitable as an evacuation depot. Furthermore, it was seven miles from the front on the first day, imposing a harrowing ride for the ambulances. This was soon made worse by the destruction of bridges. Since regimental medical men stuck with their regimental units, the large hospital was understaffed. At the end of the first day, the patients had not been evacuated from the field hospital to make room for the thousands to come. This stupidity was compounded by an opposite stupidity. When the fighting was over and no new patients were to be expected, the wounded, many of whom could not be moved without harm, were evacuated "with a dogged indifference to consequences."

The Confederate victory added further complications. A large proportion of the wounded had been left on the field over which the Confederates had become the masters, as well as over a number of regimental hospitals crowded with other wounded. On September 1, Medical Inspector Richard Coolidge, who had been sent out from Washington the day before to take control of Medical Department activities, succeeded in arranging a truce. He found Lee's medical director, Dr. Lafayette Guild, courteous and friendly, and it was agreed that the Union wounded be paroled, and might be cared for by their own surgeons until they could be taken through the lines. The Confederates restored to the Union surgeons the greater part of the captured medical supplies and agreed to share captured blankets equally; but Lee had little to offer in the way of foodstuffs and would not permit an enemy supply train to enter his lines.

Three days after the battle some 3,000 wounded men still lay where they had fallen, most of them unfed and practically all without surgical attention. Two days later they still numbered 600. The last convoy of wounded, some of whom had lain six or seven days before being picked up, left the field September 9, three days later. One of these unfortunates had been given water by the Confederates, but had gone without food for six days and seven nights. They had lain through alternating thunderstorms and blistering sunshine, suffering immeasurable agonies. Many reported "Killed in Action" must have died lingering deaths, victims of faulty organization.

The handling of the wounded was fatally slowed down by the villainous conduct of the civilian teamsters hired by the Quartermaster Corps to drive the army's ambulances. Practically every one of them ran away. Responding to the continued and desperate calls for ambulances and supplies, the Surgeon General procured a troop of cavalry which commandeered vehicles on the streets of Washington, to the number of 140 hacks, 40 omnibuses and numbers of beer and delivery trucks, and other vehicles. Government clerks and other civilian volunteers were added to the civilian surgeons arriving from everywhere in response to Secretary Stanton's pleas, and a mighty relief force started out for Centreville and the battlefield. But the drivers were of the same stamp as the earlier deserters. The vehicles carrying supplies were known to include liquor. In the darkness many of the drivers eluded the cavalry escort, broke into the liquor boxes, and turned back to Washington. Because the drivers of some of the hacks were persuaded to do their duty a few reached the battlefield. Even these, along with drivers of additional wagons and ambulances which came out on September 6 and later, behaved abominably. They refused to give water to the wounded; they refused to assist in putting them into the ambulances; they were impudent to the medical officers; they stole blankets and provisions from the scanty stores; some even went through the pockets of their helpless passengers.

From this "frightful state of disorder," Surgeon General Hammond drew the proper deductions. The Army must have an ambulance corps; and the Medical Department, rather than the Quartermaster Corps, must have control of the ambulances and the medical transport.

*Source*: George Worthington Adams, *Doctors in Blue* (New York: Henry Schuman, 1952), 3–4, 74–76.

* * *

The sorry state of medical education throughout the world was partly responsible for the poor medical care. In addition, medical knowledge and the development of hospitals in the United States lagged behind those in Europe.

## DOCUMENT 17: *Doctors in Blue*, George Worthington Adams (1952)

In evaluating the Civil War surgeons many allowances must be made. Judged by modern standards, the best of them were deplorably ignorant and badly trained. But in comparison with the older generation of practicing physicians of their own time they appear in a better light. Nearly all had diplomas from medical schools, while as recently as the second quarter of the century most American practitioners had been office-trained. This must be considered a mild distinction, based on the theory that any diploma is better than no diploma, for American medical schools were never worse than in the middle years of the nineteenth century. The standard medical course was two years of nine months each, topped off with a term of service as assistant to an active practitioner. The second year was usually given over to a repetition of the first year's lectures. In neither year was laboratory or clinical instruction given real attention. In many States dissection was legally prohibited. The backwardness and poor equipment of even the better schools is illustrated by the fact that the Harvard medical school had no stethoscope until 1868, thirty years after its invention, and no microscope until 1869. Its catalogues failed to mention these instruments until those years. Many schools were mere diploma mills, living upon the fees of their students entering practice in a society which had not even set up a State licensing system for its own protection.

Had the schools represented the most advanced knowledge of their day they could have given their students only the merest beginnings of modern scientific medicine. The long debate between "rational medicine" and empiricism, between deductive knowledge and experimentalism, was ending in a qualified victory for the latter. In Europe, with France taking the lead, modern medicine had just come to birth during the first half of the century. The post-mortem investigation of local pathological lesions, combined with careful clinical observation, proved the key which was to make possible accurate diagnosis and understanding of disease. When scientific medical statistics were introduced, and used in conjunction with the findings of the pathologists, medical men began to feel that the ground was firm beneath their feet. The work of Pasteur and Koch in bacteriology was to shed a great light on the causes for diseased tissues that had been explored by the pathologists; antisepsis in surgery as pioneered by Lister was to make great surgical triumphs possible. Both however came too late to affect the ideas and methods of the men who had to do the medical and surgical work of the Civil War.

*Source*: George Worthington Adams, *Doctors in Blue* (New York: Henry Schuman, 1952), 49–51.

---

## DOCUMENT 18: *The Social Transformation of American Medicine*, Paul Starr (1982)

---

We now think of hospitals as the most visible embodiment of medical care in its technically most sophisticated form, but before the last hundred years, hospitals and medical practice had relatively little to do with each other. From their earliest origins in preindustrial societies, hospitals had been primarily religious and charitable institutions for tending the sick, rather than medical institutions for their cure. While in Europe from the eighteenth century they played an important part in medical education and research, systematic clinical instruction and investigation were neglected in America until the founding of Johns Hopkins [in 1873]. Before the Civil War, an American doctor might contentedly spend an entire career in practice without setting foot on a hospital ward. The hospital did not intrude on the worries of the typical practitioner, nor the practitioner on the routine of the hospital.

But in a matter of decades, roughly between 1870 and 1910, hospitals moved from the periphery to the center of medical education and medical practice. From refuges mainly for the homeless poor and insane, they evolved into doctors' workshops for all types and classes of patients. From charities, dependent on voluntary gifts, they developed into market institutions, financed increasingly out of payments from patients. What drove this transformation was not simply the advance of science, important though that was, but the demands and example of an industrializing capitalist society, which brought larger numbers of people into urban centers, detached them from traditions of self-sufficiency, and projected ideals of specialization and technical competence. . . .

. . . Before anesthesia, surgery was brutal work; physical strength and speed were at a premium, so important was it to get in and out of the body as fast as possible. After Morton's demonstration of ether at the Massachusetts General Hospital in 1846, anesthesia came quickly into use, and slower and more careful operations became possible. But the range and volume of surgery remained extremely limited. Infections took a heavy toll in all "capital operations," as major surgery was so justly called: The mortality rate for amputations was about 40 percent. Very rarely did the surgeon penetrate the major bodily cavities, and then only in desperation, when every other hope had been exhausted. . . .

Change came slowly after Lister's work on antisepsis was published in 1867 because it was inherently difficult to reproduce. Many surgeons tested out his carbolic acid spray but found they were still plagued by fatal infections; ... Lister's method was not generally adopted until around 1880, soon after which it was superseded by aseptic techniques. ... It was not actually until the 1890s and early 1900s that surgery began to take off. Then, in a burst of creative excitement, the amount, scope, and daring of surgery enormously increased. Improvements in diagnostic tools, particularly the development of X-rays in 1895, spurred the advance. Surgeons began to operate earlier and more often for a variety of ills, many of them, like appendicitis, gallbladder disease, and stomach ulcers, previously considered medical rather than surgical cases.

Source: Paul Starr, The Social Transformation of American Medicine, chapter 4, "The Reconstitution of the Hospital" (New York: Basic Books, 1982), 145–146.

* * *

## MORTALITY, 1900–1950

Overall mortality declined steadily between 1900 and 1950, mainly because of the decrease in fatal infections. One might be inclined to attribute this decrease to the discovery and use of antibiotics. But the decrease was not the result of these wonder drugs; sulfanilamide was introduced only in the late 1930s and penicillin in the early 1940s, whereas the following chart shows eloquently that the decrease in mortality due to infections occurred steadily between 1900 and 1950. Rather, this decrease resulted from improvements in hygiene—better housing, water supply, sanitation, and general cleanliness.

With the waning of mortality due to infections, the major causes of death became degenerative diseases, mainly strokes and heart attacks, as well as neoplasms, that is, cancer and sarcomas (malignant growths of epithelium and connective tissue, repectively). According to U.S. Mortality Statistics, by 1990 heart disease and strokes accounted for 40.2 percent of deaths, and neoplasms for 23.5 percent.

More specific advances in medical care occurred rapidly in the first half of the twentieth century. To appreciate these advances, consider the following: If you, the reader, were twenty years old in 1998 and we assume that a generation spans thirty years, your grandparents were twenty years old in 1938. At that time, Nazism flourished in Germany, and World War II was to begin soon. Insulin treatment for diabetes was only fifteen years old; liver treatment of pernicious anemia was only eleven years old; and separation of transfused blood into different types of cells and different proteins in the plasma was only developed during

World War II. There was, of course, no immunization for poliomyelitis; epidemics occurred during many summers, and the iron lung had only been used for eleven years to aid respiration in victims of this disease. Although heart disease and strokes had become the leading causes of death by 1950, their physiopathology was poorly understood, and treatment was virtually nonexistent. Chemotherapy for cancer was in its infancy.

---

**DOCUMENT 19: Diagrammatic Representation of Death Rates from All Causes, United States, 1900–1969, by Major Categories as Indicated (in numbers per 100,000 population), Thomas M. Peery (1975)**

---

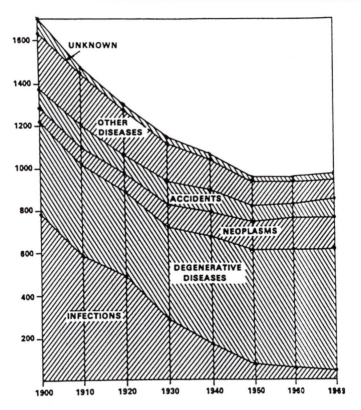

*Source*: Thomas M. Peery, "The New and Old Diseases: A Study of Mortality Trends in the United States, 1900–1969," *American Journal of Clinical Pathology* 63 (1975): 458. Copyright © 1975 by the American Society of Clinical Pathologists. Reprinted with permission.

* * *

## THE EARLY EUTHANASIA MOVEMENT

The term "euthanasia" derives from the Greek *eu*, meaning "easy," and *thanatos*, meaning "death." Today, the term usually means the act or practice of ending the life of a sick person by some active means. If the sick person has asked for euthanasia, the process is called "voluntary euthanasia'; if the invalid is put to death without his or her knowledge, it is "involuntary euthanasia."

Euthanasia is to be differentiated from withdrawing treatment that temporarily sustains life from individuals with a fatal condition, or failing to initiate such treatment. The right to withhold or withdraw treatment from a mortally ill individual was achieved as a result of court decisions and the passage of laws, which will be discussed in Parts IV and V. The beginning of the euthanasia movement is well described in a book by O. Ruth Russell.

---

## DOCUMENT 20: *Freedom to Die*, O. Ruth Russell (1975)

---

During the latter part of the nineteenth century a few books and essays appeared with the word euthanasia in the title or a chapter heading. The first of these was an essay in 1872 by S. D. Williams entitled "Euthanasia," published in England. This appears to be the first time the word euthanasia was used in the modern sense of inducing death, though William Mountford came close to it in his *Euthanasy: Or Happy Talk Towards the End of Life*, published in 1848 and in its fourth edition in 1852.

Williams' essay was followed the next year by one entitled, "The Cure for Incurables," by the Honorable Lionel A. Tollemache. Tollemache, a British philosopher, defended the thesis of Williams and systematically refuted the arguments advanced against it by its critics. These scholarly and practical essays made a highly significant contribution to thinking about euthanasia. . . .

Tollemache not only discussed the pros and cons of euthanasia but gave strong support to the idea that the laws should be changed to permit it. He quoted and supported Williams' view that "in cases of incurable and painful illness the doctors should be allowed, with the patient's consent, and after taking all necessary safeguards, to administer so strong an anaesthetic as to render all future anaesthetics superfluous; in short, there should be a sort of legalized suicide by proxy."

Tollemache added, "Any of us may one day have to bear—many of us certainly have to witness—either cancer, creeping paralysis . . . or a mortally wounded soldier who wishes to die. . . . So even from the most selfish point of view we all have an interest that this question should be speedily discussed." He said we must consider also the friends who, besides the immediate suffering of nursing the sick man, often permanently impair their constitutions and nervous systems.

In his rebuttal of the argument that there would be abuses if euthanasia were made legally permissible, Tollemache questioned the right of the state to forbid the sick man to choose his own way of "severing himself from his friends," and he said "if we rejected all reforms which might lead to contingent and remote evils, no reform whatever would be passed and we should be in a state of . . . stagnation." He envisaged adequate safeguards to prevent the abuse of power in the proposed legislation.

An 1887 book by Dr. William Munk, a Fellow of the Royal College of Surgeons, was entitled *Euthanasia: or Medical Treatment in Aid of an Easy Death.* Another was *Euthanasia: the Aesthetics of Suicide,* by Baron Harden-Hickey in 1894.

In Munk's book, . . . the word euthanasia was used in its original meaning, an easy or good death; the author made a plea that the dying patient be made as comfortable as possible, using opium when necessary to relieve pain. . . .

During the first three decades of the twentieth century, although several articles were written denouncing euthanasia, little was written in support of it except for one very significant article in 1901 by a prominent British physician, Dr. Charles E. Goddard, entitled, "Suggestions in Favor of Terminating Absolutely Hopeless Cases of Injury and Disease."

Dr. Goddard, who later became Medical Officer of Health for Harrow, England, advocated euthanasia not only for people dying from incurable and painful disease who demanded relief from their suffering, but also for certain cases of hopeless idiots, imbeciles, and monstrosities; these latter he described as "Those who, having no will power nor intelligence of their own, and being a burden to themselves and especially to their friends and society, [and] of course, absolutely incapable of improvement." He said their cases should be considered and their fate determined by a "Committee of Experts," who, being convinced of the eligibility for such relief, would arrange the proper method for the termination of their miserable existence.

Dr. Goddard said there was need for a new attitude on the part of the public regarding this "somewhat gruesome subject." He thought the first step should be by the medical profession. He said,

I am satisfied of this, that when once it was recognized that it was lawful to accept the means of relief at all, it would be gratefully accepted by thousands of suffering creatures in the years to come as a God-given escape. It would be regarded as a providential help in a time of terrible need. I am sure more than half the opposition will arise from cruel prejudice. Some of us are old enough to remember in our practice people who were prejudiced against the use of anaesthetics on the supposition that pain was never intended by the Almighty to be avoided in this way.

... The advocacy of euthanasia by Dr. Charles Eliot Norton of Harvard, a distinguished scholar and humanitarian, brought forth denunciation in a January 6, 1906 editorial in the *New York Times* which said that Norton had been moved by an "unfortunate impulse," and called euthanasia a "curious delusion." In spite of this climate of opinion, a bill for the legalization of euthanasia for certain incurable sufferers was introduced in the legislature of the state of Ohio, January 23, 1906. This appears to have been the first such bill introduced into the legislature of any English-speaking country....

The Ohio bill would have provided that when an adult of sound mind had been fatally hurt or was so ill that recovery was impossible, or if he was suffering from extreme physical pain without hope of recovery, his physician, if not a relative and if not interested in any way in his estate, might ask him in the presence of three witnesses if he wished to die. If he indicated that he did, then three other physicians were to be summoned in consultation and if they agreed that the case was hopeless, they were to make arrangements to put the person out of pain and suffering with as little discomfort as possible.

A motion to reject the bill was defeated by a vote of 19 yeas to 79 nays, so the bill was given a first reading and referred to the Committee on Medical Jurisprudence, but it was finally defeated by a vote of 23 to 79. Much publicity and much hostility ensued....

An editorial in the *New York Times* on January 25, 1906, called the Ohio proposal "something considerably worse than ignorant folly—something that verges close upon, if not into, the criminal." Ironically, the following day the *Times* reported the assertion of Dr. Walter Kempster of Milwaukee that he had given a fatal dose of morphine to a woman who had been fatally burned. He said, "There are others to whom a law providing death might be applied with benefit. If such a measure is contemplated it should include in its provisions such members of the community as are suffering from incurable diseases, lunatics, and idiots." ...

In 1912, Sara Harwis of New York, suffering almost constant pain and distress from an incurable disease, created a sensation when she announced that she was sending a petition to the Legislature of the State of New York asking for such a relaxation of the homicide laws as would permit her physician to put her painlessly to death. Her petition was not granted, but it was widely publicized and the press reported much hostility to it.

In 1917, at the sixth annual convention of the American Association of Progressive Medicine in Chicago, Dr. William A. Guild of Des Moines advocated legalized euthanasia for the aged, infirm, and those suffering from incurable maladies. A resolution calling for a commission to submit to every state legislature a proposal for legalization of euthanasia was adopted by a vote of 87 to 24. But apparently the desired action was not taken since Dr. Guild presented the same proposal in 1931 to the Illinois Homeopathic Medical Association, and again no action seems to have been taken.

In July 1917 Dr. Harry J. Haiselden of Chicago allowed a baby girl born with a microcephalic head to die when he could have saved her life. Forty doctors had looked at the child and agreed with Dr. Haiselden's decision. In a November trial which acquitted him, Dr. Haiselden was supported by 15 doctors. He said he had followed the same course in a similar case in 1915.

It seems clear that at this time the climate of medical opinion regarding the legalization of euthanasia was not favorable, but the debates stimulated by Dr. Goddard and the Ohio bill seemed to indicate that perhaps the winds of change might be stirring, as indeed, they were.

*Source*: O. Ruth Russell, *Freedom to Die: Moral and Legal Aspects of Euthanasia* (New York: Human Sciences Press, 1975), 57–69.

* * *

## THE EUTHANASIA MOVEMENT IN GREAT BRITAIN AND THE UNITED STATES

In 1931, a highly regarded British physician, C. Killick Millard, was very active in organizing a movement in Great Britain to legalize euthanasia for the dying who requested it. Largely as a result of his activity, the Voluntary Euthanasia Legalization Society was formed in 1935. Supporters of the society included such notables as Julian Huxley, James Jeans, H. G. Wells, G. Bernard Shaw, A. A. Milne, Dr. William R. Inge, former dean of St. Paul's Cathedral and his successor. In the United States, the subject of euthanasia continued to be discussed, for example, in a debate published in *Forum* magazine in 1935.

## DOCUMENT 21: "The Right to Die: A Debate. I. Legalize Euthanasia!" Abraham L. Wolbarst; "II. Life Is Sacred," James J. Walsh (1935)

I—Legalize Euthanasia! by ABR. L. WOLBARST

The question as usually submitted limits the discussion of legal euthanasia to those "incurables whose physical suffering is unbearable to themselves." That limitation is rather unfortunate, because the number of incurables within this category is actually and relatively extremely small. Very few incurables have or express the wish to die. However great their physical suffering may be, the will to live, the desire for life, is such an overwhelming force that pain and suffering become bearable and they prefer to live. Nevertheless, there are those who earnestly wish to end their suffering through death, and their plight deserves the most serious consideration. . . .

To be sure, the problem is not a simple one, for who is there among us so wise and farseeing that he can assume the responsibility for ending the life of another human? Those of us who have lived long enough and have seen enough of disease know that certain individuals possess an exceptional degree of vitality and occasionally recover from injuries and disease which would kill others. . . . Doctors are only human beings, with few if any supermen among them. They make honest mistakes, like other men, because of the limitations of the human mind. They might conceivably agree on legal euthanasia in a certain case, only to find, on autopsy, that they had made a wrong diagnosis.

Notwithstanding these doubtful aspects of euthanasia, I am strongly in favor of it in certain well-defined circumstances, especially for those whose sufferings are unbearable to themselves. We consider it an act of mercy to end the suffering of our dumb animals; is it not equally merciful to end the suffering of a human being? Should he be allowed to suffer merely because he happens to be human? . . .

Today, however, the law does not permit that humane act to be carried out, nor do the ethics of the medical profession. If it became known that a doctor, touched by the suffering of his patient, deliberately hastened the end to relieve him of his agony, that doctor soon would find himself behind prison bars, charged with murder. He might make a good defense, of course, and an intelligent jury might acquit him, but there is no certainty of that. Within the past few years, several so-called mercy slayers have called public attention to this subject by reason of their trials before the bar of justice.

If legal euthanasia has a humane and merciful motivation, it seems to me the entire question should be considered from a broad angle. There are times when euthanasia is strongly indicated as an act of mercy even though the subject's suffering is not "unbearable to himself," as in the case of an imbecile. . . .

For my own part, I should insist upon euthanasia if ever I found myself incurably afflicted, helpless, suffering pain and torture endlessly and uselessly, and a burden to those about me. A painless death would be far preferable to painful lingering which eventually must end the same way. I should consider my voluntary passing the greatest manifestation of my affection for those near and dear to me.

## II—Life Is Sacred by JAMES J. WALSH

The question with which Dr. Wolbarst opens this discussion is whether those "incurables whose physical suffering is unbearable to themselves" should not, if they request it, be legally put to painless death, thus saving suffering not only for the victims but for those around them. I thoroughly agree with him that, if the question be strictly limited to the consideration of patients who come under this formula, there will be very few indeed to take advantage of any relief afforded by the State in the matter and that they would be sufferers not from physical agony but from mental anguish. . . .

On the other hand, I have often heard neurotic patients wish that they might be taken out of existence because they could no longer bear up under the pain that they were suffering. As a matter of fact, they were suffering not physical but mental pain. They were overcome mainly by self-pity. Above all, they were sympathy seekers and they wanted to produce the impression on those around them that no one had ever suffered quite so much as they. Of physical pain there was almost no trace, but they were hysterically ready, so they claimed, to welcome death as a relief from their intolerable condition. They had a number of long adjectives that they liked to use. . . .

Suffering is one of the great mysteries of life, and we do not know the meaning of it. Many people have insisted that, because of the presence of suffering and evil in the world, there cannot be a beneficent Creator; but see what suffering has done for men. The man who has himself suffered is sympathetic toward others and has a rounded-out, human character that makes him what Francis Bacon would call a "full man." . . .

Life is a mystery. It is one of the seven riddles of the universe. With matter, motion, law, sensation, consciousness, and free will, it constitutes an historic septenate of mystery. Life was given to us as a precious treasure to be used to the best advantage. It is the Creator's gift, not to be thrown back into the Giver's face until He asks for it.

To leave God out of the reckoning and to deny the existence of the Creator is, in the present state of scientific knowledge and its attitude toward the spiritual world, to stultify one's intelligence and to refuse to follow our human reason and logic to its legitimate conclusion. Surely all this great universe around us did not come by accident and did not set itself in order by chance. To take one's own life is to violate that order. To take it because of pain and suffering which one is exaggerating is the act of a coward and has always been so proclaimed by men. It is not pain but the yielding to self-pity that brings men and women to the point where they take their own lives. There are heroic men and women who face death and suffering calmly and who are made heroes by the suffering to which they are subjected. This is the real answer to the question of legal euthanasia.

If a patient with an incurable and painful disease begged me to do something to end his agony, my immediate response would be very much the same as if a young unmarried woman who was pregnant should ask me to help her avoid the disgrace of giving birth to a child, by producing an abortion. Life is too mysteriously significant to be at the mercy of even its owner, much less one who has a special duty with regard to it.

*Source*: Abraham L. Wolbarst and James J. Walsh, "The Right to Die: A Debate," *Forum* 94, no 6 (December 1935) 330–334.

* * *

A bill to legalize voluntary euthanasia was introduced in the Nebraska legislature on February 13, 1937, but did not pass.

## DOCUMENT 22: "Mercy Death Bill Filed in Nebraska," *New York Times* (February 14, 1937)

LINCOLN, Neb., Feb. 13—A 70 year-old woman physician has forced into the open an issue which has been debated bitterly for years.

Through the efforts of Dr. Inez Celia Philbrick, retired University of Nebraska faculty member, Nebraska's unicameral Legislature will consider a bill to legalize euthanasia or, "mercy death."

Sponsor of the bill is Senator John H. Comstock of Lincoln, whose mother was attended at his birth by Dr. Philbrick. Mr. Comstock, 32, a Republican and graduate of the University of Nebraska Law School says he has received many letters from other States in support of the measure, none in opposition.

Dr. Philbrick asserts she represents a group of physicians in her efforts in behalf of the bill. The measure would permit a district judge, on application of any adult suffering a painful, incurable disease, to appoint a commission of two physicians and a lawyer to recommend action.

During seventeen years, Dr. Philbrick taught 2,600 girls in a course on sex hygiene at the University of Nebraska, until June, 1936, when she retired. She has delivered 2,100 babies. She believes in birth control, sterilization of degenerates and criminal defectives and foresees State medicine.

She resigned from the American Medical Society after thirty years' membership because she didn't like "the commercial basis upon which medicine is being practiced."

In the face of criticism by clergymen and the legislative committee of the Nebraska State Medical Association, she insists euthanasia does not conflict with the Oath of Hippocrates, which includes this statement, "I will give no deadly medicine to any one if asked, nor suggest any such counsel."

Dr. Philbrick, in a radio speech in defense of the bill, said that "it seems not to have occurred to the minds of many of the profession that the Oath of Hippocrates, dating from the fourth century B. C., may in some particulars be more honored in the breach than in the observance; that it may need amendment to meet the thought and needs of the twentieth century A.D."

Dr. A. L. Miller, only physician member of the Legislature and a fellow of the American College of Surgeons, declined to introduce the bill. He said he believed the bill had merit, but was "twenty-five years too soon." Opposition of the Medical Association committee was based on the view that "science is not sufficiently advanced to be sure that death must ensue."

*Source*: "Mercy Death Bill Filed in Nebraska," *New York Times* (February 14, 1937).

* * *

The cause of euthanasia was taken up by a liberal Unitarian minister, Charles Francis Potter. He was a biblical expert in the 1925 trial of John Scopes, a teacher who was charged with violating a Tennessee law that prohibited teaching the theory of evolution. On January 16, 1938, Potter announced the formation of the National Society for the Legalization of Euthanasia in New York City. (A few years later, its name was changed to the Euthanasia Society of America.)

## DOCUMENT 23: "National Euthanasia Society Formed; Mercy-Killing Advocates Plan Legislation," Announcement of the Formation of the Euthanasia Society (1938)

Announcement was made Jan. 16, 1938, of the formation in New York City of a National Society for the Legalization of Euthanasia, commonly known as "mercy-killing." The group forming the Board of Directors and the Advisory Board of the new society includes over fifty eminent American and British men and women with representatives from the legal, medical, educational, ministerial, and literary professions. Members of the faculties of Harvard, Cornell, Ohio State, California, Chicago, Smith, McGill, Duke, Vermont, Wisconsin, Indiana, and Oxford Universities are included.

The purposes of the Society embrace not only the conducting of a national campaign of education on the subject and the maintenance of a central headquarters for information and free literature, but also the preparation and introduction of bills into state legislatures and at Washington.

The establishing of the Euthanasia Society is in response to a real need increasingly recognized by the thoughtful people of this country. I have in my office letters from over fifty eminent men and women of this country and England enthusiastically accepting my invitation to serve on the Advisory Board of the Euthanasia Society. These letters afford us a cross-section view of public sentiment. Only a few declinations were received and most of these were due to the fact that individuals did not want to expose to criticism the institutions with which they are connected. . . .

Personally, my experiences as a clergyman for many years have forced me to recognize the necessity for laws permitting euthanasia in certain cases and under proper restrictions. I have seen many middle-aged and elderly persons, mostly women, dying in prolonged agony from such diseases as cancer. They have begged me to bring them secretly some quick-acting poison pills to put them out of their misery.

More than that, I have known of cases where whole families have been forced to endure the terrible mental anguish of watching the tortured breathing of loved ones for weeks before the last gasp. The mental effect upon relatives of sufferers is of incalculable harm.

Those opponents of euthanasia who claim that a sufferer is only a coward if he or she wishes to end his life, forget that most such sufferers are much more concerned about the anguish they are causing their dear ones than they are about their own pain.

I sense a growing demand on the part of thoughtful people every-where that the ancient taboos should be lifted in order that the supreme mercy be no longer withheld from those who will certainly die within a few weeks or months but are kept alive only to suffer increasing anguish.

*Source*: Euthanasia Society archives, presently held by Choice In Dying, Washington, DC.

* * *

The Euthanasia Society of America initially failed to indicate that euthanasia should be voluntary, and speeches by Potter suggested that it might be applied to mentally incompetent persons.

To better understand the attitude toward the mentally defective and insane requires some knowledge of the eugenics movement, which advocated improvement in human behavior through control of inherited characteristics. This movement sprang from so-called social Darwinism, which was the mistaken application of Darwinian principles of natural selection to the economic and social positions of human beings.

---

## DOCUMENT 24: *Social Darwinism in American Thought,* Richard Hofstadter (1955)

---

During these same years when social Darwinism was under increasingly strong criticism among social theorists, it was being revived in a somewhat new guise in the literature of the eugenics movement. Accompanied by a flood of valuable genetic research carried on by physicians and biologists, eugenics seemed not so much a social philosophy as a science; but in the minds of most of its advocates it had serious consequences for social thought.

The theory of natural selection, which had assumed the transmission of parental variations, had greatly stimulated the study of heredity. Popular credulity about the scope and variety of hereditary traits had been almost boundless. Darwin's cousin, Francis Galton, had laid the foundations of the eugenics movement and coined its name during the years when Darwinism was being sold to the public. In the United States, Richard Dugdale had published in 1877 his study of *The Jukes,* which, although its author gave more credit to environmental factors than did many later eugenists, had nevertheless offered support to the common view that disease, pauperism, and immorality are largely controlled by inheritance. . . . It was not until the turn of the century that the eugenics movement took organized form, first in England and then in the United States. Eugenics then grew with such great rapidity that by 1915 it had reached the dimensions of a fad. While eugenics has never since been so widely discussed, it has proved to be the most enduring aspect of social Darwinism. . . .

The National Conference on Race Betterment in 1914 showed how thoroughly the eugenic ideal had made its way into the medical profession, the colleges, social work, and charitable organizations. The ideas of the movement began to receive practical application in 1907, when Indiana became the first state to adopt a sterilization law; by 1915 twelve states had passed similar measures.

Doubtless the rapid urbanization of American life, which created great slums in which were massed the diseased, the deficient, and the demented, had much to do with the rise of eugenics. The movement was also favored by a growing interest in philanthropy and increasing endowments for hospitals and charities and appropriations for public health. Especially stimulating to the study of mental disease and deficiency was the rapid expansion of American psychiatry after 1900. As more and more diseased and defective families in great cities came to the attention of physicians and social workers, it was easy to confuse the rising mass of known cases with a real increase. The influx of a large immigrant population from peasant countries of central and southern Europe, hard to assimilate because of rustic habits and language barriers, gave color to the notion that immigration was lowering the standard of American intelligence; at least so it seemed to nativists who assumed that glib command of English is a natural criterion of intellectual capacity. The apparent economic deceleration at the end of the century was also seen by many observers as the beginning of a national decline; and it was in accordance with the habits of a Darwinized era to find in this apparent social decline a biological deterioration associated with the disappearance of "the American type." . . .

Early eugenists tacitly accepted that identification of the "fit" with the upper classes and the "unfit" with the lower that had been characteristic of the older social Darwinism. Their warnings about the multiplication of morons at the lower end of the social scale, and their habit of speaking of the "fit" as if they were all native, well-to-do, college-trained citizens, sustained the old belief that the poor are held down by biological deficiency instead of environmental conditions. Their almost exclusive focus upon the physical and medical aspects of human life helped to distract public attention from the broad problems of social welfare.

*Source*: Richard Hofstadter, *Social Darwinism in American Thought*, rev. ed. (Boston: American Historical Association; Beacon Press, 1944; revised edition, 1955), 161–163 (references omitted).

\* \* \*

The focus on euthanasia of insane and mentally defective persons decreased over the next few years for several reasons. A poll among New
York State physicians indicated that more of them were in favor of
euthanasia for terminally ill persons than for so-called idiots and defectives. It seemed more likely that a bill could be passed that permitted
only mercy killing of hopelessly ill persons without mentioning institutionalized demented individuals. Finally, there was great revulsion
when Americans learned about the killing of defective individuals by
the Nazis.

## DOCUMENT 25: *Doctors of Infamy*, Alexander Mitscherlich and Fred Mielke (1949)

*The granting of "dying aid" in the case of incurable mental patients and*
*malformed or idiot children may be considered to be still within the legitimate*
*sphere of medical discussion. But as the "winnowing process" continued, it*
*moved more and more openly to purely political and ideological criteria for death,*
*whether the subjects were considered to be "undesirable racial groups," or*
*whether they had merely become incapable of supporting themselves. The cam-*
*ouflage around these murderous intentions is revealed especially by proof that*
*in the concentration camps prisoners were selected by the same medical con-*
*sultants who were simultaneously sitting in judgment over the destiny of mental*
*institution inmates. A sworn statement by the defendant Waldemar Hoven,*
*formerly camp physician at the Buchenwald concentration camp, sets forth,*
*among other things:*

In 1941 I learned that a so-called "euthanasia program" for the extermination of the feeble-minded and crippled in Germany had gone into
effect. The camp commandant, Koch, at the time assembled all the SS
officers in positions of authority in the camp and announced that he had
received secret orders from Himmler to the effect that all feeble-minded
and crippled camp inmates were to be killed. The commandant declared
that on orders from higher authority in Berlin all Jewish prisoners in the
Buchenwald concentration camp were to be included in this program of
extermination. In compliance with these orders some 300 or 400 Jewish
prisoners of various nationalities were shipped to the euthanasia station
at Bernburg for extermination.

*Source*: Alexander Mitscherlich and Fred Mielke, *Doctors of Infamy: The Story of*
*the Nazi Medical Crimes* (New York: Henry Schuman, 1949), 117–118.

\* \* \*

## ATTEMPTS TO LEGALIZE EUTHANASIA IN THE UNITED STATES

During the 1940s, the Euthanasia Society essentially had two activities: (1) to spread its message as widely as possible in speeches, on the radio, and in articles principally for magazines, and (2) to promote legislation permitting voluntary euthanasia. For example, according to the *Euthanasia Society Bulletin,* in March 1949 an audience of 421 people heard Dr. Howard Wilcox Haggard of Yale and Dr. Charles Francis Potter, President of the Euthanasia Society, speak at the Town Hall in New York City on the need for legalizing voluntary euthanasia. In the mid-1940s the society drew up a law that it hoped would be passed in New York State.

---

## DOCUMENT 26: Proposed New York State Law on Voluntary Euthanasia (1947)

---

### AN ACT TO AMEND THE PUBLIC HEALTH LAW, AND THE PENAL LAW, IN RELATION TO VOLUNTARY EUTHANASIA

*The People of the State of New York, represented in Senate and Assembly, do enact as follows:*

Section One

Chapter forty-nine of the laws of nineteen hundred nine, entitled *An act in relation to the public health, constituting chapter forty-five of the consolidated laws,* is hereby amended by adding thereto a new article, to be article fifteen, to read as follows:

*Article 15*
*VOLUNTARY EUTHANASIA*

Section 300. Definitions.
      301. Who may receive euthanasia.
      302. Jurisdiction of courts.
      303. Application to court.
      304. Investigation and report of committee appointed by court.
      305. Administration of euthanasia.
      306. Immunity from criminal or civil liability.

---

*Sec. 300. Definitions.* As used in this article:

"Euthanasia" means the termination of human life by painless means for the purpose of ending severe physical suffering.

"Patient" means the person desiring to receive euthanasia.

"Physician" means any person licensed to practice medicine in the state of New York.

*Sec. 301. Who may receive euthanasia.* Any person of sound mind over twenty-one years of age who is suffering from severe physical pain caused by a disease for which no remedy affording lasting relief or recovery is at the time known to medical science may have euthanasia administered.

The desire to anticipate death by euthanasia under these conditions shall not be deemed to indicate mental impairment.

*Sec. 302. Jurisdiction of courts.* Any judge of a court of record of the city or county, or any justice of the Supreme Court of the judicial district, in which the patient resides or may be, to whom a petition for euthanasia is presented, shall have jurisdiction of and shall grant euthanasia upon the conditions and in conformity with the provisions of this article.

*Sec. 303. Application to court.* A petition for euthanasia must be in writing signed by the patient in the presence of two witnesses who must add their signatures and the post-office addresses of their domicile. Such petition must be made in the following form:

To the_____Court

I_____residing at_____hereby declare as follows:

I am_____years of age and am suffering severe physical pain caused, as I am advised by my physician, by a disease for which no remedy affording lasting relief or recovery is at this time known to medical science.

I am desirous of anticipating death by euthanasia and hereby petition for permission to receive euthanasia.

The names and addresses of the following persons are as follows or, if unknown to me, I so state:

Father_____

Mother_____

Spouse_____

Children_____

Uncles_____

Aunts_____

Signed_____

In the presence of

_____residing at_____

_____residing at_____

Date_____

Such petition must be accompanied by a certificate signed by the patient's attending physician in the following form:

To the_____Court

I_____of_____

do hereby certify as follows:

I have attended the patient,_____

since_____

It is my opinion and belief that the patient is suffering severe physical pain caused by a disease for which no remedy affording lasting relief or recovery is at the present time known to medical science.

The disease from which the patient is suffering is known as

_____

I am satisfied that the patient understands the nature and purpose of the petition in support of which this certificate is issued and that such disease comes within the provisions of section three hundred one of article fifteen of the Public Health Law.

Signature_____

Date_____Medical Qualifications_____

If, for any reason, the patient is unable to write, he may execute the petition by making his mark which shall be authenticated in the manner provided by law.

*Sec. 304. Investigation and report of committee appointed by court.* The judge or justice to whom a petition for euthanasia has been presented shall appoint a committee of three competent persons, who are not opposed to euthanasia as herein provided, of whom at least two must be physicians and members of a county or district medical society, who shall forthwith examine the patient and such other persons as they deem advisable or as the court may direct and, within five days after their appointment, shall report to the court whether or not the patient understands the nature and purpose of the petition and comes within the provisions of section three hundred one of this article. The court must either grant or deny the petition within three days of the coming in of such report, exclusive of Saturdays and Sundays.

The said committee shall serve without compensation.

If the said committee or any two members thereof report in the affirmative the court shall grant the petition unless there is reason to believe that the report is erroneous or untrue, in which case the court shall state in writing the reason for denying the petition.

From an order denying a petition for euthanasia an appeal shall lie to the appellate division of the supreme court.

*Sec. 305. Administration of euthanasia.* When the petition has been granted as herein provided, euthanasia shall be administered in the presence of the committee, or any two members thereof, appointed according to section 304 of this article, by a person chosen by the patient or by said committee, or any two members thereof, with the patient's consent; but no person shall be obliged to administer or to receive euthanasia against his will.

*Sec. 306. Immunity from criminal or civil liability.* A person to whom euthanasia has been administered under the conditions of this act shall not be deemed to have died a violent or unnatural death nor shall any physician or person who has administered or assisted in the administration thereof be deemed to have committed any offense criminal or civil, or be liable to any person whatever for damages or otherwise.

Section Two

The penal law is hereby amended by adding thereto a new section, to be section ten hundred fifty-six, to read as follows:

*Sec. 1056. Application of article to euthanasia.* Death resulting from euthanasia administered pursuant to and in accordance with the provisions of article fifteen of the public health law shall not constitute a crime or be punishable under any provisions of this act.

Section Three

This act shall take effect immediately.

*Source*: New York State law proposed in 1947.

\* \* \*

In the hope of influencing the New York State legislature, the Euthanasia Society publicized a statement on the ethical aspects of the legalization of voluntary euthanasia signed by fifty religious leaders of New York City. They included Dr. Henry Sloan Coffin, president of Union Theological Seminary, and Dr. David E. Roberts and Dr. Henry P. Van Dusen, its deans; Dr. Guy Emery Shipler, editor of the *Churchman*; Dr. Harry Emerson Fosdick, pastor of the Riverside Church; Dr. George Paul T. Sargent, rector of St. Bartholomew's Episcopal Church; and Dr. Ralph W. Sockman, of the Methodist Christ Church. Physicians were also solicited by a distinguished committee; 1,100 New York State physicians signed the following petition.

## DOCUMENT 27: Petition to the Legislature of the State of New York from Physicians (1947)

**Whereas**, large numbers of our population, notwithstanding the advance of medical science, suffer from painful diseases for which neither prevention, cure, nor lasting relief has been found, and

**Whereas**, the proportion of the aged in our population, who are subject to the painful, chronic, degenerative diseases, is rapidly increasing and the death rate from cancer reached a new high in 1946, and

**Whereas**, many incurable sufferers, facing months of agony, attempt crude, violent methods of suicide; while in other cases distraught relatives of hopeless incurables who plead for merciful release, secretly put them out of their misery and thereby render themselves liable to prosecution as murderers, and

**Whereas**, to permit the termination of useless, hopeless suffering at the request of the sufferer is in accord with the humane spirit of this age, therefore be it

**Resolved** that voluntary euthanasia (merciful release petitioned for by an incurable sufferer) should be permitted by law, brought out into the open and safeguarded against abuse rather than, as at present, practiced illegally, surreptitiously and without supervision or regulation; and be it further

**Resolved** that we, the undersigned, members of the Committee of 1776 Physicians for Legalization of Voluntary Euthanasia in New York State, hereby petition the legislature of the State of New York to amend the law to permit voluntary euthanasia for incurable sufferers, when authorized by a Court of Record, upon receipt of a signed and attested petition from the sufferer and after investigation of the case by a medical committee designated by the Court.

*Source*: Euthanasia Society archives, presently held by Choice In Dying, Washington, DC.

\* \* \*

In 1949, a petition signed by 387 Protestant and Jewish clergy of New York State was presented to the New York State legislature; 63 percent of the signers were from outside the boroughs of New York City. The proposed New York State law as well as bills proposed in Connecticut and New Jersey in the 1950s failed to reach the floor of the legislatures.

## DOCUMENT 28: Petition to the Legislature of the State of New York from Ministers (1949)

**We, the undersigned Ministers of Religion**, taking note of the fact that a distinguished company of a thousand physicians of New York State have courageously advocated the legalization of voluntary euthanasia, desire to affirm our conviction also that the ending of the physical existence of an individual at his request, when afflicted with an incurable disease which causes extreme suffering is, under proper safeguards, not only medically indicated, but also in accord with the most civilized and humane ethics and the highest concepts and practices of religion.

**Our profession** takes us constantly into the presence of sickness and death. Every one of us has seen suffering which has passed beyond any possibility of an ennobling effect upon character and has become protracted torture, when the only merciful prayer would be that the end might come speedily. We have seen the degradation and disintegration of personality through the prolonging of existence by the administration of deadening drugs.

**Since humanity** was endowed by its Creator with powers that entail the responsibility to determine human destiny, powers which are increasingly exercised in the light of growing knowledge, we believe we must not shirk the responsibilities of mercy.

**We believe** in the sacredness of the human personality, but not in the worth of mere existence or "length of days." We no longer believe that God wills the prolongation of physical torture for the benefit of the soul of the sufferer. For one enduring continual and severe pain from an incurable disease, who is a burden to himself and his family, surely life has no value.

**We believe** that such a sufferer has the right to die, and that society should grant this right, showing the same mercy to human beings as to the sub-human animal kingdom. "Blessed are the merciful."

**Resolved**, therefore, that we, the undersigned ministers of religion in New York State, hereby petition the Legislature of the State of New York to amend the law to permit voluntary euthanasia for incurable sufferers, when authorized by a Court of Record, upon receipt of a signed and attested petition from the sufferer, and after investigation of the case by a medical committee designated by the Court.

*Source*: Euthanasia Society archives, presently held by Choice In Dying, Washington, DC.

* * *

In 1952, the British and American Euthanasia Societies hoped to gain support from the United Nations Commission on Human Rights by drafting a petition signed by 356 prominent Britons and 2,157 prominent Americans. About one-third of the American signatories were physicians, one-third were clergymen, and one-third were prominent in the fields of science, law, education, and the arts. Although Eleanor Roosevelt, the chairperson of the commission, was sympathetic, she thought that it was an inopportune time to present the petition. It was never resubmitted.

## DOCUMENT 29: Petition to the United Nations for Amendment of the Declaration of Human Rights to Include the Right of Incurable Sufferers to Voluntary Euthanasia, (1952)

If the rights proclaimed in the Declaration of Human Rights as approved by the United Nations' General Assembly are to be fully realized and enjoyed by mankind, it is essential that a further right be recognized and observed—the right of incurable sufferers to euthanasia or merciful death.

In Article 5, the Declaration states, "No one shall be subjected to torture." This freedom cannot be fully assured unless sufferers from the torture of prolonged and painful incurable disease, for which no lasting relief is known, may legally secure release by death.

According to the preamble of the Declaration, we aspire to "a world in which human beings shall enjoy . . . freedom from fear. . . ." Then let us relieve them from fear of a slow, painful death, by granting them the right to prompt release from incurable suffering, should they ever be subjected to it.

The preamble further declares that "the recognition of the inherent dignity . . . of all members of the human family is the foundation of freedom. . . ." But the dignity of the human being is degraded, his personality is disintegrated, by suffering that breaks down his self-control, or by the repeated administration of deadening drugs for the temporary relief of such suffering.

In Articles 3 and 18 the Declaration states, "Everyone has the right to life, liberty and the security of person . . . to freedom of . . . conscience and religion." But the *right* to life does not mean the obligation to live:— a humane society will not condemn its members to live when life is nothing but prolonged suffering. By granting incurables the right to merciful release, society would confer no power upon the state to deprive anyone of life, liberty or security of person. Whether the individual sufferer would avail himself of the the [*sic*] right would depend entirely upon his own volition; he would have complete freedom to act in accordance with the dictates of his own conscience or religion.

Inasmuch as this right is, then, not only consonant with the rights and freedoms set forth in the Declaration of Human Rights but essential to their realization, we hereby petition the United Nations to proclaim the right of incurable sufferers to euthanasia.

*Source*: Euthanasia Society archives, presently held by Choice In Dying, Washington, DC.

\* \* \*

## OPPOSITION TO THE EUTHANASIA MOVEMENT

While many among the more liberal Protestant and Jewish clergy endorsed the euthanasia movement, the Catholic hierarchy and more conservative Protestant and Jewish communities were strongly opposed to it, as the following newspaper articles demonstrate.

## DOCUMENT 30: "Euthanasia Critics Lauded by Cardinal," *New York Herald Tribune* (May 7, 1950)

He Praises Stand of World Medical Association

A statement by Francis Cardinal Spellman commending the World Medical Association for condemning euthanasia will be published today and next Sunday by the Roman Catholic press of forty-eight nations, according to word received here yesterday from the National Catholic Welfare Conference in Washington. The Cardinal's statement was the result of a cablegram to the World Medical Association's headquarters a few days ago from Copenhagen, where its legislative council adopted a resolution decrying the theory that physicians might put their patients out of pain by death.

The world association called this doctrine "contrary to public interest

and to medical ethical principles as well as to natural and civil rights."
It urged national medical associations to adopt similar resolutions.

In the light of this action, Cardinal Spellman said: "The condemnation
of euthanasia by the World Medical Association should be highly commended by all moral-minded people.

"It is, in fact, a reaffirmation that the members of this association accept as rules of their daily practiced [sic] the commandment of God,
'Thou Shalt not kill,' and the promises which they made in their Hippocratic oath.

"The world has impatiently awaited such a pronouncement of moral
and ethical principles by the medical profession ever since its reputation
was besmirched by the assertions of the euthanasiasts that many physicians were secretly practicing mercy killing of the sick, and that most
physicians approved of such practices, which alleged facts were advanced as reasons for legalizing medical murder."

*Source*: "Euthanasia Critics Lauded by Cardinal," *New York Herald Tribune*, May
7, 1950.

---

## DOCUMENT 31: "Presbyterian Council Opposes Mercy Killing," *Jacksonville, Illinois, Journal* (May 24, 1951)

Cincinnati, May 23—(AP)—The General Council of the Phesbyterian
[sic] Church in the U.S.A. today expressed official opposition to a movement to legalize mercy killing.

Dr. Jesse H. Baird, San Francisco, council chairman, said the general
assembly, which meets tomorrow, will be asked to take action.

The assembly will be requested "to issue such a statement on the Presbyterian attitude toward this problem as will inform our church of the
serious danger inherent in the movement."

The council pointed out many Protestant clergymen, "including members of our own church," have signed petitions advocating the legalizing
of mercy killing.

"Euthanasia is in direct conflict with the interpretation of the Sixth
Commandment and legislation would open the door to more dangerous
and vicious practices," the council said in a report.

"Any encouragement given by our church to practice euthanasia or to
legislation permitting it, would be contrary to our standards and dangerous to the well being of the nation."

*Source*: "Presbyterian Council Opposes Mercy Killing," *Jacksonville, Illinois, Journal*, May 24, 1951.

* * *

Many physician groups also opposed euthanasia. For example, the New York State Medical Society, representing some 25,000 physicians in the state, adopted a resolution stating its opposition.

---

## DOCUMENT 32: Resolution of the New York State Medical Society (1950)

---

Life is God-given and precious and the art and science of medicine will some day discover the cure for diseases now incurable—therefore, be it resolved that the Medical Society of the State of New York go on record as being unalterably opposed to euthanasia and to any legislation that will legalize euthanasia.

*Source*: Resolution of the New York State Medical Society, quoted in the *Los Angeles, California, Tidings*, May 19, 1950.

* * *

### MERCY KILLINGS

A number of so-called mercy killings took place between 1938 and 1953. These were deaths caused by a relative or close friend who could not bear the patient's suffering. Such deaths were given considerable newspaper publicity. A typical example is the case of Carol Paight.

---

## DOCUMENT 33: "Cancer Haunted Paight Family," *New York Journal-American* (September 28, 1949)

---

STAMFORD, Conn., Sept. 28, (AP)—A grief-stricken mother asked sympathy and understanding today for pretty Carol Paight who fatally shot her cancer-ridden father in his hospital bed rather than see him suffer.

Mrs. Mary Nolan Paight, reining her grief and anxiety, disclosed that Police Sergt. Carl W. Paight was the third member of her family to become victim of the malady and said:

"Carol knew the terrible pain of the victim of cancer and the terrible strain on those who have to stand by and wait for death of their loved ones."

She said she was thankful for the hundreds of messages of comfort and consolation which have come in the wake of the tragic case, and added that "all I ask is that sympathy and understanding be given Carol."

## CHARGED WITH HOMICIDE

Carol, charged with homicide, waits action by a Fairfield County grand jury. Police Chief John B. Brennan quoted Carol as saying she shot her father "because I didn't want to see him suffer."

Mrs. Paight said that her husband's sister, Mrs. Agnes Paight Coulson, died of cancer when Carol was a child.

"Carl and I often talked of the dread disease in front of Carol without realizing she was storing our talk in her memory," said Mrs. Paight, a New York City school teacher for many years.

"Five years ago when my aunt, Mrs. Alice Dyer, died of cancer," she continued, "Carol was old enough to realize what the disease does."

Carol, 20-year-old college student, was with her mother last Friday, when Dr. William E. Smith reported to them that Sergeant Paight had inoperable cancer.

## PRAYED AT CHURCH

Mrs. Paight said she and Carol had returned to the hospital after praying at St. Mary's Church that surgeons would not find malignancy.

"The news was shocking to both of us," she said, "but it did something to Carol."

"Carol became hysterical and pleaded again and again that 'Daddy not be told he had cancer.' "

Carol left the hospital with her mother after the talk with Dr. Smith, only to return later with her father's service revolver and shoot him through the head. Paight died several hours later.

*Source*: "Cancer Haunted Paight Family," *New York Journal-American*, September 28, 1949.

* * *

A jury made up entirely of parents did not acquit Carol Paight, but found her temporarily insane, although the state prosecution made much of the fact that she fired a practice shot from her father's revolver to be sure she knew how to operate the gun. Applause in the courtroom greeted the verdict. The following editorial sums up the attitude of many.

## DOCUMENT 34: "Murder, Mercy and the Law," *New York Daily News* (October 2, 1949)

The other day in Stamford, Conn., a 20-year-old girl named Carol Paight was informed by physicians that her father, Police Sergt. Carl Paight, was hopelessly riddled with cancer.

The girl was devoted to her father. She brooded for a while over the pain he might suffer before the end should come in due course. Then she slipped into the hospital room where he was still under an anesthetic after an exploratory operation, and, using the officer's own service revolver, fired one bullet into his head. He died four hours later.

A couple of days after that, in Scituate, Mass., a 15-year-old boy named Francis E. Whorf confessed to having killed his father, by drilling him with a bullet behind one ear while the elder Whorf lay sleeping.

The boy explained that he had done the deed "for the good of the family." It seems the father had beaten up his wife at least once recently, had done time in an institution for alcoholics, and was generally a nuisance around the house.

Here we have two cases of mercy killing. The girl killed her father to save him from a more or less slow and agonizing death from cancer. The boy shot his father as, in his view, an act of mercy for the rest of the family.

What makes these cases especially grim is the extreme likelihood that both of the slain men were better off dead than alive, when you look at the tragedies from a detached point of view.

There was no hope for Sergt. Paight, stricken with cancer discovered too late for an operation to cure him. Young Whorf's father was undoubtedly a burden to his family, and quite conceivably a burden to himself.

The Paight killing proceeded from a daughter's deep affection for a stricken father, the Whorf affair from a boy's heartfelt concern for his mother and brother.

In both cases there were all the elements of true tragedy—pity, terror, the irony of Fate, the helplessness of poor human beings caught up by forces which they can only half understand.

Whenever one of these mercy killings comes to light—as do a considerable number of them each year—a lot of warmhearted people clamor that the law ought to make exceptions in such cases.

Pressures are brought on the prosecuting attorney either not to ask [for] an indictment at all or to hint broadly to the jury, if the case comes to trial, that the state wants no more than a minimum sentence or an acquittal. Most prosecutors, so far as we know, habitually resist such pressure, and pursue the matter as energetically as if it were just an ordinary murder.

We believe that any prosecutor who acts in this manner is to be commended and deserves the gratitude of the community he serves. What other course can be followed without the gravest consequences to society in general?

Suppose it became part of our unwritten law that mercy killers could count on mercy from the authorities? Such private executions would almost surely increase greatly in number per year in this country. Also, many a coldblooded, sordid murder of an unwanted old person or baby would be dressed up to look like a mercy killing, and it seems a certainty that a considerable percentage of killers would go scot free.

In self-defense, society has always had to have laws against murder, and as strict enforcement of those laws as possible, men and women being what they are.

Begin making exceptions, so that people can safely take the law into their own hands, under some circumstances, and the end result could be a breakdown of what law and order we still have in the United States. To be blunt, we don't have too much law and order now.

Even the backers of euthanasia—painless death for hopelessly ill persons—do not suggest that families do the putting-away on their own initiative. Under proposed euthanasia statutes, the patient would have to request release, and the request would be passed upon by more than one physician. Euthanasia laws still seem a long way off, because of strong opposition from various religious groups.

Until and unless such measures are enacted, it looks to us as if public officials have no choice but to prosecute every deliberate killer under the law as written, pitiful though the circumstances in some cases undeniably are.

*Source*: "Murder, Mercy and the Law," Editorial, *New York Daily News*, October 2, 1949.

\* \* \*

In 1954 the *Euthanasia Society Bulletin* published a summary of the fate of twenty-six so-called mercy killers.

## DOCUMENT 35: "What Is the Fate of 'Mercy Killers'?" *Euthanasia Society Bulletin* (November–December 1954)

In 26 cases of which we have complete records, 10 committed suicide; four were committed to a House of Correction; two were committed to an insane asylum, but immediately released; two were sentenced to death, but the sentence was suspended; one was committed to a state hospital for the insane; one was sentenced to death, but the sentence was commuted to life imprisonment; three were acquitted on the formal charge of temporary insanity; one was acquitted on the absurd assumption that the sufferer had been dead already when her doctor injected air into her veins; one was sentenced to two years in prison, but immediately released on probation; and one was sentenced to 6–15 years in prison, but was released after five years.

In not a single case was the penalty of death actually inflicted. Courts do not enforce the law, and it should be amended.

*Source*: "What Is the Fate of 'Mercy Killers'?" *Euthanasia Society Bulletin* 4, no. 12 (November–December 1954).

* * *

Luis Kutner, the lawyer who proposed the living will (see Part IV), discussed the legal aspects of mercy killing. A portion of his discussion follows.

---

## DOCUMENT 36: "Due Process of Euthanasia: The Living Will, a Proposal," Luis Kutner (1969)

---

Clearly, although conceptually the law does not treat mercy killing differently from other cases involving the taking of human life, in practice an exception does exist. Prosecutors, judges and juries do approach a mercy killing case differently. Public opinion simply does not reflect the same revulsion against an act of mercy killing that it does towards other instances of murder. Therefore, society is not prone to inflict the same type of punishment. Although there may be opposition to mercy killing in principle, there is sympathy for the mercy killer. Significantly, in *People v. Roberts*, one of the few cases where a mercy killer was convicted of first degree murder and sentenced to life imprisonment, the decision was rendered by a judge without a jury.

Invariably, because of the human interest element involved, a mercy killing case will receive wide press coverage and focus public attention. The tendency is for public sympathy to side with the defendant. . . . Although objection may be made as to this treatment of mercy killers, it is necessary to separate what may be regarded as the "ought" from the "is." The judicial process as it "is," deals differently with mercy killers. The defendant may be not prosecuted, found innocent because of insanity, or found guilty of a lesser offense then [*sic*] murder and given a light sentence. . . .

This survey indicates that the law effecting [*sic*] euthanasia in practice differs from its conceptual basis in that, in practice, the judicial process treats a mercy killer differently from a murderer with malice. The criminal code is in need of adaptation to account for this situation. The suggested approach is to adopt the standard of motive as indicated by the codes of other legal systems. The punishment for an accused who killed at the request of the victim, where the victim was suffering from an incurable disease and was in great pain, would be milder than in other incidents of homicide. A somewhat harsher, but still mild punishment, would be inflicted upon the accused who killed where the victim did not request to be killed or was incapable of giving his rational consent, but was suffering from an apparent physical or mental affliction and there was no element of malice or personal gain. Such an approach would accord with notions of due process. It is submitted that to subject the accused to life imprisonment or execution would constitute excessively cruel and inhumane punishment in contravention to the eighth amendment of the Constitution.

*Source*: Luis Kutner, "Due Process of Euthanasia: The Living Will, a Proposal," *Indiana Law Journal* 44 (1969): 539–554 (notes omitted).

## FURTHER READING

Clendening, Logan. *Source Book of Medical History*. New York: Dover Publications, 1960.
President's Commission for the Study of Ethical Problems in Medicine and Biomedical and Behavioral Research. *Deciding to Forego Life-Sustaining Treatment*. Washington, DC: U.S. Government Printing Office, 1981.
Russell, O. Ruth. *Freedom to Die: Moral and Legal Aspects of Euthanasia*. New York: Human Sciences Press, 1975.

# Part III

# Changes in Medical Care and the Way We Die: The Euthanasia Movement, 1953– 1965

## THE IMPACT OF CHANGES IN MEDICAL CARE ON THE END OF LIFE

Although the causes of death and the mortality rate changed very little between 1950 and 1965 (see Document 19 in Part II), the ability of physicians to prolong the lives of desperately ill persons increased during that period and thereafter. It became possible to provide artificial ventilation for prolonged periods when respiration failed. Cardiopulmonary resuscitation could often restart the heartbeat and breathing when they had ceased. Patients could be fed by infusion or, for indefinite periods, by gastric intubation. Fluids and blood products were readily available to maintain the circulation of blood. Chemotherapy could prolong the life of many cancer patients.

This increased ability to maintain the life of mortally ill patients created a dilemma for physicians: When, if ever, should they stop treatment? The following article by Dr. Edward H. Rynearson was published in a special issue of a journal devoted to care of patients dying of cancer.

## DOCUMENT 37: "You Are Standing at the Bedside of a Patient Dying of Untreatable Cancer," Edward H. Rynearson (1959)

Because I wish to personalize my remarks and define my parameters, I have adopted a title which emphasizes that I address myself to the INDIVIDUAL physician who is seeing an INDIVIDUAL patient dying of a cancer for which every conceivable avenue of treatment has been explored with total failure, and this patient, moreover, is suffering excruciating pain and is pleading for release. There are too many instances, in my opinion, in which patients in such a situation are kept alive indefinitely by means of tubes inserted into their stomachs, or into their veins, or into their bladders, or into their rectums—and the whole sad scene thus created is encompassed within a cocoon of oxygen which is the next thing to a shroud. Certain tissue cultures have kept cells living for so many years that they have fulfilled their usefulness and have been thrown out; we have used much of the information thus gained in an inverse manner, meaning that with all the fluids, vitamins, electrolytes, protein supplements, antibiotics, hormones and other agents available to us now we can keep people suffering for an indeterminate number of months. Moreover, although the point is not related to the subject of cancer, we all know of many instances in which persons have been kept alive for years in a near-decerebrate state after massive damage to the brain caused by a stroke, an injury or infection.

The present piece has nothing to do with euthanasia, nor am I talking about any patient in whom there is any question as to the diagnosis. I refer to the patient who is almost in extremis; this unfortunate state has been established beyond any doubt, for the physician and his associates are in unanimous agreement, and there is no question in anyone's mind as to the prognosis. This patient already has undergone surgical exploration, chemotherapy, radiation therapy—and perhaps, also, if the resources of surgery have been pushed to the ultimate—castration, adrenalectomy and hypophysectomy. Despite all the impressive ministrations science can provide, he is still dying and is still suffering. There simply is no other treatment to apply now, for there is no treatment for death (and may I add that in my opinion many of the so-called extraordinary measures are not often indicated). Neither can the true physician bolster the onus of his own doubts and uncertainties by transferring them to the shoulders of the dying person's relatives or friends. . . .

. . . In a situation of the dying patient, one has to consider:

1. The philosophies of the one who is dying, of the living family and of the medical attendants.

2. The fact that society itself has traditional values which are accorded to life and death and which must be taken into account; however, these values should be of less importance than those very personal values as decided by the patient and his family.

3. The fact that there are certain unconscious elements, such as the feeling on the part of some relatives that they are somehow guilty in the presence of impending death, and that this ill-founded sense of guilt needs to be defended by prolongation of the life of the victim; superstitions may be at hand which need to be propitiated, or a personal anxiety born of a relative's identification with the dying person may need to be ameliorated somehow.

One must also remember that religious values interwoven in the process of death sometimes are viewed in different ways:

1. In some cases death is viewed as a punishment—an end, rather than a beginning.

2. In other cases death is accepted as a natural terminus—simple, factual, unemotional.

3. Sometimes death is viewed as a reward—a beatific vision, union with the eternal and so on.

It need not be emphasized here that all cultures, from the most primitive to the most advanced, have death rites and that in our country these rites can take all forms, for we have at least the residuum of all cultures. What then should be the components of the care of the dying patient?

1. He should die with dignity, respect and humanity.

2. He should die with minimal pain.

3. He should have the opportunity to recall the love and benefits of a lifetime of sharing; he and his family and friends should visit together, if the patient so wishes.

4. He should be able to clarify relationships—to express wishes—to share sentiments.

5. The patient and relatives should plan intelligently for the changes which death imposes upon the living.

6. The patient should die in familiar surroundings, if possible; if not, then quietus should take place in surroundings made as near homelike as possible.

7. Finally, but importantly, there should be concern for the feelings of the living.

If these two things are certain: first, that the patient is dying of a malignant process for which there can be no treatment, and second, that the patient, his relatives and his spiritual adviser are aware of the situation, then what I am suggesting is that the physician should do all he can to alleviate the patient's suffering and make no effort to prolong his life.

In discussing this conviction, I have received three comments or questions. The first is: "You are trying to play God." I reject this charge, for I believe that it is actually the physician who, by using extraordinary measures, prolongs life and suffering is the one who "plays God."

Second is the query: "What do physicians do?" Well, that has been answered innumerable times, and many of the instances in question are in my own practice and among my own friends. Most physicians do not ask for anything more than kindness and comfort; they are likely specifically to oppose "heroic measures."

Every physician worthy of the name shrinks from the "I:it" relationship with his patient and, rather, embraces the "I:thou" apposition, for his daily labors remind him only too forcefully that one day he, too, may be the patient.

Third is the question: "What would you do if this occurred in your own family?" I have had the answer to such a problem for some years gone by, for the travail and misfortune I am speaking about did occur to a member of my immediate family. We kept her in her own bed in her own home and made certain she suffered as little as possible until she was released by death.

I conclude by saying that when I am at the bedside of a patient dying of untreatable cancer, I make the decisions I have recorded here. But now YOU are standing at another bedside and YOU must make YOUR decision.

*Source*: Edward H. Rynearson, "You Are Standing at the Bedside of a Patient Dying of Untreatable Cancer," *CA–Bull. Cancer Progr.* 9 (1959): 85–87.

* * *

Pope Pius XII courageously confronted a portion of the issue of when to stop treatment in an address to the International Congress of Anesthesiologists in 1957.

## DOCUMENT 38: "The Prolongation of Life," Pope Pius XII (1957)

Does [the doctor] have the right, or is he bound, in all cases of deep unconsciousness, even in those that are considered to be completely hopeless . . . , to use modern artificial respiration apparatus . . . ? . . . In most cases this situation arises, not at the beginning of resuscitation attempts, but when the patient's condition, after a slight improvement at first, remains stationary and it becomes clear that only automatic artificial respiration is keeping him alive. . . .

The solution to this problem, already difficult in itself, becomes even more difficult when the family—themselves Catholic perhaps—insist that the doctor in charge, especially the anesthesiologist, remove the artificial respiration apparatus in order to allow the patient, who is already virtually dead, to pass away in peace. . . .

. . . normally one is held to use only ordinary means—according to circumstances of persons, places, times, and culture—that is to say, means that do not involve any grave burden for oneself or another. . . . On the other hand, one is not forbidden to take more than the strictly necessary steps to preserve life and health, as long as he does not fail in some more serious duty. . . .

The rights and duties of the doctor are correlative to those of the patient. The doctor, in fact, has no separate or independent right where the patient is concerned. In general he can take action only if the patient explicitly or implicitly, directly or indirectly, gives him permission. The technique of resuscitation which concerns us here does not contain anything immoral in itself. Therefore the patient, if he were capable of making a personal decision, could lawfully use it and, consequently, give the doctor permission to use it. On the other hand, since these forms of treatment go beyond the ordinary means to which one is bound, it cannot be held that there is an obligation to use them nor, consequently, that one is bound to give the doctor permission to use them.

The rights and duties of the family depend in general upon the presumed will of the unconscious patient if he is of age and "sui juris". Where the proper and independent duty of the family is concerned, they are usually bound only to use ordinary means.

Consequently, if it appears that the attempt at resuscitation constitutes in reality such a burden for the family that one cannot in all conscience impose it upon them, they can lawfuly insist that the doctor should discontinue these attempts, and the doctor can lawfully comply.

*Source*: Pope Pius XII, "The Prolongation of Life," *The Pope Speaks* 4, no. 4 (1958).

\* \* \*

## EUTHANASIA

During the period 1953–65, the Euthanasia Society of America functioned as an educational organization, providing speakers to organizational meetings and on the radio. No further attempts were made to pass legislation in this field. However, the increased ability to maintain life in mortally ill patients provided a new impetus to the discussion of euthanasia. Two influential books published in the mid-1950s contained chapters on euthanasia. One of these books was entitled *Morals and Medicine*, by Joseph Fletcher, professor of pastoral theology and Christian ethics at the Episcopal Theological School in Cambridge, Massachusetts, who was in favor of voluntary euthanasia.

---

## DOCUMENT 39: *Morals and Medicine*, Joseph Fletcher (1954)

Euthanasia, the deliberate easing into death of a patient suffering from a painful and fatal disease, has long been a troubling problem of conscience in medical care. For us in the Western world the problem arises, *pro forma*, out of a logical contradiction at the heart of the Hippocratic Oath. Our physicians all subscribe to that oath as the standard of their professional ethics. The contradiction is there because the oath promises two things: first, to relieve suffering, and second, to prolong and protect life. When the patient is in the grip of an agonizing and fatal disease, these two promises are incompatible. Two duties come into conflict. To prolong life is to violate the promise to relieve pain. To relieve the pain is to violate the promise to prolong and protect life. . . .

. . . In a limited space, perhaps the best procedure will be to speak directly to the ten most common and most important objections [to euthanasia]. Therefore, suppose we deal with them as if they stood one by one in a bill of particulars.

1. It is objected that euthanasia, when voluntary, is really suicide. If this is true, and it would seem to be obviously true, then the proper question is: have we ever a right to commit suicide? Among Catholic moralists the most common ruling is that "it is never permitted to kill oneself intentionally, without explicit divine inspiration to do." Humility requires us to assume that divine inspiration cannot reasonably be expected to occur either often or explicitly enough to meet the requirements of medical euthanasia. A plea for legal recognition of "man's inalienable right to die" is placed at the head of the physicians' petition to the New York State Assembly. Now, has man any such right, however limited and imperfect it may be? Surely he has, for otherwise the hero or martyr and all those who deliberately give their lives are morally at fault. It might be replied that there is a difference between the suicide, who is directly seeking to end his life, and the hero or martyr, who is seeking directly some other end entirely, death being only an undesired by-product. But to make this point is only to raise a question as to what

purposes are sufficient to justify the loss of one's life. If altruistic values, such as defense of the innocent, are enough to justify the loss of one's life (and we will all agree that they are), then it may be argued that personal integrity is a value worth the loss of life, especially since, by definition, there is no hope of relief from the demoralizing pain and no further possibility of serving others. To call euthanasia egoistic or self-regarding makes no sense, since in the nature of the case the patient is not choosing his own good rather than the good of others.

Furthermore, it is important to recognize that there is no ground, in a rational or Christian outlook, for regarding life itself as the *summum bonum*. . . . In the personalistic view of man and morals, asserted through-out these pages, personality is supreme over mere life. To prolong life uselessly, while the personal qualities of freedom, knowledge, self-possession and control, and responsibility are sacrificed is to attack the moral status of a person. It actually denies morality in order to submit to fatality. And in addition, to insist upon mere "life" invades religious interests as well as moral values. For to use analgesic agents to the point of depriving sufferers of consciousness is, by all apparent logic, incon-sistent even with the practices of sacramentalist Christians. The point of death for a human person *in extremis* is surely by their own account a time when the use of reason and conscious self-commitment is most meritorious; it is the time when a responsible competence in receiving such rites as the viaticum and extreme unction would be most necessary and its consequences most invested with finality.

2. It is objected that euthanasia, when involuntary, is murder. . . . peo-ple with a moral rather than a legal interest—doctors, pastors, patients, and their friends—will never concede that malice means only premedi-tation, entirely divorced from the motive and the end sought. These fac-tors are entirely different in euthanasia from the motive and the end in murder, even though the means—taking life—happens to be the same. If we can make no moral distinction between acts involving the same means, then the thrifty parent who saves in order to educate his children is no higher in the scale of merit than the miser who saves for the sake of hoarding. . . .

3. What of the common religious opinion that God reserves for himself the right to decide at what moment a life shall cease? . . . As to this doc-trine, it seems more than enough just to answer that if such a divine-monopoly theory is valid, then it follows with equal force that it is immoral to lengthen life. . . . Prolonging life, on this divine-monopoly view, when a life appears to be ending through natural or physical causes, is just as much an interference with natural determinism as mer-cifully ending a life before physiology does it in its own amoral way. . . .

4. It is also objected by religious moralists that euthanasia violates the Biblical command, "Thou shalt not kill." It is doubtful whether this kind

of Biblicism is any more valid than the vitalism we reject. Indeed, it is a form of fundamentalism, common to both Catholics and reactionary Protestants. . . .

Certainly those who justify war and capital punishment, as most Christians do, cannot condemn euthanasia on this ground. We might point out to the fundamentalists in the two major divisions of Western Christianity that the beatitude "Blessed are the merciful" has the force of a commandment too! The medical profession lives by it, has its whole *ethos* in it. But the simplest way to deal with this Christian text-proof objection might be to point out that the translation "Thou shalt not kill" is incorrect. It should be rendered, as in the responsive decalogue of the *Book of Common Prayer*, "Thou shalt do no murder," i.e., unlawful kill-ing. . . .

5. Another common objection in religious quarters is that suffering is a part of the divine plan for the good of man's soul, and must therefore be accepted. . . . If this simple and naive idea of suffering were a valid one, then we should not be able to give our moral approval to anesthetics or to provide any medical relief of human suffering. . . .

6. It is frequently pointed out, as an objection to euthanasia, that pa-tients pronounced incurable might recover after all, for doctors can and do make mistakes. This seems, frankly, like a fundamentally obstruc-tionist argument. It takes us back to the evasion based on fallibility with which we had to deal in the question of truth-telling. Doctors are indeed finite creatures. So they may also err in recommending and carrying out operations, or in other forms of treatment. As far as the accuracy of their advice is concerned, we have to trust them, although it is always our right to doubt their advice and to change doctors. If reluctance to trust them were a common attitude pervading medical relationships generally, it would spell the doom of medical care. Also, it is sometimes added that if we will just hang on something may turn up, perhaps a new discovery which will save us after all. Although this objection really evades the point at issue, it has a very great importance when seen in its own perspective. We always have ground for hope that many of the conditions which have called for euthanasia in the past will no longer do so. . . .

And there are, of course, occasional incidents of totally unexpected, last-minute recovery from "hopeless" illnesses. An actual case would be that of the hospital chaplain who once stood by at a "certain" death and a horrible one from pemphigus. The doctors had even advised that the patient's family be called in for a last visit. Then, at the last moment, a new penicillin drug was flown in from another city, and the patient was saved. Such things happen, yes. But all we need to say to this objection to euthanasia is that by no stretch of the imagination, in a typical situ-ation, can we foresee a discovery that will restore health to a life already running out. A patient dying of metastatic cancer may be considered already dead, though still breathing. In advanced cases, even if a cure were to be found, toxemia has in all likelihood damaged the tissues and organs fatally.

7. It is said, with some truth, that patients racked by pain might make impulsive and ill-considered requests for euthanasia, if it were morally and legally approved. To this there are two rejoinders: first, that a careful law, such as that of the Euthanasia Society, would provide that there must be medical advice that death is certain, which rules out any hasty euthanasia in non-fatal illnesses; and, second, that the law would provide an interval between application and administration. The law should not permit euthanasia to be done on the spur of the moment, and the patient should be free to withdraw his request at any time. The requirement that the disease must be of a fatal character is needed to guard against unconscious wishes for destruction which are to be seen sometimes, although rarely, in patients. The confirmation of the patient's and the attending physician's decisions by disinterested parties is a sufficient bulwark against impulsive action. This might also be the place to emphasize that a doctor is always free to refuse to administer medical euthanasia, as a patient ought to be free to request it. . . .

Connected with this is this further objection: what if the patient can no longer speak or even gesture intelligibly? Can we be sure we always understand the patient's real desire, his choice for or against death, especially in cases where his condition is nearly unconscious or comatose? We all know that communication is not solely verbal. The provision that the request must come from the patient in a documentary form is introduced in proposals like that of the Euthanasia Society out of great caution, presumably in the fear that a gesture or other sign might be misinterpreted. A restriction like this will also exclude the possibility of a doctor's carrying out euthanasia when the patient had expressed a desire for it but the formalities could not be fulfilled before his physical powers to apply had failed. . . .

8. Sometimes we hear it said that the moral and legal approval of euthanasia would weaken our moral fiber, tend to encourage us to minimize the importance of life. . . . It is very hard to find any real hope of taking hold of an objection like this, with its broad value-terms such as "moral fiber" and "the importance of life." It could just as easily be reasoned that to ask for euthanasia, to leave voluntarily for the unknown, would call for courage and resolution and faith, and would encourage us to live with faith and without fear of the unknown. . . .

9. It is objected that the ethics of a physician forbids him to take life. We have already recognized that fact *as a fact*, but the issue is raised precisely because there are cases when the doctor's duty to prolong and protect life is in conflict with his equal duty to relieve suffering. As a

matter of fact, this dilemma is actually inescapable and inherent in the medical care of many terminal illnesses anyway, at the technical as well as the moral level. If the physician's obligation is both to relieve pain and prolong life, how then can he use analgesics, which bring relief but have the necessary effect of hastening death? . . .

10. Finally, it is objected that doctors do not want euthanasia made legal. It is not at all uncommon to hear doctors admit that they generally engage in the practice, in one way or another. . . . From time to time there are reports, undocumentable but from usually reliable sources, of medical meetings such as one recently in the Middle West at which a speaker asked for a show of hands from those who have never administered euthanasia. Not a hand was raised. . . .

There are three other objections closely allied to these we have examined. They may deserve just a word or two. First, it is said that medical euthanasia would weaken medical research, that it would take away the incentive to find cures for painful maladies. This is nonsense because doctors are already practicing euthanasia and yet their fight against fatal diseases is mounting, not flagging. . . . Second, it is objected that the heirs or enemies of an invalid might use euthanasia to hasten his death. To this we reply that the legal requirement of a written application by the sufferer, and of both legal and medical investigations, would be a safeguard. He would have far more protection than is provided for many patients now committed for treatment of mental disorder. . . . Third, it is claimed that once we legalize mercy deaths the application of the principle will be widened disastrously to cover non-fatal illnesses. But why is it, then, that although legal killing by capital punishment has been in vogue a long time, yet it has been narrowed rather than extended in scope? In fact it has been narrowed a great deal from the days when people were hanged for stealing a few shillings.

*Source:* Joseph Fletcher, *Morals and Medicine* (Princeton, NJ: Princeton University Press, 1954), 172, 190–207 (notes omitted).

* * *

The second influential book was entitled *The Sanctity of Life and the Criminal Law,* by Glanville Williams, a British jurist. It was based on the Charpentier Lectures given at Columbia University and the Association of the Bar of the City of New York.

## DOCUMENT 40: *The Sanctity of Life and the Criminal Law,* Glanville Williams (1957)

[I]f it is true that euthanasia can be condemned only according to a religious opinion, this should be sufficient at the present day to remove the prohibition from the criminal law. . . .

The religious objection is principally the familiar one that killing falls under the ban of the Sixth Commandment. . . . [However, t]he true translation of the Sixth Commandment is not "Thou shalt not kill" but "Thou shalt do no murder," as the Book of Common Prayer has it; and it is only by a stretch of words that a killing with the patient's consent, to relieve him of inexpressible suffering, can morally be described as murder. If wholesale killing in war and the punitive killing of criminals are not "murder," surely a killing done with the patient's consent and for his benefit as an act of mercy can claim to be excluded from this ugly word. . . . Even on the religious hypothesis of a soul, to release the soul from the tortured body and set it at liberty is surely to confer a benefit upon it and not an injury.

*Source*: Glanville Williams, *The Sanctity of Life and the Criminal Law* (New York: Alfred A. Knopf, 1957), 312–314.

\* \* \*

Yale Kamisar, associate professor of law at the University of Minnesota Law School, wrote a lengthy reply to Williams's views on euthanasia.

## DOCUMENT 41: "Some Non-religious Views against Proposed 'Mercy-Killing' Legislation," Yale Kamisar (1958)

*If* a person is *in fact* (1) presently incurable, (2) beyond the aid of any respite which may come along in his life expectancy, suffering (3) intolerable and (4) unmitigable pain and of a (5) fixed and (6) rational desire to die, I would hate to have to argue that the hand of death should be stayed. But abstract propositions and carefully formed hypotheticals are one thing; specific proposals designed to cover everyday situations are something else again.

I see the issue, then, as the need for voluntary euthanasia versus (1) the incidence of mistake and abuse; and (2) the danger that legal machinery initially designed to kill those who are a nuisance to themselves may someday engulf those who are a nuisance to others. . . .

[T]he simple negative proposal to remove "mercy killings" from the ban of the criminal law is strenuously resisted on the ground that it offers the patient far too little protection from not-so-necessary or not-so-merciful killings. On the other hand, the elaborate affirmative proposals of the euthanasia societies meet much pronounced eye-blinking, not a few guffaws, and sharp criticism that the legal machinery is so drawn-out, so complex, so formal and so tedious as to offer the patient far too little solace.

*Source*: Yale Kamisar, "Some Non-religious Views against Proposed 'Mercy-Killing Legislation," *Minnesota Law Review* 42 (1958) 969–1042 (excerpts from pages 975, 976, 979).

## FURTHER READING

Fletcher, Joseph. *Morals and Medicine*. Princeton, NJ: Princeton University Press, 1954.

Russell, O. Ruth. *Freedom to Die: Moral and Legal Aspects of Euthanasia*. Rev. ed. New York: Human Sciences Press, 1977.

# Part IV

# Advance Directives: Their Legalization and Implementation

Improvements in sanitation, the discovery of antibiotics and chemotherapy, and the development of techniques for mechanical ventilation and artificial nutrition and hydration increased people's life spans enormously. For many individuals, this meant living to a reasonably healthy and comfortable old age. But for some, life became miserable, and for patients who were unconscious, it became meaningless. The wish to control one's fate, especially when one could no longer speak for oneself, led to the development of living wills or advance directives, that is, documents that leave instructions for one's treatment.

## THE ORIGINAL LIVING WILL

Luis Kutner (1908–1993) was a Chicago human rights lawyer who promoted his strong beliefs in human rights in several ways. He was a cofounder of Amnesty International in London, he campaigned for a worldwide habeas corpus code, and he was instrumental in obtaining the release of persons who had been unjustly held in prisons or mental hospitals. He conceived the "living will," a term that he coined. A living will is a document that states one's wishes about medical treatment at the end of life if one is unable to communicate them directly.

## DOCUMENT 42: "Due Process of Euthanasia: The Living Will, a Proposal," Luis Kutner (1969)

The law provides that a patient may not be subjected to treatment without his consent. But when he is in a condition in which his consent cannot be expressed, the physician must assume that the patient wishes to be treated to preserve his life. His failure to act fully to keep the patient alive in a particular instance may lead to liability for negligence. But it may well be that a patient does not desire to be kept in a state of indefinite vegetated animation. How then can the individual patient retain the right of privacy over his body—the right to determine whether he should be permitted to die, to permit his body to be given to the undertaker?

Where a patient undergoes surgery or other radical treatment, the surgeon or the hospital will require him to sign a legal statement indicating his consent to the treatment. The patient, however, while still retaining his mental faculties and the ability to convey his thoughts, could append to such a document a clause providing that, if his condition becomes incurable and his bodily state vegetative with no possibility that he could recover his complete faculties, his consent to further treatment would be terminated. The physician would then be precluded from prescribing further surgery, radiation, drugs or the running of resuscitating and other machinery, and the patient would be permitted to die by virtue of the physician's inaction.

The patient may not have had, however, the opportunity to give his consent at any point before treatment. He may have become the victim of a sudden accident or a stroke or coronary. Therefore, the suggested solution is that the individual, while fully in control of his faculties and his ability to express himself, indicate to what extent he would consent to treatment. The document indicating such consent may be referred to as "a *living will*," "a declaration determining the termination of life," "testament permitting death," "declaration for bodily autonomy," "declaration for ending treatment," "body trust," or other similar reference.

The document would provide that if the individual's bodily state becomes completely vegetative and it is certain that he cannot regain his mental and physical capacities, medical treatment shall cease. A Jehovah's Witness whose religious principles are opposed to blood transfusions could so provide in such a document. A Christian Scientist could, by virtue of such a document, indicate that he does not wish any medical treatment.

The document would be notarized and attested to by at least two witnesses who would affirm that the maker was of sound mind and acted of his own free will. The individual could carry the document on his person at all times, while his wife, his personal physician, a lawyer or confidant would have the original copy.

*Source*: Luis Kutner, "Due Process of Euthanasia: The Living Will, a Proposal," *Indiana Law Journal* 44 (1969): 539–554 (excerpt from pages 550–551) (notes omitted).

\* \* \*

After Kutner spoke at a meeting of the Euthanasia Society of America in 1967, the Euthanasia Society drew up a living will in response to his proposal. In 1967 the society formed the Euthanasia Educational Fund (later the Euthanasia Educational Council). The council reported that it had distributed a quarter of a million copies of the living will by 1973.

## DOCUMENT 43: Living Will Distributed by the Euthanasia Society (1972)

TO MY FAMILY, MY PHYSICIAN, MY CLERGYMAN, MY LAWYER—

If the time comes when I can no longer take part in decisions for my own future, let this statement stand as the testament of my wishes:

If there is no reasonable expectation of my recovery from physical or mental disability, I, _____ request that I be allowed to die and not be kept alive by artificial means or heroic measures. Death is as much a reality as birth, growth, maturity and old age—it is the one certainty. I do not fear death as much as I fear the indignity of deterioration, dependence and hopeless pain. I ask that drugs be mercifully administered to me for terminal suffering even if they hasten the moment of death.

This request is made while I am in good health and spirits. Although this document is not legally binding, you who care for me will, I hope, feel morally bound to follow its mandate. I recognize that it places a heavy burden of responsibility upon you, and it is with the intention of sharing that responsibility and of mitigating any feelings of guilt that this statement is made.

Signed _____

Date _____

Witnessed by: _____

_____

*Source*: Euthanasia Society archives, held by Choice In Dying, Washington, DC.

* * *

## STATEMENTS IN SUPPORT OF PATIENTS' RIGHTS

### Statement of Health Care Personnel

In January 1973, the American Hospital Association produced a bill of rights for patients that is still widely posted in hospitals. It included the following statement.

## DOCUMENT 44: *A Patient's Bill of Rights*, American Hospital Association (1973)

The patient has the right to receive from his physician information necessary to give informed consent prior to the start of any procedure and/or treatment. The patient has the right to refuse treatment to the extent permitted by law and to be informed of the medical consequences of his action.

*Source*: American Hospital Association, *A Patient's Bill of Rights* (Chicago: American Hospital Association, 1973).

* * *

### Statement of Physicians

In April 1973, the House of Delegates of the Connecticut State Medical Society approved a resolution suggesting that a healthy person be entitled to sign a statement asking not to be kept alive by "artificial means or heroic measures" in the event that he contracted a terminal "physical or mental and spiritual disability" and was unable to make decisions about his own future. The delegation introduced its recommendation at the 122nd Annual Convention of the American Medical

Association, which referred the matter to the Judicial Council. In December 1973, the House of Delegates of the American Medical Association adopted the following statement.

## DOCUMENT 45: Statement of the American Medical Association House of Delegates (1973)

The intentional termination of the life of one human being by another—mercy killing—is contrary to that for which the medical profession stands and is contrary to the policy of the American Medical Association. The cessation of the employment of extraordinary means to prolong the life of the body when there is irrefutable evidence that biological death is imminent is the decision of the patient and/or his immediate family. The advice and judgment of the physician should be freely available to the patient and/or his immediate family.

*Source*: American Medical Association, Proceedings of the House of Delegates, 27th Clinical Convention, Anaheim, California, December 2–5, 1973. Cited in O. Ruth Russell, *Freedom to Die* (Human Sciences Press, 1975), 160.

\* \* \*

### Statement of a Public Opinion Maker

The columnist Abigail Van Buren, author of the widely distributed newspaper column "Dear Abby," was a steadfast champion of the living will. An example of an early column follows. Requests for living will forms from tens of thousands of readers were vital in sustaining the Euthanasia Society and its successor organizations for many years.

## DOCUMENT 46: "Dear Abby" Column (April 1, 1973)

DEAR ABBY: I hear they are trying to pass a law making it legal to let people die just by discontinuing treatment. They say it will be used so old people who are incurably sick won't have to linger and suffer after all hope for recovery is gone.

The thought of this is frightening. WHO will decide who is old enough and sick enough?

If you know anything about "euthanasia"—which in plain English means "mercy killing"—please state your views.

CONCERNED

DEAR CONCERNED: "Euthanasia" literally means "the good death," and I am all for it. I believe it is cruel and senseless to prolong life by artificial means when there is no hope for recovery.

The right to die with dignity should be everybody's right. The Euthanasia Education Council has made available "A Living Will." It reads as follows:

"To My Family, My Phsycian [sic], My Clergyman, My Lawyer—If the time comes when I can no longer take part in decisions for my own future, let this statement stand as the testament of my wishes:

"If there is no reasonable expectation of my recovery from physical or mental or spiritual disability, I (name) request that I be allowed to die and not be kept alive by artificial means or heroic measures. Death is as much a reality as birth, growth, maturity, and old age—it is the one certainty. I do not fear death as much as I fear the indignity of deterioration, dependence, and hopeless pain. I ask that drugs be mercifully administered to me for terminal suffering even if they hasten the moment of death.

"This request is made while I am in good health and spirits. Although this document is not legally binding, you who care for me will, I hope, feel morally bound to follow its mandates. I recognize it places a heavy burden of responsibility upon you, and it is with the intention of sharing that responsibility and of mitigating any feelings of guilt that this statement is made."

Sign document in the presence of witnesses, and give it to your family physician, attorney, and-or a member of your family. (Better yet, obtain three copies, and give each one a copy. I did.)

*Source*: Abigail Van Buren, "Dear Abby" syndicated column, "Some Thoughts on 'A Good Death,' " *Universal Press Syndicate*, April 1, 1973. Taken from a DEAR ABBY column by Abigail Van Buren. Reprinted with permission of UNIVERSAL PRESS SYNDICATE. All rights reserved.

\* \* \*

## LEGALIZING THE LIVING WILL

In 1968, Dr. Walter Sackett, a Catholic physician who was also a member of the Florida legislature, introduced a bill making living wills legally binding. Other states subsequently introduced similar bills, but none was passed until Governor Edmund G. ("Jerry") Brown, Jr., of California signed the first so-called Natural Death Act in 1976. The impetus for passage of the law was the highly publicized struggle over the withdrawal of artificial respiration from Karen Ann Quinlan, who was in a persistent vegetative state (details of her case are discussed in

Part V). The following year, seven more states passed similar laws, and other states followed.

As of December 31, 1998, forty-seven states and the District of Columbia had living will statutes. In the other three states, the validity of living wills is protected by constitutional and common law. Most of the statutes require that the patient be unable to make his or her own treatment decisions. Typically, the patient must be in a "terminal condition," "permanently unconscious," or "persistently vegetative" before the living will may become operative. An example of such a law follows.

## DOCUMENT 47: West Virginia Living Will Law (1994)

§16-30-3. Executing a living will.

(a) Any mentally competent person eighteen years of age or older may execute at any time a living will governing the withholding or withdrawal of life-prolonging intervention from himself or herself. A living will made pursuant to this article shall be: (1) In writing; (2) executed by the declarant or by another person in the declarant's presence at the declarant's express direction if the declarant is physically unable to do so; (3) dated; (4) signed in the presence of two or more witnesses at least eighteen years of age; and (5) signed and attested by such witnesses whose signatures and attestations shall be acknowledged before a notary public as provided in subsection (d) of this section.

(b) In addition, a witness may not be:

(1) The person who signed the living will on behalf of and at the direction of the declarant;

(2) Related to the declarant by blood or marriage;

(3) Entitled to any portion of the estate of the declarant according to the laws of intestate succession of the state of the declarant's domicile or under any will of the declarant or codicil thereto: Provided, That the validity of the living will shall not be affected when a witness at the time of witnessing such living will was unaware of being a named beneficiary of the declarant's will;

(4) Directly financially responsible for declarant's medical care;

(5) The attending physician; or

(6) The declarant's health care representative, proxy or successor health care representative.

(c) It shall be the responsibility of the declarant to provide for notification to his or her attending physician and other health care providers of the existence of the living will. An attending physician, when presented with the living will, shall make the living will or a copy of the living will a part of the declarant's medical records.

(d) At the time of admission to any hospital or extended care facility, each person shall be advised of the existence and availability of living will and medical power of attorney forms and shall be given assistance in completing such forms if the person desires: Provided, That under no circumstances may admission to a hospital or extended care facility be predicated upon a person having completed either a medical power of attorney or living will.

(e) The living will may, but need not, be in the following form, and may include other specific directions not inconsistent with other provisions of this article. Should any of the other specific directions be held to be invalid, such invalidity shall not affect other directions of the living will which can be given effect without the invalid direction and to this end the directions in the living will are severable.

"LIVING WILL

"Living will made this . . . . . . . . . day of . . . . . . . . (month, year). I, . . . . . . . . . . , being of sound mind, willfully and voluntarily declare that in the absence of my ability to give directions regarding the use of life-prolonging intervention, it is my desire that my dying shall not be artificially prolonged under the following circumstances:

"If at any time I should be certified by two physicians who have personally examined me, one of whom is my attending physician, to have a terminal condition or to be in a persistent vegetative state, I direct that life-prolonging intervention that would serve solely to artificially prolong the dying process or maintain me in a persistent vegetative state be withheld or withdrawn, and that I be permitted to die naturally with only the administration of medication or the performance of any other medical procedure deemed necessary to keep me comfortable and alleviate pain.

"SPECIAL DIRECTIVES OR LIMITATIONS ON THIS DECLARATION: (If none, write "none".)

"It is my intention that this living will be honored as the final expression of my legal right to refuse medical or surgical treatment and accept the consequences resulting from such refusal.

"I understand the full import of this living will.

"Signed . . . . . . . . . . . . . . . . . . . . . . . . . . . . . . . . . . . . . . . . . . . . . . . . . . . . . . . . . . . . . . . . . . .

"Address. . . . . . . . . . . . . . . . . . . . . . . . . . . . . . . . . . . . . . . . . . . . . . . . . . . . . . . . . . . . . . . . . . . . .

. . . . . . . . . . . . . . . . . . . . . . . . . . . . . . . . . . . . . . . . . . . . . . . . . . . . . . . . . . . . . . . . . . . . . . . . . . .

"I did not sign the declarant's signature above for or at the direction of the declarant. I am at least eighteen years of age and am not related to the declarant by blood or marriage, entitled to any portion of the estate of the declarant according to the laws of intestate succession of the state of the declarant's domicile or to the best of my knowledge under any will of declarant or codicil thereto, or directly financially responsible for declarant's medical care. I am not the declarant's attending physician or the declarant's health care representative, proxy or successor health care representative under a medical power of attorney.

"Witness .................................................................

"Address.................................................................

.................................................................

"Witness .................................................................

"Address.................................................................

.................................................................

"STATE OF.................................................................

"COUNTY OF.................................................................

"The foregoing instrument was acknowledged before me this.........
(date) by the declarant and by the two witnesses whose signatures appear above.

"My commission expires:.......................

"
.................................................................

Signature of Notary Public."
(1984, c. 134; 1991, c. 85.)

### §16-30-4. Revocation.

(a) A living will may be revoked at any time only by the declarant or at the express direction of the declarant, without regard to the declarant's mental state by any of the following methods:

(1) By being destroyed by the declarant or by some person in the declarant's presence and at his direction;

(2) By a written revocation of the living will signed and dated by the declarant or person acting at the direction of the declarant. Such revocation shall become effective only upon delivery of the written revocation to the attending physician by the declarant or by a person acting on behalf of the declarant. The attending physician shall record in the declarant's medical record the time and date when he or she receives notification of the written revocation; or

(3) By a verbal expression of the intent to revoke the living will in the presence of a witness eighteen years of age or older who signs and dates a writing confirming that such expression of intent was made. Any verbal revocation shall become effective only upon communication of the revocation to the attending physician by the declarant or by a person acting on behalf of the declarant. The attending physician shall record, in the declarant's medical record, the time, date and place of when he or she receives notification of the revocation.

(b) There is no criminal or civil liability on the part of any person for failure to act upon a revocation made pursuant to this section unless that person has actual knowledge of the revocation. (1984, c. 134; 1991, c. 85.)

§16-30-5. Physician's duty to confirm, communicate and document terminal condition or persistent vegetative state; medical record identification.

(a) An attending physician who has been notified of the existence of a living will executed under this article, without delay after the diagnosis of a terminal condition or persistent vegetative state of the declarant, shall take the necessary steps to provide for confirmation, written certification and documentation of the declarant's terminal condition or persistent vegetative state in the declarant's medical record.

(b) Once confirmation, written certification and documentation of the declarant's terminal condition is made, the attending physician shall verbally or in writing inform the declarant of his or her terminal condition or the declarant's health care representative, next of kin or other responsible person, if the declarant lacks capacity to comprehend such information and shall document such communication in the declarant's medical record.

(c) All inpatient health care facilities shall develop a system to visibly identify a person's chart which contains a living will as set forth in this article. (1984, c. 134; 1991, c. 85.)

§16-30-6. Competency and intent of declarant.

(a) The desires of a capable declarant at all times supersede the effect of the living will.

(b) If a person is incapacitated at the time of the decision to withhold or withdraw life-prolonging intervention, the person's living will executed in accordance with section three [§16-30-3] of this article is presumed to be valid. For the purposes of this article, a physician or health facility may presume in the absence of actual notice to the contrary that a person who executed a living will was of sound mind when it was executed. The fact that a person executed a living will is not an indication of the person's mental incapacity. (1984, c. 134; 1991, c. 85.)

§16-30-7. Liability and protection of living will; transfer.

(a) No health care provider or employee thereof who in good faith and pursuant to reasonable medical standards causes or participates in the withholding or withdrawing of life-prolonging intervention from a person pursuant to a living will made in accordance with this article shall, as a result thereof, be subject to criminal or civil liability.

(b) An attending physician who cannot comply with the living will of a declarant pursuant to this article shall, in conjunction with the health care representative, next of kin of the declarant or other responsible person, effect the transfer of the declarant to another physician who will honor the living will of the declarant. Transfer under these circumstances does not constitute abandonment. (1984, c. 134; 1991, c. 85.)

*Source*: West Virginia Natural Death Act, W. Va. Code §16-30-1 to §16-30-10 (Michie, 1995).

* * *

## MEDICAL POWER OF ATTORNEY: HEALTH CARE AGENT APPOINTED BY THE PATIENT

A living will cannot define all of the circumstances that may arise when the principal becomes incapacitated. For example, the living will may state broadly that the patient does not want to be placed on a ventilator, but there are circumstances under which the patient can recover completely if this particular medical treatment is used temporarily.

The difficulty of establishing in advance when medical treatment should be withheld or withdrawn led to the development of the medical power of attorney, also known as a health care proxy or durable power of attorney for health care. This document enables an individual to appoint a health care agent to consult with the patient's physician and make decisions when the patient no longer has the capacity to do so. Note that an advance directive may be either a living will or a document that appoints a health care agent or surrogate.

A health care agent can respond to unanticipated changes and can base decisions not only on written or verbal expressions of treatment wishes, but also on general knowledge of the principal as an individual. As of December 31, 1998, forty-nine states and the District of Columbia had laws that permit a health care agent to make medical decisions regarding life-sustaining treatment for an incapacitated patient.

Despite the value of a health care proxy, a living will can be very useful for several reasons:

- Not everyone has someone to serve as a health care agent.
- If the agent and alternate agent become unavailable or unwilling to serve, the living will can serve as a guide to medical decision making.
- If the agent's decisions are challenged, the living will can provide evidence that the agent is acting in good faith.
- The living will can reassure the agent that he or she is following the wishes of the principal and ease the burden of decision making to some degree.

The following is an example of forms that fulfill Florida's requirements for appointing a health care surrogate and executing a living will.

---

**DOCUMENT 48:** Florida Advance Directives (1998)

---

# FLORIDA DESIGNATION OF HEALTH CARE SURROGATE

---

Name:_____
       *(Last)*                 *(First)*                 *(Middle Initial)*

In the event that I have been determined to be incapacitated to provide informed consent for medical treatment and surgical and diagnostic procedures, I wish to designate as my surrogate for health care decisions:

Name:_____

Address: _____

_____ Zip Code: _____

Phone: _____

If my surrogate is unwilling or unable to perform his or her duties, I wish to designate as my alternate surrogate:

Name: _____

Address: _____

_____ Zip Code: _____

Phone: _____

I fully understand that this designation will permit my designee to make health care decisions and to provide, withhold, or withdraw consent on my behalf; to apply for public benefits to defray the cost of health care; and to authorize my admission to or transfer from a health care facility.

Additional instructions (optional):

I further affirm that this designation is not being made as a condition of treatment or admission to a health care facility. I will notify and send a copy of this document to the following persons other than my surrogate, so they may know who my surrogate is:

Name: _____

Address: _____

Name: _____

Address: _____


Signed: _____

Date: _____


Witness 1:

    Signed: _____

    Address: _____


Witness 2:

    Signed: _____

    Address: _____

# FLORIDA LIVING WILL

Declaration made this _____ day of _____, 19_____.

I, _____, willfully and voluntarily make known my desire that my dying not be artificially prolonged under the circumstances set forth below, and I do hereby declare:

If at any time I have a terminal condition and if my attending or treating physician and another consulting physician have determined that there is no medical probability of my recovery from such condition, I direct that life-prolonging procedures be withheld or withdrawn when the application of such procedures would serve only to prolong artificially the process of dying, and that I be permitted to die naturally with only the administration of medication or the performance of any medical procedure deemed necessary to provide me with comfort care or to alleviate pain.

It is my intention that this declaration be honored by my family and physician as the final expression of my legal right to refuse medical or surgical treatment and to accept the consequences for such refusal.

In the event that I have been determined to be unable to provide express and informed consent regarding the withholding, withdrawal, or continuation of life-prolonging procedures, I wish to designate, as my surrogate to carry out the provisions of this declaration:

Name: _____

Address: _____

_____ Zip Code: _____

Phone: _____

I wish to designate the following person as my alternate surrogate, to carry out the provisions of this declaration should my surrogate be unwilling or unable to act on my behalf:

Name: _____

Address: _____

_____ Zip Code: _____

Phone: _____


Additional instructions (optional):




I understand the full import of this declaration, and I am emotionally and mentally competent to make this declaration.

Signed: _____


Witness 1:

    Signed: _____

    Address: _____

Witness 2:

    Signed: _____

    Address: _____

*Source*: Florida Designation of Health Care Surrogate and Florida Living Will, 1996. Choice In Dying, Inc., 1035 30th St., Washington, DC 20007.

\* \* \*

## LAWS THAT PERMIT HEALTH CARE DECISIONS TO BE MADE BY A SURROGATE WHO WAS NOT APPOINTED BY THE PATIENT

Many individuals who have lost the capacity to make their own decisions have neither executed a living will nor appointed someone to make health care decisions for them. As of December 31, 1998, twenty-eight state and the District of Columbia had passed surrogate-decision-making laws that permit someone close to the incapacitated individual to make health care decisions for him or her in the absence of an advance directive. The laws usually describe the order in which the surrogate must be chosen. Most of these provisions are found within the state's advance-directive legislation.

---

## DOCUMENT 49: New Mexico Surrogate-Decision-Making Law (1995)

---

### DECISIONS BY SURROGATE.—

A. A surrogate may make a health-care decision for a patient who is an adult or emancipated minor if the patient has been determined according to the provisions of Section 24-7A-11 NMSA 1978 to lack capacity and no agent or guardian has been appointed or the agent or guardian is not reasonably available.

B. An adult or emancipated minor, while having capacity, may designate any individual to act as surrogate by personally informing the supervising health-care provider. In the absence of a designation or if the designee is not reasonably available, any member of the following classes of the patient's family who is reasonably available, in descending order of priority, may act as surrogate:

(1) the spouse, unless legally separated or unless there is a pending petition for annulment, divorce, dissolution of marriage or legal separation;

(2) an individual in a long-term relationship of indefinite duration with the patient in which the individual has demonstrated an actual commitment to the patient similar to the commitment of a spouse and in which the individual and the patient consider themselves to be responsible for each other's well-being;

(3) an adult child;

(4) a parent;

(5) an adult brother or sister; or

(6) a grandparent.

C. If none of the individuals eligible to act as surrogate under Subsection B of this section is reasonably available, an adult who has exhibited special care and concern for the patient, who is familiar with the patient's personal values and who is reasonably available may act as surrogate.

D. A surrogate shall communicate his assumption of authority as promptly as practicable to the patient, to members of the patient's family specified in Subsection B of this section who can be readily contacted and to the supervising health-care provider.

E. If more than one member of a class assumes authority to act as surrogate and they do not agree on a health-care decision and the supervising health-care provider is so informed, the supervising health-care provider shall comply with the decision of a majority of the members of that class who have communicated their views to the provider. If the class is evenly divided concerning the health-care decision and the supervising health-care provider is so informed, that class and all individuals having lower priority are disqualified from making the decision.

F. A surrogate shall make a health-care decision in accordance with the patient's individual instructions, if any, and other wishes to the extent known to the surrogate. Otherwise, the surrogate shall make the decision in accordance with the surrogate's determination of the patient's best interest. In determining the patient's best interest, the surrogate shall consider the patient's personal values to the extent known to the surrogate.

G. A health-care decision made by a surrogate for a patient shall not be made solely on the basis of the patient's pre-existing physical or medical condition or pre-existing or projected disability.

H. A health-care decision made by a surrogate for a patient is effective without judicial approval.

I. A patient, at any time, may disqualify any person, including a member of the patient's family, from acting as the patient's surrogate by a signed writing or by personally informing a health-care provider of the disqualification. A health-care provider who is informed by the patient of a disqualification shall promptly communicate the fact of disqualification to the supervising health-care provider and to any health-care institution at which the patient is receiving care.

J. Unless related to the patient by blood, marriage or adoption, a surrogate may not be an owner, operator or employee of a health-care institution at which the patient is receiving care.

K. A supervising health-care provider may require an individual claiming the right to act as surrogate for a patient to provide a written declaration under penalty of perjury stating facts and circumstances reasonably sufficient to establish the claimed authority.

*Source*: New Mexico Uniform Health Care Decisions Act, 1995.

## DOCUMENT 50: Map of States with Surrogate Decision-Making Laws (June 1998)

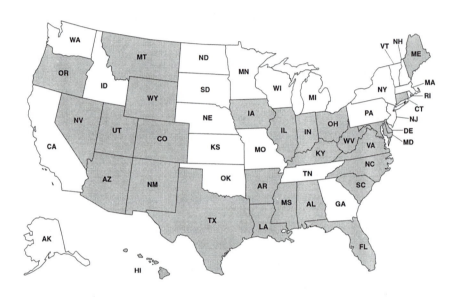

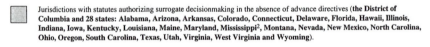 Jurisdictions with statutes authorizing surrogate decisionmaking in the absence of advance directives (**the District of Columbia and 28 states: Alabama, Arizona, Arkansas, Colorado, Connecticut, Delaware, Florida, Hawaii, Illinois, Indiana, Iowa, Kentucky, Louisiana, Maine, Maryland, Mississippi[2], Montana, Nevada, New Mexico, North Carolina, Ohio, Oregon, South Carolina, Texas, Utah, Virginia, West Virginia and Wyoming**).

☐ States without statutes authorizing surrogate decisionmaking (**22 states: Alaska, California, Georgia, Idaho, Kansas, Massachusetts, Michigan, Minnesota, Missouri, Nebraska, New Hampshire, New Jersey, New York[1], North Dakota, Oklahoma, Pennsylvania, Rhode Island, South Dakota, Tennessee, Vermont, Washington and Wisconsin**).

[1] New York does authorize surrogate decisionmaking for do-not-resuscitate order decisions.

[2] Effective July 1, 1998.

© 1998 Choice In Dying, Inc. 1035 30th Street, NW. Washington, DC 20007

\* \* \*

Some individuals have no one who is willing or available to serve as a surrogate. The New York State Task Force on Life and the Law has recommended policies to guide decision making for such patients.

## DOCUMENT 51: "Treatment Decisions for Patients without Surrogates," Tracy Miller, Carl H. Coleman, and Anna Maria Cugliari (1997)

### Decisions About Major Medical Treatment

For decisions about major medical treatment, defined to include those treatments that entail significant risk, discomfort, debilitation, or invasion of bodily integrity and for which physicians ordinarily seek informed consent, the attending physician would decide about treatment in consultation with other health care professionals involved in the patient's care. . . .

### Decisions About Life-Sustaining Treatment

Under the Task Force's proposal, the attending physician would also initiate decisions to forgo life-sustaining treatment. The physician must determine, in consultation with other health care professionals caring for the patient, that the decision accords with the patient's wishes and interests. In addition, decisions to forgo life-sustaining treatment would be authorized only if the treatment imposes an "excessive burden" on the patient and the patient is terminally ill or permanently unconscious, or if the patient has an incurable or irreversible condition and the treatment would "involve such pain, suffering, or other burden that it would reasonably be deemed inhumane or excessively burdensome under the circumstances." These are the same standards that would guide decisions for patients who have family members or others to decide on their behalf.

If these standards are satisfied, the attending physician must consult a second physician who independently decides whether to concur in the recommendation to withhold or withdraw treatment. In addition, the decision must be reviewed and approved by a multi-disciplinary committee within the healthcare facility. The committee would seek to determine if the standards for the decision have been met. Is any information available about the patient's wishes and is the decision consistent with those wishes? Does the patient meet the medical standards for the decision? In evaluating the physician's recommendations, the committee would in effect provide the kind of consideration that a surrogate would offer, if available. . . .

### CONCLUSION

No data are available about the number of patients who have no surrogate, their personal circumstances, or how decisions are made for them. The scarcity of data itself reflects the lack of public attention to the needs of these patients. The small number of court cases seeking guardians to decide about medical care or judicial approval for particular treatment decisions for patients who have no family or other surrogate, in comparison with the potentially large population of these patients, especially in the nations' nursing homes, suggests that physicians often decide about treatment for these patients without legal authorization. This leaves a significant gap between law and practice. It also undermines the well-being of patients, some of whom may receive unnecessary treatment while others may not receive treatment they need. For many, decisions will be made without the consultation or explicit guidelines that shape decisions for other patients.

The proposal by the Task Force on Life and the Law offers a useful model for healthcare providers and policymakers. If implemented, it would require careful study and evaluation, but it holds out the possibility of removing legal barriers to needed care and providing a sound facility-based approach to decisions about life-sustaining treatment for socially isolated patients. Whether state policymakers adopt this approach or consider other options, the challenges presented by caring for elderly patients without surrogates must be publicly explored and debated, especially as our health care system becomes increasingly cost conscious. The fact that incapacitated patients who have no surrogate are often voiceless makes public debate about their needs more, not less, critical.

*Source*: Tracy E. Miller, Carl H. Coleman, and Anna Maria Cugliari, "Treatment Decisions for Patients without Surrogates. Rethinking Policies for a Vulnerable Population," *Journal of the American Geriatrics Society* 45 (1997): 369–374 (notes omitted).

* * *

## LIMITATIONS OF ADVANCE DIRECTIVES

Along with their common provisions, the state statutes governing advance directives have common shortcomings. Perhaps the most problematic are the definitions that the statutes give to the qualifying medical conditions. Terms such as "permanent coma," "permanent unconsciousness," "senility," "dementia," and "persistent vegetative state" may evade clear definition. More important, it may be constitutionally impermissible for a legislature to arbitrarily limit the conditions under which an advance directive can have effect. It is unclear what state interest could justify allowing advance directives in some, but not all, cases in which a person permanently loses decision-making capacity. Rather than amending living-will statutes with restrictive qualifying medical conditions, many states have passed medical-power-of-attorney acts that unconditionally permit an agent to refuse life support on an incompetent principal's behalf. This creates an inconsistency in which an agent can act in cases in which the principal could not give advance instructions on his or her own behalf.

Another problem is the limitation of the applicability of a woman's advance directive during pregnancy in thirty-three states as of December 31, 1998. In 1992, the U.S. Supreme Court reaffirmed the principle that "viability marks the earliest point at which the state's interest in fetal life is constitutionally adequate to justify a legislative ban" on a woman's right to end her pregnancy (*Planned Parenthood of Southeastern Pennsylvania v. Casey*). Therefore, pregnancy exclusions in advance-directive or medical-power-of-attorney statutes, particularly those that prohibit withholding or withdrawing life support at any time in the course of a pregnancy, may be unconstitutional.

## FEDERAL LAW RELATING TO ADVANCE DIRECTIVES

The decision of the U.S. Supreme Court regarding termination of life support for Nancy Cruzan (see Part V) emphasized the importance of communicating one's wishes about end-of-life treatment. In an attempt to promote the use of advance directives, the federal Patient Self-Determination Act (PSDA) was sponsored by Senators John C. Danforth of Missouri and Daniel P. Moynihan of New York, and Representative Sander Levin of Michigan, passed in 1990, and implemented in 1991. This law mandates that all health care facilities that receive Medicaid or Medicare funds, that is, hospitals, long-term-care facilities, hospices, home-care facilities, and health maintenance organizations, do the following:

---

## DOCUMENT 52: Patient Self-Determination Act (1990)

---

"(A) to provide written information to each such individual concerning—

"(i) an individual's rights under State law (whether statutory or as recognized by the courts of the State) to make decisions concerning such medical care, including the right to accept or refuse medical or surgical treatment and the right to formulate advance directives (as defined in paragraph (3)), and "(ii) the written policies of the provider or organization respecting the implementation of such rights;

"(B) to document in the individual's medical record whether or not the individual has executed an advance directive;

"(C) not to condition the provision of care or otherwise discriminate against an individual based on whether or not the individual has executed an advance directive;

"(D) to ensure compliance with requirements of State law (whether statutory or as recognized by the courts of the State) respecting advance directives at facilities of the provider or organization; and

"(E) to provide (individually or with others) for education for staff and the community on issues concerning advance directives.

Subparagraph (C) shall not be construed as requiring the provision of care which conflicts with an advance directive.

*Source: Omnibus Budget Reconciliation Act (OBRA), 42 U.S.C. 1395cc(a) et seq. (1990).*

\* \* \*

The following document describes the experience of a woman whose father suffered a stroke.

## DOCUMENT 53: "Live and Let Die," Harriet Brickman (July 2, 1995)

My parents have always been clear about "quality of life" issues. They, and most of their friends, want protection from what they call an undignified death and have prepared living wills and proxy arrangements for making health care decisions in case they are incapacitated. The difficulty is that "heroic" and "extraordinary" measures are neither medical nor legal terms. The medical profession and the insurance industry are grappling with these issues, but increasingly the decisions fall to the family.

There was no choice but to go to the hospital, they decided. . . .

None of the medical staff inquired about his living will. And the drama that was playing out across the hall suggested that the document was not adequate insurance against invasive care. An 87-year-old woman with intestinal cancer and a benign brain tumor was being prepared for brain surgery despite her living will and the protests of her family. The daily battles spilled out of her room and down the corridors.

We had no such battles, but my father's situation was not unequivocal.

Though emotionally excruciating, the process went relatively smoothly for several reasons—including the fact that the two doctors most involved were aware of my father's views. Most important, the family spoke with a consistent, firm voice. Even a whiff of dissent would have made things very different.

My parents were in accord and my mother was able to speak for my father. We were there virtually all the time, monitoring his care and questioning procedures. Clarity was important; any relaxation into euphemism could undo our efforts. Repetition was useful; patience essential.

I had arrived two days after my father's admission, when his condition had worsened and he could no longer speak for himself. But he squeezed my hand as I embraced him and there was a trace of smile.

That was all the time we had before the troops pressed into the small room—the neurologist, the resident, two interns and several medical students. They discussed treatment and rehabilitation: perhaps his speech would return; eventually he might be able to move with the aid of a walker. They wanted him to get well. Relatively well. We did not. We knew that whatever the physical possibilities, the consequences of not being able to express himself, feed or clean himself, write or play the piano would be too much for him.

It became apparent that there would be no private moment to discuss my father's situation with the doctor. And that was central to the way his case was handled. We spoke openly, as a family. With my mother beside me, I said that neither my mother nor my father had the physical or emotional stamina to endure rehabilitation. Her quiet, unflinching affirmation was powerful. The brisk medical discussion came to an uncomfortable halt.

That evening, the presiding neurologist returned to talk. . . . The doctor again outlined my father's prognosis.

You've got to realize, I said, that your best hopes are my father's worst nightmare. My mother concurred. The doctor seemed to understand.

The next morning, the troops regrouped. My mother and I listened carefully to an intense discussion about what drugs to commence to prevent "failure." Finally, I asked whether failure meant heart failure. Yes, they said, it did.

My mother's eyes were wide with disbelief, an expression my father adored in her. Tell them what you're thinking, I prompted. Is there any reason to prevent heart failure, she asked? Isn't it a relatively expedient and painless way to die? Yes, they acknowledged, and left.

By the next day, my father was rarely responsive. Tests showed a spreading intercranial bleeding. We agreed to withdraw his medications, in the expectation that he would not survive without the menu of drugs he'd been taking for years. Yet the next day we were asked if we wanted a temporary feeding tube placed through his nose or a more permanent tube surgically constructed through his stomach. Why, we asked?

They constantly probed for cracks in our position. Had my father actually expressed these wishes? Did other family members feel the same way? In fact, there were family members not quite so firm in their resolve, but they had the wisdom to voice their concerns within the family, away from the medical staff.

My father did not die from lack of medications. His heart did not fail and he didn't have another stroke. Finally, we stopped giving him even fluids, a decision we were allowed to make in stages. He became less and less responsive, though of course no one can gauge what he was able to perceive. My mother and I tended him for seven more days, matching his breaths with our own, grateful for the gift of transition.

It is hard to let go of someone you have loved so intensely. It would have been harder not to let go. Being nursed through an illness is a blessing. For my father, being nursed for months or years toward death would have been an assault. He was spared the tragedy he most feared, a life ended in advance of death. He wanted, he always said, to live until he died.

*Source*: Harriet Brickman, "Live and Let Die," *New York Times Magazine*, July 2, 1995, 14.

\* \* \*

Despite considerable favorable publicity, only about 20 percent of individuals have executed advance directives. The following articles describe some of the research that has been carried out to determine what proportion of the population has executed advance directives and how this number might be increased.

## DOCUMENT 54: "Living Will Completion in Older Adults," Keith L. Stelter, Barbara A. Elliott, and Candace A. Bruno (1992)

This survey was given to all people who ate at one of the 10 local nutrition sites at the senior centers in a midwestern community [Duluth, MN] on a November day in 1990....

...Of the 245 surveys that were completed and returned, 214 were used for data analysis. Thirty-one surveys were eliminated because the respondent was less than 65 years of age....

...The average age of our study group was 73 years, with a range from 65 to 90 years of age. The majority of our subjects were female (60%), lived alone (53%), were white (96%), and considered their health to be good or excellent (69%). The sample was fairly well educated; 49% had completed high school or held a general education diploma. . . .

Of the 214 subjects with usable responses, 15% already had executed an LW, 66% planned to complete an LW, and 86% wanted to have an LW. These proportions are the same as those reported in other national and random samples. . . .

Two characteristics described those who already had an LW: they were highly educated and did not consider the LW form too long for its purpose. The older adults who planned to complete an LW identified two barriers impeding them: family issues and a need for assistance in completing the form. The majority of the older adults (61%) desired that their physicians initiate discussions with them about an LW.

*Conclusions.* Conclusions from these data yield recommendations for health care providers toward implementing the act; physician-initiated discussions, community programs, and available information and assistance are needed.

*Source*: Keith L. Stelter, Barbara A. Elliott, and Candace A. Bruno, "Living Will Completion in Older Adults," *Archives of Internal Medicine* 152 (1992): 954–959.

---

## DOCUMENT 55: "Knowledge, Attitudes, and Behavior of Elderly Persons Regarding Living Wills," Elizabeth R. Gamble, Penelope J. McDonald, and Peter R. Lichstein (1991)

---

Fifty-two percent (39) of these subjects said they were familiar with living wills and 64% (48 persons) correctly summarized what the North Carolina living will says. When asked about preferences for medical care in the setting of a terminal illness, 86% (65 persons) stated a desire to receive basic medical care or comfort care only. Although their preferences were consistent with the provisions of a living will, none had signed the living will document provided by the state of North Carolina, and only two (3%) had discussed a living will with their physician. Seventy (93%) wanted their family or spouse to make decisions about terminal care if they themselves were unable to participate, and discussions between these persons and their chosen proxies actually occurred 45% (34/75) of the time. Eighty-one percent (61 persons) stated a desire to discuss end-of-life care with their physicians, but a minority (eight [11%]) had actually talked with their physicians, and these discussions were usually initiated by the patient (five of eight). We conclude that living will legislation is congruent with the desire of many elderly persons to limit medical care in terminal illness. However, this elderly population did not make use of living wills as a means of indicating their wishes.

*Source*: Elizabeth R. Gamble, Penelope J. McDonald, and Peter R. Lichstein, "Knowledge, Attitudes, and Behavior of Elderly Persons Regarding Living Wills," *Archives of Internal Medicine* 151 (1991): 277–280.

* * *

The study by Laura C. Hanson and Eric Rodgman was unusually large; although it was based on data collected in 1986, the results are in general agreement with those of later studies.

## DOCUMENT 56: "The Use of Living Wills at the End of Life," Laura C. Hanson and Eric Rodgman (1996)

**Methods**: We analyzed the 1986 National Mortality Followback Survey, a random sample of all US deaths linked to a survey about decedents' use of living wills, their social and health status, and their use of medical services. Decedents with and without living wills were compared for differences in social and health characteristics and use of medical services.

**Results**: There were 16678 decedents; 9.8% had a living will. Rates of use were higher for decedents who were white (10.7%), were female (11.0%), had private insurance (13.8%), had incomes of $22000 or more (14.5%), or had college educations (18.7%). The use of living wills was lower among blacks (2.7%), Medicaid recipients (6.3%), those with incomes of less than $5000 (7.5%), or those with less than 8 years of education (4.0%). Health was also related to use of living wills. Functionally independent persons were unlikely to have a living will (5.5%); use increased with dependency. Cognitive impairment made it less likely that a decedent had a living will (6.7%). Persons who died of cancer (16.4%) or pulmonary disease (11.4%) were more likely to have one. All demographic and health characteristics remained significant in multivariate analyses. Controlling for health status, decedents with living wills used more physician visits (five to nine vs two to four, $P < .001$) and hospital days (37 vs 30, $P < .001$). Although more likely to use hospices (19.5% vs 8.4%, $P < .001$) and half as likely to receive cardiopulmonary resuscitation or ventilatory support, they were still 20% more likely to die in the hospital.

**Conclusions**: Patients who are black, poorly educated, underinsured, or cognitively impaired are least likely to prepare a living will. Decedents with living wills forgo specific treatments, but remain intensive users of routine medical services.

*Source*: Laura C. Hanson and Eric Rodgman, "The Use of Living Wills at the End of Life," *Archives of Internal Medicine* 156 (1996): 1018–1022.

* * *

## SOME CULTURAL AND RELIGIOUS RESPONSES TO ADVANCE DIRECTIVES

### Responses of Different Ethnic Groups

Another exhaustive study compared knowledge about and completion of advance directives among European Americans, Mexican Americans, African Americans, and Korean Americans.

---

## DOCUMENT 57: "Ethnicity and Advance Care Directives," Sheila T. Murphy et al. (1996)

---

### Discussion

Of the 271 respondents who knew what an advance care directive is (that is, they could provide a correct definition of a living will or a durable power of attorney for health care), seventy-seven (28 percent) actually possessed such a document. Rates of possession among subjects with knowledge, however, varied dramatically across ethnic groups. European Americans had the highest percentage of individuals who possessed an advance directive (40 percent of those with knowledge). By comparison, only 22 percent of the Mexican Americans, 17 percent of the African Americans, and 0 percent of the Korean Americans with knowledge possessed an advance directive. . . .

### Conclusion

The intent of this research is not to identify one set of moral rules for each ethnic group nor to encourage physicians to respond in a stereotypical fashion to their patients based on their ethnicity. It is important to note that although common patterns characterize individuals of the same ethnic group, nevertheless, substantial variance exists within each ethnic group. Our findings, however, together with those of the SUPPORT study,[1] suggest that the process of end-of-life decision making is more complex than previously imagined. The concept of advance care documents may appeal only to certain subsets of the population, limiting the clinical usefulness of living wills and durable powers of attorney for health care. Increasing knowledge of and access to advance care directives may not necessarily increase the completion across all ethnic groups. For members of ethnic groups who tend to avoid discussing death with patients, or who believe that decisions about the use of life support should be made by the family, other avenues of communication about these issues must be found. Rather than narrowly focusing on increasing the completion rate of formal advance directives, we need to listen to the diverse voices of the communities we serve and then to adapt our practices to fit their needs better.

This is perhaps easier to advise than to achieve. One alternative may be to promote the durable power of attorney for health care as an all-purpose way to appoint a substitute decision maker—not just for end-of-life decisions, but for any situation where a person is unable to make decisions for himself/herself. This would decouple the durable power of attorney for health care from its exclusive association with the dying process and recast it as a method of identifying an appropriate surrogate whenever an individual is mentally incapacitated, be it temporarily (for example, after trauma or major surgery) or permanently (as in a persistent vegetative state). A more generic "appointment" document of this sort might have been more acceptable to the Mexican American and Korean American respondents in our study because it might have avoided the need for specific discussions about death and dying (which were perceived as potentially harmful to the patient) and because it might be more compatible with the family-centered decision-making style that these groups tend to favor.[2] It is not clear, however, that this type of advance directive would be accepted by the African American community. Among African Americans, the reasons for completing formal advance directives seem to be more complex, and may involve issues such as distrust of the medical profession or of legal documents, and the belief that such decisions are best left in the hands of God. These, and other issues, are currently being explored in the qualitative portion of this study.

Much energy and time has been devoted to promoting advance directives as a means to improve the care of dying patients. The results of our study, however, cast doubt on the appropriateness of these documents, at least as they are currently formulated, for many patients. Our findings suggest the need for a critical analysis of the value of advance directives and alternative mechanisms to ensure that the strongly felt preferences of patients, when they exist, are not disregarded.

## NOTES

1. The SUPPORT Principal Investigators, "A Controlled Trial to Improve Care for Seriously Ill Hospitalized Patients," *JAMA*, 274 (1995): 1591–98.

2. L. J. Blackhall et al., "Ethnicity and Attitudes toward Patient Autonomy," *Journal of the American Medical Association* 274 (1975): 820–825.

*Source*: Sheila T. Murphy, Joycelynne M. Palmer, Stanley Azen, Geyla Frank, Vicki Michel, and Leslie J. Blackhall, "Ethnicity and Advance Care Directives," *Journal of Law, Medicine & Ethics*, 24 (1996): 108–117 (references omitted). Reprinted with the permission of the American Society of Law, Medicine & Ethics.

* * *

The cultural differences that suggest why African Americans are unlikely to complete advance directives are further explored in the following article.

## DOCUMENT 58: "Mistrust, Racism, and End-of-Life Treatment," Case Study with Commentary, Eric L. Krakauer and Robert D. Truog (1997)

Mr. Miller was a sixty-year-old African American nursing home resident from a working-class background. He had multiple medical problems, including insulin-dependent diabetes mellitus, a history of two myocardial infarctions, and multiple strokes that had left him demented and aphasic for the previous nine years. Throughout his life his access to health care had been inconsistent. He held several part-time jobs, most of which included no health care benefits. He had received care at the outpatient clinic of a city hospital when he could afford to take time off, or at the emergency room.

Five months ago he had been diagnosed with metastatic colon cancer during exploratory surgery for an abdominal mass. After the surgery, he was left with a permanent colostomy and two tubes protruding from his abdomen, one for feeding and one to drain his urine. Due to his poor health and functional status, the oncologist, Dr. Bonhom, recommended against chemotherapy and radiation therapy. Family members who visited Mr. Miller—two of his children and several grandchildren—appeared to agree, but expressed no interest in preparing an advance directive. In fact, they responded defensively whenever Dr. Bonhom raised the topic. After nearly five months in the hospital Mr. Miller was discharged to his nursing home.

One week later he was sent to the emergency room because of difficulty breathing. On arrival, he was in shock and hardly breathing. He was found to have pneumonia, a bladder infection, and multiple skin ulcers; one of these infections gave rise to an overwhelming blood infection. Dr. Schuler, the European-American resident caring for Mr. Miller in the emergency room, described the situation to Mr. Miller's son. He said that because Mr. Miller was so gravely ill life support would be of no benefit; it would only harm him. He apologized for having to convey this news and proposed that Mr. Miller be given the utmost in comfort care but no life-support measures. The son disagreed with Dr. Schuler and became very upset. Avoiding eye contact with the resident, he repeatedly questioned the assessment of his father's condition and wanted to know why the machines could not be used to keep him alive. Unpersuaded by the resident's responses, he demanded that "everything be done."

The resident said he would review the situation with the emergency room attending. Within earshot of the son, the attending, also a European American, gave a clear response: no intubation, no CPR, no ICU transfer. He and Dr. Schuler agreed that these would be futile treatments. Dr. Schuler sent Mr. Miller to the oncology floor, where Dr. Bonhom assumed responsibility for his care. Dr. Bonhom, however, decided against a do-not-resuscitate order. He decided to respect the son's request, for it was his sense that the son's demand for aggressive life support and the family's refusal to consider an advance directive were based on a fundamental mistrust of "the system." Mr. Miller was intubated and sent to the intensive care unit. He was placed on a breathing machine. Catheters were inserted into large blood vessels to permit close monitoring of his vital signs and administration of powerful drugs to support his sagging blood pressure. During his first day, he became deeply comatose in spite of the treatment. Over the course of the week, all of Mr. Miller's major organs failed. Yet the son, joined now by the entire family, remained adamant that aggressive life support be continued. When, on the eighth hospital day, Mr. Miller's condition had not improved, the family finally agreed to Dr. Bonhom's proposal that life support be withdrawn and a do-not-resuscitate order written. Mr. Miller was extubated and he expired.

Was Dr. Schuler's refusal to respect the son's request for life support justifiable? Was Dr. Bonhom's concern about the issue of mistrust an appropriate consideration in his treatment decision? To what extent can racism and other societal injustices be addressed in the care of individuals?

## Commentary by Eric L. Krakauer

This case shows how mistrust related to social inequalities, racism, and cultural difference may be an important consideration in negotiating a conflict between family and physicians over end-of-life care and in determining whether intensive care is an appropriate therapeutic option for dying patients. The best way to handle conflict over end-of-life care is to prevent it through advance discussion with the patient or surrogate, goal setting, and preparation of advance directives. Yet we see in this case how goal setting and advance directives themselves may have cultural meanings and become the source of conflict. . . .

Although his intentions were good, Dr. Schuler failed to take into account the historical, social, and cultural contexts of this case. As working-class African Americans, Mr. Miller and his family belong to a different culture from that of the physicians in this case. The difference separating these cultures has been historically determined by the enslavement of African Americans, by systematic segregation and discrimination, in short, by institutionalized racism. Moreover, there is a long history of medical racism in this country, notoriously exemplified by the Tuskegee Syphilis Study. And there is abundant evidence that even today African Americans continue to be denied medical services available to others. The social separation and abuse that produced this cultural difference also appears to have generated mistrust of European-American physicians and the health care system. . . .

Mistrust generated by past and present racial discrimination appears to have complicated the conversation between Mr. Miller's family and his physicians. Such mistrust is not unreasonable, may be deeply felt, and is often highly relevant to decisions about end-of-life care. It is as legitimate a cultural factor as religious belief. As such, Dr. Bonhom acted appropriately when he factored this mistrust into his treatment decision. Physicians and other clinicians must become aware of the mistrust many African Americans feel toward the medical establishment and take it seriously. This awareness may help them recognize that demands for aggressive life support made by African Americans may be an expression of mistrust. This does not mean that physicians should desist from strongly recommending comfort care as an alternative to life support if they believe that life support would be futile or more burdensome than beneficial. They should, however, make special efforts to win the trust of patients and families, even when their requests seem unreasonable. This endeavor might require that they acknowledge the history of racism in American medicine and express an understanding of minority patients' and families' fears about discriminatory withholding of medical resources. Physicians should not tolerate such discriminatory rationing among colleagues and should remain reflective about their own practice patterns. In doing so, they will be better able to reassure patients and families that they will not illegitimately withhold information or resources and that they will work out treatment plans in dialogue with families. A family's wishes may still, on occasion, be overridden and futility invoked. But this should be done only after a careful search for and consideration of all relevant cultural, religious, and personal factors, only after bona fide efforts to win the family's trust have failed, and only if the patient's comfort and dignity are severely compromised by life support treatment.

### Commentary by Robert D. Truog

This case raises powerful issues about race, power, and social injustice that go well beyond the realm of medicine. Nevertheless, even while the societal solution to these problems is far from clear, these situations are common enough in clinical settings that physicians and nurses need guidance for dealing with them in ways that are both culturally sensitive and ethically defensible. . . .

Dr. Bonhom's transfer of Mr. Miller to intensive care is surely well intended. He believes that systematic discrimination against African Americans in this country justifies differential treatment of some patients, even if only to provide the time to build more cooperative, trusting relationships with patients and family members. Yet in trying to serve the goals of justice, he has committed a grave injustice. The benefits garnered by his conciliatory response are realized not by Mr. Miller but by his son and family, and perhaps Dr. Bonhom himself.

Respecting patient autonomy and prioritizing patient benefit over competing interests have been emphasized in the bioethics literature and often serve as trump values in traditional bioethical analysis; however, in practice third-party interests often come to have significant weight. This is particularly true as patients approach death and it becomes clear that the only "surviving" interests will be those of the family and loved ones. Indeed, thoughtful and compassionate clinicians often will orchestrate the death of a patient specifically to ensure that the patient's loved ones are left with the "least worst" memories possible. Bioethical paradigms that emphasize care and community are better suited for justifying these approaches than more traditional forms of analysis. But it is not at all clear that even from a "care" perspective one could justify subjecting Mr. Miller to aggressive life-support treatment. Concerns about the family's perception of the treatment decision, even when this perception is rooted in grave historical injustices, should not trump compassionate patient care.

Although I view Dr. Bonhom's efforts to address social justice issues within the care of individual patients misguided, I also reject Dr. Schuler's hasty invocation of futility. Instead, a procedural intervention, such as a clinical team meeting or an ethics committee consult, should have been instituted promptly to consider the complexities of the case and to ensure that Mr. Miller did not suffer needlessly. Although the time necessary to institute such an approach would probably still have required placing Mr. Miller on life support, the basis of this decision would have been a commitment to determining what was of benefit to Mr. Miller, not a commitment to more abstract concerns of justice. With his immediate interests driving the decision-making process, it is highly unlikely that Mr. Miller would have been kept on life support for so many days. The decision to treat him with aggressive life support even for a short time should be seen as an unfortunate but unavoidable harm, not as an ethically appropriate option based upon considerations of racial justice.

*Source*: Eric L. Krakauer and Robert D. Truog, "Mistrust, Racism, and End-of-Life Treatment," *Hastings Center Report*, May–June 1997, 23–25.

\* \* \*

### Responses of Religious Groups

The Congregation for the Doctrine of the Faith drew up a document in 1980 that was approved by Pope John Paul II. After a section prohibiting "the killing of an innocent human being," it presented guidelines regarding "extraordinary" means for prolonging life. The Catholic Health Association issued a subsequent statement on terminal illness in 1982. That statement follows.

## DOCUMENT 59: Vatican Document on Euthanasia (1980)

1. "If there are no other sufficient remedies, it is permitted, with the patient's consent, to have recourse to the means provided by the most advanced medical techniques, even if these means are still at the experimental stage and are not without a certain risk. By accepting them, the patient can even show generosity in the service of humanity."

2. "It is also permitted, with the patient's consent, to interrupt these means, where the results fall short of expectations. But for such a decision to be made, account will have to be taken of the reasonable wishes of the patient and the patient's family, as also of the advice of the doctors who are specially competent in the matter. The latter may in particular judge that the investment in instruments and personnel is disproportionate to the results foreseen; they may also judge that the techniques

applied impose on the patient strain or suffering out of proportion with the benefits which he or she may gain from such techniques."

3. "It is also permissible to make do with the normal means that medicine can offer. Therefore one cannot impose on anyone the obligation to have recourse to a technique which is already in use but which carries a risk or is burdensome. Such a refusal is not the equivalent of suicide; on the contrary, it should be considered as an acceptance of the human condition, or a wish to avoid the application of a medical procedure disproportionate to the results that can be expected, or a desire not to impose excessive expense on the family or the community."

4. "When inevitable death is imminent in spite of the means used, it is permitted in conscience to take the decision to refuse forms of treatment that would only secure a precarious and burdensome prolongation of life, so long as the normal care due to the sick person in similar cases is not interrupted. In such circumstances the doctor has no reason to reproach himself with failing to help the person in danger."

*Source*: News release from the Archdiocese of New York, June 17, 1980.

---

## DOCUMENT 60: "Christian Affirmation of Life: A Statement on Terminal Illness," Catholic Health Association (1982)

Christians believe that through death life is merely changed, not taken away and that death need not be resisted with every possible means. Dying is a natural part of life that should be made as comfortable as possible for the patient and should not be unnecessarily prolonged. Not unduly prolonging the dying process affirms belief in eternal life.

Patients have a legal and moral right to choose what will be done to care for them. It is their right to decide to what extent, if at all, physicians may treat their diseases. In order that patients be able to exercise this right, they should be fully advised of the diagnosis, the prognosis, the proposed treatment, other therapeutic options, and the risks and benefits of each course of action.

When a patient is unable to make decisions regarding treatment, others, usually the next of kin, must do so, and they must make these judgments in accordance with the patient's legitimate wishes, if they are known. The "Christian Affirmation of Life" is provided as a means of indicating one's desires regarding treatment for terminal illness. It is not a legal document but one of moral persuasion. In states where law gives binding effect to such declarations if a particular format is used, the state form can also be used.

*Source*: Catholic Health Association of the United States, "Christian Affirmation of Life: A Statement on Terminal Illness," 1982.

*  *  *

Orthodox Jews, unlike Conservative and Reform Jews, closely follow Jewish law (Halakha); its many restrictions about the treatment of dying persons have necessitated the development of a Halakhic living will.

---

## DOCUMENT 61: *Judaism and Healing,* David Bleich (1981)

Jewish teaching with regard to these questions is shaped by the earlier-stated belief that not only is human life in general of infinite and inestimable value, but that every moment of life is of infinite value as well. Accordingly, obligations with regard to treatment and cure are one and the same, whether the person's life is likely to be prolonged for a matter of years or merely for a few seconds. An exception is made only for the case of a person in a state of *gesisah,* i.e., a moribund patient (as defined by Halakhah) in whom the death process has actually begun. Thus, even on the Sabbath, efforts to free a victim buried under a collapsed building must be continued even if the victim is found in such circumstances that he cannot survive longer than a brief period of time. . . .

Life with suffering is regarded as being, in many cases, preferable to cessation of life and with it elimination of suffering. . . .

. . . Any positive act designed to hasten the death of the patient is equated with murder in Jewish law, even if death is hastened only by a matter of moments. No matter how laudable the intentions of the person performing an act of mercy-killing may be, his deed constitutes an act of homicide.

*Source*: David Bleich, *Judaism and Healing* (Hoboken, NJ: KTAV Publishing House, 1981).

*  *  *

A number of Protestant groups have published resolutions about the use of advance directives. Two examples follow.

---

## DOCUMENT 62: Resolution Concerning Death with Dignity, United Methodist Church (1996)

*Death with Dignity*—We applaud medical science for efforts to prevent disease and illness and for advances in treatment that extend the mean-

ingful life of human beings. At the same time, in the varying stages of
death and life that advances in medical science have occasioned, we recognize the agonizing personal and moral decisions faced by the dying,
their physicians, their families, and their friends. Therefore, we assert the
right of every person to die in dignity, with loving personal care and
without efforts to prolong terminal illnesses merely because the technology is available to do so.

*Source*: Resolution 65L on Social Principles, United Methodist Church, 1996.

---

## DOCUMENT 63: Resolution Concerning the Rights and Responsibilities of Christians Regarding Human Death, United Church of Christ (1991)

*WHEREAS*, we live in an era of complex biomedical technologies, with
various means to maintain or prolong physical life and postpone inevitable death;

*WHEREAS*, there are ever-increasing anxieties about a prolonged dying
process with irreversible deterioration, and its potentially devastating
effects on the dignity of the dying person, the emotional and physical
well-being of families, as well as the responsible Christian stewardship
of resources;

*WHEREAS*, technology advances more quickly than public policy, and
public opinion is often ahead of legislative enactment;

*WHEREAS*, individuals have increasing responsibilities in these life and
death decisions, but often lack adequate information regarding available
options;

*WHEREAS*, life is sourced in God, and recognizing that our faith calls
for commitment and work for the quality of human life with mercy,
justice and truth;

*WHEREAS*, affirming that the gift of abundant life is more than the
avoidance of death, and that over-regard for the body, without proper
concern for the needs of the person or the human spirit, can become a
kind of biological idolatry; we are convinced that what is required is a
balanced appreciation of the whole person;

*WHEREAS*, General Synod 12 of the United Church of Christ has supported the legal recognition of living wills and General Synod 9 addressed the rights and responsibilities of Christians regarding human death; and

*WHEREAS*, we support the right and responsibility of individuals to choose their own destiny, and recognize the need for safeguards to protect persons who cannot make life and death choices for themselves.

*THEREFORE, BE IT RESOLVED*, the Eighteenth General Synod supports the rights of individuals, their designees and their families to make decisions regarding human death and dying.

*BE IT FURTHER RESOLVED*, the Eighteenth General Synod affirms the right of individuals to die with dignity and not have their lives unnecessarily prolonged by extraordinary measures if so chosen.

*BE IT FURTHER RESOLVED*, the Eighteenth General Synod calls on Christians to offer love, compassion and understanding to those who are faced with difficult life-ending decisions.

*BE IT FURTHER RESOLVED*, the Eighteenth General Synod calls upon the churches to study and discuss life-ending issues. . . .

*BE IT FURTHER RESOLVED*, the Eighteenth General Synod encourages the enactment of legislation safeguarding these rights, including the rights of those who are unable to make decisions for themselves.

*Source*: Resolution adopted by the United Church of Christ, 1991.

* * *

## ATTEMPTS TO INCREASE THE NUMBER OF COMPLETED ADVANCE DIRECTIVES

Numerous attempts have been made to increase the number of persons who have executed advance directives. Some groups have given patients written material; an example is the study by Susan Rubin and her colleagues, who carried out a randomized controlled trial of the effect of distributing an educational pamphlet on the completion of durable powers of attorney at the Kaiser Permanente Medical Center in San Francisco.

## DOCUMENT 64: "Increasing the Completion of the Durable Power of Attorney for Health Care," Susan M. Rubin et al. (1994)

**Objective.**—Wider use of written advance directives may prevent many ethical dilemmas about life-sustaining interventions for patients who have lost decision-making capacity. We investigated whether a simple educational intervention increased patient completion of the durable power of attorney for health care.

**Design.**—A randomized, controlled trial.

**Setting.**—A health maintenance organization.

**Subjects.**—All patients aged 65 years and older and discharged from a hospital between January 1991 and May 1991 (n=1101) were randomized to either an intervention group or a control group.

**Intervention.**—An educational pamphlet on the durable power of attorney for health care and a durable power of attorney for health care form were mailed to all patients in the intervention group. The control group received conventional care only.

**Main Outcome Measure.**—Completion of the durable power of attorney for health care form.

**Results.**—There were no significant baseline differences between the intervention group and the control group. Following our intervention, 18.5% of the subjects in the experimental group completed a durable power of attorney for health care form, compared with 0.4% of the control group ($P<.0001$).

**Conclusions.**—A simple educational intervention significantly increased the completion of the durable power of attorney for health care. Our findings should stimulate further efforts to empower patients to make informed decisions about their health care.

*Source*: Susan M. Rubin, William M. Strull, Michael F. Fialkow, Sarah J. Weiss, and Bernard Lo, "Increasing the Completion of the Durable Power of Attorney for Health Care: A Randomized, Controlled Trial," *Journal of the American Medical Association* 271 (1994): 209–212.

\* \* \*

A more effective method of education involves personal counseling.

---

## DOCUMENT 65: "Marked Improvement in Recognition and Completion of Health Care Proxies," Diane E. Meier et al. (1996)

---

**Background**: Advance directives provide a means for patients to retain influence on their medical care should decisional capacity be lost. Several studies have now demonstrated that advance directives that are completed in the ambulatory care setting are rarely available and recognized when patients are admitted to the acute care hospital.

**Objective**: To evaluate a generalizable model for improving recognition of previously completed advance directives and for promoting appointment of health care proxies in hospitalized patients.

**Methods**: Hospitalized elderly patients were randomly assigned to receive the intervention or usual care (n=190). Intervention patients with capacity were counseled by hospital patient representatives about advance directives and encouraged to complete health care proxies. Patients with existing proxies had this information noted in their charts. For patients without capacity, counselors reviewed their charts for proxy documentation and if absent, contacted patients' next of kin and private physicians to determine proxy status. Usual care patients were not contacted by patient representatives.

**Results**: Forty-eight percent of intervention patients completed a new proxy or had a previously completed proxy identified compared with 6% of controls ($P<.001$). For patients with capacity, 22% of intervention patients had a previously appointed proxy agent identified compared with 6% of controls ($P<.001$). Thirty-six percent of intervention patients appointed a proxy decision maker compared with 0% of controls ($P<.02$). For patients without capacity, 31% of intervention patients had previously appointed proxies identified compared with 6% of controls ($P<.001$).

**Conclusions**: Counseling by hospital patient representatives is an effective and generalizable means of improving recognition and execution of advance directives in the acute care hospital.

*Source*: Diane E. Meier, Barbara R. Fuss, Donna O'Rourke, Shari A. Baskin, Moshe Lewis, and R. Sean Morrison, "Marked Improvement in Recognition and Completion of Health Care Proxies: A Randomized Controlled Trial of Counseling by Hospital Patient Representatives," *Archives of Internal Medicine* 156 (1996): 1227–1232.

* * *

A number of interesting suggestions about encouraging completion of advance directives were made by Susan Evans and Peter Clarke.

---

## DOCUMENT 66: "Rethinking How We Communicate about Advance Directives," Susan Evans and Peter Clarke (1992)

---

We will share five challenges to the "obvious" facts about how best to urge people to execute, or just to think carefully about advance directives. Attempts thus far have produced a discouraging chain of results. ... We have plunged blindly into advanced planning for medical procedures without contemplating the surprises that might lie in store.... We can share five puzzles we are uncovering about people's attitudes toward advance directives and the issues they arouse....

*Puzzle number one.* Many of the people we have interviewed do not want to discuss end-of-life matters with physicians. Many people do not have a personal relationship with their doctor or report that they don't see the same physician from visit to visit.... *Puzzle number two.* People want the living will and durable power of attorney forms to be legally binding. Providing them on tear-off pads or selling them over-the-counter in the hospital gift shop shatters their authenticity.—*Puzzle number three.*—Confusion reins [*sic*] about procedures and terminology. And the misperception has taken firm root that a verbal statement, casually shared with one or two others, is adequate to ensure that wishes are honored.—*Puzzle number four.* We find sharp gender differences in decision-making strategies. Men fear giving control to anyone else, and they worry that by nominating a proxy, say their wife—they will saddle her with too heavy a burden. Women talk in terms of negative consequences of not completing an advance directive, such as a lack of tidiness in one's affairs. *Puzzle number five*—If logistical considerations force us to use hospitals and other care facilities to deliver the message, why not focus on the time of discharge rather than patient entry? As patients convalesce, they and family and close friends are susceptible to issues surrounding health care planning. Materials could be given to patients and their family with encouragement to study them at home.

*Source*: Susan Evans and Peter Clarke, "Rethinking How We Communicate about Advance Directives: Hidden Errors in Our Assumptions about Planning for Care," paper presented at the conference, "Communications and the Self-

Determination Act: Strategies for Meeting the Educational Mandate," Annenberg Washington Program and the American Association of Critical Care Nurses, Washington, DC, November 9–10, 1992.

* * *

## RESPONSES OF PHYSICIANS TO ADVANCE DIRECTIVES

The large and widely quoted SUPPORT study (Study to Understand Prognoses and Preferences for Outcomes and Risks of Treatments) dealt in part with attempts to increase the efficacy of advance directives. The conclusion of the article that dealt with this follows.

---

## DOCUMENT 67: "Advance Directives for Seriously Ill Hospitalized Patients," Joan Teno et al. (1997)

---

In these seriously ill patients, ADs [advance directives] did not substantially enhance physician-patient communication or decision-making about resuscitation. This lack of effect was not altered by the PSDA or by the enhanced efforts in SUPPORT, although these interventions each substantially increased documentation of existing ADs. Current practice patterns indicate that increasing the frequency of ADs is unlikely to be a substantial element in improving the care of seriously ill patients. Future work to improve decision-making should focus upon improving the current pattern of practice through better communication and more comprehensive advance care planning.

*Source*: Joan Teno, Joanne Lynn, Neil Wenger, Russell S. Phillips, Donald P. Murphy, Alfred F. Connors, Jr., Norman Desbiens, William Fulkerson, Paul Bellamy, and William A. Knaus for the SUPPORT Investigators, "Advance Directives for Seriously Ill Hospitalized Patients: Effectiveness with the Patient Self-Determination Act and the SUPPORT Intervention," *Journal of the American Geriatrics Society* 45 (1997): 500–507.

* * *

Editorial comments on this article emphasize the important role that should be played by a discussion between the patient and the physician.

## DOCUMENT 68: "Advance Directives and SUPPORT," Joseph J. Fins (1997)

. . . It is important to understand the physician's role because patients expect guidance from their physicians and seldom initiate prospective planning unilaterally. This suggests that advance care planning occurs in the context of relationships between the patient, the surrogates, and the physician. Looking at advance directive documentation without acknowledging the relationships that both sustain and inform them will lead us to confuse pre-existing documents for pre-existing *relationships*.

The authors note rightly that "advance directives cannot be expected to function well unless they arise from effective communication between patient and physician." Given this, it is not surprising that the intervention enhanced advance directive documentation but that these "documented" directives failed to influence care. These documents may not have been sustained by therapeutic relationships that have the power to direct care. Important life choices are not made in a formulaic or episodic manner but within the context of families and trusting relationships with clinicians.

SUPPORT's findings suggest that preferences regarding end of life decisions require more than documentation to be integrated into care decisions. They need an institutional setting that promotes dialogue, fosters continuity of care at the end of life, encourages the discovery of pre-existing preferences, and acknowledges the legitimacy of palliation.

Unfortunately, investigators have constructed a study design—and intervention—that makes good communication difficult. The way the patient is asked about resuscitation exemplifies how options were communicated:

As you know, there are a number of things doctors can do to try to revive someone whose heart has stopped beating, which usually includes a machine to help breathing. Thinking of your current condition, what would you want your doctors to do if your heart ever stops beating? Would you want your doctors to try to revive you, or would you want your doctors not to try to revive you?

The question is too narrowly cast. If the patient is simply asked whether she wants to be resuscitated, without being given an alternative palliative care option, the response is predictable. This reinforces the false belief that there are just two options at the end of life: resuscitation or "doing nothing." Posing the question in this way will bias responses that will lead to decisions to do "something" over "nothing." To truly assess patient preferences about resuscitation, patients need to be informed more fully about the likelihood of a successful resuscitation, its morbidity, and other care alternatives. When clinicians present resuscitation choices robustly, patients overwhelmingly decide to forgo resuscitation.

SUPPORT investigators should be commended for undertaking this randomized clinical trial. They have demonstrated the value of rigorous empirical research in clinical ethics. Nonetheless, we should recognize that the object of their study is anthropologically complex. When we interpret quantitative findings about care at the end of life, we must examine critically both the cultural assumptions that inform study design and the conclusions. It may be tempting to distill the many deficiencies in end of life care identified in SUPPORT into a critique of advance directives. However, as clinicians, we should remind ourselves that the failure is ours and not the fault of advance directives. Shifting responsibility away from ourselves indicates our own denial of death and avoidance of much needed dialogue at the bedside of dying patients. It is too easy to scapegoat advance directives when it is clear that advance directives are going to be only as good as our efforts to obtain them.

Advance care planning will become effective only when we are more comfortable discussing end of life care and when we understand the cultural determinants that have made American medicine so hesitant to accept human finitude. For as Dr. Stead reminds us, "You have to know the culture of the system as well as the science of the system in order for things to work at all."

*Source*: Joseph J. Fins, "Advance Directives and SUPPORT," *Journal of the American Geriatrics Society* 45 (1997): 519–520 (references omitted).

* * *

Many physicians not only fail to discuss end-of-life planning with their patients, but also fail to carry out the patient's wishes, whether expressed through a living will or by appointment of a health care agent. The following letter from an agent who had great difficulty in having her mother's wishes carried out describes such a situation poignantly.

## DOCUMENT 69: "A Letter from a Patient's Daughter," Elisabeth Hansot (1996)

My mother, Georgia Hansot, died recently in the intensive care unit of a major hospital in the eastern United States. She was 87 years old. This is an account of the 5 days she spent in the hospital from the point of view of her daughter, a 57-year-old professional woman who was charged with her mother's power of attorney for health care. . . .

This essay could as easily be entitled "There Are No Villains Here." Medical personnel, trained to save lives and not to let patients die, exerted themselves to that end. Hospital staff and the families of other patients in the intensive care unit, as time and ability allowed, tried to comfort. Nonetheless, those 5 days were among the loneliest and most disorienting that I have ever experienced.

As I think back on it, I am astounded that I had so little inkling of how hard it would be to help my mother have the death she wanted. . . .

Entrusted with a general power of attorney and a power of attorney for health care, I believed that I could make decisions on her behalf as she would want them made if she were to become incapacitated. As it turned out, I was woefully unprepared for what was in store for her and for me.

On a spring morning in April, my mother abruptly became ill and was promptly admitted to the local hospital. When I arrived in the late afternoon, she was resting comfortably after a long day of diagnostic tests. Because she had been tired by the day's ordeal, I stayed only briefly, promising to be back early in the morning with newspapers and books. I left my number with the nurse, in case of an emergency.

At 2:00 the next morning, I was awakened by a call from the night nurse. My mother had suddenly taken a turn for the worse and was being transferred to intensive care. I arrived on the hospital floor just as the gurney was being wheeled into the unit. My mother's face was covered by an oxygen mask, but she was able to respond to my voice with an exclamation. It was the last time she would be able to do so.

I tried to accompany her into the intensive care unit but could not. The physician in charge firmly instructed me to stay outside until my mother was "taken care of." An hour later, when I was allowed to see her, she was attached to a respirator and had a feeding tube inserted down her throat.

What had happened? My mother had left a carefully updated power of attorney for health care with her physician, her lawyer, and her offspring, reaffirming her determination not to have her life prolonged by artificial means. Exactly the opposite of what she had wished had occurred; the living will had become invisible just when it was needed most. My mother's physician, it turned out, had not notified the medical team of her advance directive, and the hospital, despite a 1990 federal law that mandates such inquiries, did not ask my mother whether she had such a document. And I, in turn, had neglected to check that the physicians and nurses knew about her desire not to have heroic measures used to prolong her life.

Over the ensuing 5 days, I came to understand how serious the results of these omissions were. I found that I was dealing with a bewildering array of medical specialists trained to prolong lives, not to let patients die. During the first day that my mother was in the intensive care unit, I asked her physician to make it clear to the attending medical personnel that she had given me durable power of attorney for health care. He readily complied. I was told that my mother had had a stroke and that she would not recover from her hemiparalysis. The physicians hoped to fit her with a tracheostomy tube and send her to a nursing home. From my many conversations with my mother about quality of life and medical care, I knew that she did not want such a life. Yet my mother's wishes, as they were understood by her family physician and her daughter, were now subject to the approval of strangers: the cadre of cardiologists, neurologists, and pulmonologists who attended her.

None of these specialists knew my mother, and they all had their convictions about how to do best by her. Most notably, they varied in the latitude with which they were willing to interpret her wishes (I had become her spokesperson; my only sibling, an older brother, was out of the country). The variance was widest between my mother's wishes and those of the attending pulmonologist: He made it clear that his approach was conservative in such matters. He found it nearly impossible to accept that my mother would prefer death to living with hemiparalysis and a tracheotomy. Over the next several days, our conversations became terser and tenser as he raised such questions as whether perhaps I was an ageist, or an ideologue interested only in abstract principles. I asked the family physician whether another pulmonologist could attend the case, only to be told that all of the pulmonologists accredited to the hospital shared similar beliefs.

My stress built over the ensuing 5 days as my mother's distress was palpable. She successfully tore out her feeding tube only to have it reinserted and her restraints tightened. An attempt to remove my mother from the ventilator failed; her swollen larynx prevented her from breathing on her own. I had agreed to the removal on the condition that I be allowed to stay with her during the attempt. Afterward, the pulmonologist declared himself pleased that he had been able to reinsert her breathing tube, barely in time. He seemed, however, unaware of how agitated this process had left her. I asked that she be sedated, and an obliging nurse obtained permission for this.

The hospital increasingly came to feel like alien territory, full of medical strangers intent on maintaining my mother's vital signs at all costs. During her ordeal, my mother became increasingly frantic. She continually leaned against her restraints, trying to get her hand close enough to her feeding tube to tear it out again. My sense of being trapped in a nightmare intensified.

In the long days that I spent with her, I learned to read her increasing anguish through her refusals to have her mouth swabbed or to have the secretions in it suctioned dry. One afternoon, she rapped her cuffed hand angrily against the bed bars to get my attention, then motioned toward the tubes that she clearly wished to have removed. The next day, when I was holding her hand, she squeezed mine so hard that I winced in pain, and after that a breakthrough came: We were able to devise a mode of talking to each other.

In response to a yes or no question, my mother nodded or shook her head. Once this mode of communication was clearly established, I was able to ask my mother twice—with her nurse as a witness, and with 4 hours between each question—whether she wished to die. My very clear-headed and determined mother thus was able, finally, to assert herself for the necessary last time. The nurse informed the physicians of what she had seen. Then the wait began. The hours dragged by as the specialists were persuaded, one by one, to give their consent. Finally, a technician was allowed to pull the tube from my mother's throat. None of the physicians who had attended her was present. . . .

In the weeks that followed my mother's ordeal, I listened, with the rest of the United States, to accounts of the deaths of Richard Nixon and Jacqueline Onassis. Because both of them had living wills, the commentators explained, their lives would not be prolonged by mechanical means. Angry and frustrated at the way my mother had died, I wondered: Do you have to be notable to be heard in our society?

All told, I think that my mother was fortunate. In the long run, her wishes were followed; 5 days in the intensive care unit compares favorably with the experiences of many other elderly persons. But the experience was harrowing, for her and for me. What is routine for hospital staff is all too often the first experience of its kind for critically ill patients and their families. I had a very steep and painful learning curve. This essay is written in the hope that hospitals will devise procedures so that patients and their families can, with less pain and perplexity than I experienced, decide when and how death arrives.

*Source*: Elisabeth Hansot, "A Letter from a Patient's Daughter," *Annals of Internal Medicine* 125 (1996): 149–151.

\* \* \*

The following document is a thoughtful discussion of Ms. Hansot's difficulties by two sensitive physicians.

## DOCUMENT 70: "Whose Death Is It, Anyway?" Timothy Gilligan and Thomas A. Raffin (1996)

### Autonomy

Patient autonomy is, in principle, a cornerstone of the legitimacy of Western medicine. Legally, a person's right to control his or her body is sacrosanct, and forcing medical care on an unwilling patient is akin to battery. Although patients do not have the right to demand interventions that are clearly futile, physicians do not have the right to impose interventions, even if medically indicated, contrary to the patient's wishes. The legal history establishing a competent patient's right to refuse medical interventions has been well documented elsewhere. Although we appreciate the concern that Ms. Hansot's physicians showed for the preservation of life, the actions of these physicians violated the patient's right to decide for herself what quality of life was acceptable. The hospital was legally required to ascertain whether Ms. Hansot had completed an advance directive or similar document but failed to do so. Then, the physicians put a tube down the patient's throat, connected her to a mechanical ventilator, and placed her in physical restraints so that she could not emancipate herself. Despite clear evidence from the patient and the patient's legally designated agent that Ms. Hansot did not want her life prolonged in this manner, it took 5 days for the physicians to relent and bring their interventions into accord with the patient's desires. That these physicians acted with the best of intentions makes Ms. Hansot's experience no less painful.

Withholding and withdrawing life support from patients has gained widespread acceptance in the medical community and the legal system, but we still see far too many patients trying desperately to cut short the process of dying, only to have their best efforts rebuffed by physicians. This unwanted medicine is an arrogant usurpation of patients' rights and serves neither the interests of the patient nor those of medicine as a profession. In ancient Greece, the Hippocratic Corpus stated that one of the primary roles of medicine was to refrain from treating hopelessly ill persons, lest physicians be thought of as charlatans. This caveat still applies today. . . .

### Communication, Listening, and Caring

Communication and listening skills are prerequisites for good physician-patient relationships, and they give the physician a chance to learn what an illness means to the patient and the patient's family. Good communication skills make patients feel less lost in the hospital environment and more cared for by their physicians. Effective communication is particularly important in the intensive care unit, which is an alien environment for patients and their loved ones. It is filled with monitors and unfamiliar sounds, and the patients are often obscured by a sea of wires and tubing. Visitors may find themselves overwhelmed not only by the gravity of the patient's malady but also by the foreign stimuli. If the patient's loved ones must make life-and-death decisions on the patient's behalf, they will probably have feelings of grief, guilt, and confusion. Caring physicians who take the time to make emotional, human contact with patients and their families can greatly ease the burden that these persons feel at times of crisis.

Reading Dr. Hansot's account of her mother's last days of life, we ask ourselves what happened to the humanistic aspect of medicine in this case. One of the roles of physicians is to give solace and support to patients' families during times of serious illness. That the pulmonologist accused Dr. Hansot of being an ageist preoccupied with abstract principles when she was trying to realize her mother's wishes is to us a double violation of the principle of nonmaleficence: The physician not only did harm to the patient by prolonging her suffering but did harm to the patient's daughter by gratuitously insulting her and causing her anguish. We believe that much of Dr. Hansot's and Ms. Hansot's distress could have been avoided if the physicians had made a greater effort to listen to their patient and her daughter. . . .

### Beyond Better Communication

. . . The problem of poor communication also reflects ongoing ambivalence and uncertainties about power and control in the physician-patient relationship. As the physician has gradually taken on a less paternalistic role in Western medicine, more emphasis has been placed on patient autonomy. This shift in emphasis has moved the balance of power in the direction of the patient. Educating patients about their diseases and available therapeutic options empowers them to participate more fully in medical decision making, but it also may threaten the physician's sense of authority. Physicians may feel that they, with their greater medical knowledge and experience, are in a better position to make decisions about health care. Moreover, when it comes to difficult decisions about end-of-life care, physicians may believe that they can relieve the patient's family of guilt, regret, and confusion by making tough choices on their own. However, treatment decisions are influenced not only by outcome probabilities but also by physicians' personal values and priorities. Because it is the patient's life that is at stake, we believe that the patient's voice must be heard and the patient's values must be honored.

The case of Ms. Hansot raises an additional question about power: Was the physicians' disregard for their patient's wishes influenced by the fact that Ms. Hansot and her daughter were women? We will never know the answer, but it is an important question to ask. In the legal world, for example, a study of appellate court decisions in right-to-die cases found that the courts consistently portrayed female patients as less capable of rational decision making than male patients. And the issue is not just that men devalue women's voices; it is much more complicated. Feminist psychologists have observed that women are often more interested in the truths of relationships than in the dictates of abstract principles, in the knowledge derived from human connections rather than the knowledge derived from impersonal reasoning. When Dr. Hansot confronted her mother's physicians, a series of power dynamics were put into play. Dr. Hansot was a non-medical person questioning medical professionals; she was a woman questioning men, and she was posing the facts of her relationship with her mother against the facts of medicine presented by the physicians. The pulmonologist accused Dr. Hansot of preoccupation with abstract principles, but it seems to us that just the opposite was true. It was the pulmonologist himself who was preoccupied with the general medical principle that life is good and death is bad. Dr. Hansot was preoccupied with the knowledge of her mother's wishes, which she had obtained through a close, lifelong relationship. We are arguing not that one perspective is superior to the other but that the power differential in the physician-patient relationship can represent a deeper problem that impedes communication and interferes with optimal medical care. . . .

## Other Obstacles to Communication

Physicians may also fail to communicate with patients or ignore their requests to limit care because of the stress and emotional discomfort associated with confronting death. Physicians may be uncomfortable with their own mortality and hence may avoid spending much time with dying patients. Moreover, having been trained to prolong life and overcome disease, they may feel like failures when they allow a patient to die if that patient's life could have been prolonged with life support. In this regard, withholding or withdrawing life-sustaining care can be one of the most difficult actions that a physician has to take. Physicians who feel that they are unable to take such action probably should not work in critical care.

Discomfort with death may also explain one of the more disturbing aspects of Ms. Hansot's case: the feelings of abandonment experienced by the patient and her daughter. Why did the physician of record leave it to Dr. Hansot to determine that it was indeed possible to communicate with the intubated patient? Why were none of Ms. Hansot's physicians present at the time of death? There is an unfortunate tendency in hospitals to avoid engaging the humanity of critically ill patients near the end of life. The focus of intensive-care-unit rounds can quickly turn from the patient to the flow sheet of vital signs and laboratory values. When this happens, the patient is denied some of the most important benefits that medicine has to offer, and the physicians are denied one of their most meaningful roles, that of bedside caregiver.

Finally, physicians may fear the legal ramifications of withholding or withdrawing life support. These ramifications are complicated and still evolving, and they vary from state to state; we cannot explore them in detail in this context. What is clear is that physicians have no legal right to provide health care contrary to the wishes of the legally competent patient. . . .

### Death as a Colleague

The failure to determine and respect the end-of-life wishes of patients is an obstacle to improving the quality of medical care, an obstacle that will require doctors to come to terms with death and adjust their vision of their role in patients' lives. . . .

Dr. Hansot's account of her interactions with her mother's pulmonologist suggests problems encountered all too often in medicine: It is easier to keep patients alive on ventilators than to grapple with withdrawing support, and it is easier to define success in terms of life and death than to try to determine the quality of life that is meaningful to an individual patient. To the physicians attending Ms. Hansot, sending a hemiparetic patient with a tracheostoma out of the hospital to live in a nursing home counted as success. Ms. Hansot, however, had indicated that she wanted to be allowed to die. The patient in this case recognized death as a friend; her physicians were unable to accept death as a colleague.

### Conclusion

Dr. Hansot presents a troubling picture of medicine. She portrays physicians who are so preoccupied with the preservation of life that they can no longer see the broader human context of their work, physicians who have lost sight of one of the privileges and responsibilities of medicine: to offer some humanity at moments of suffering and loss. Most disturbing, the physicians felt that they had the right to force a sick, elderly woman to undergo the frightening and uncomfortable experience of mechanical ventilation when she clearly wished to be allowed to die.

*Source*: Timothy Gilligan and Thomas A. Raffin, "Whose Death Is It, Anyway?" *Annals of Internal Medicine* 125 (1996): 137–141 (references omitted).

\* \* \*

A study of the attitudes of 687 physicians and 759 nurses was carried out at five varied hospitals in widely separated areas of the United States (Mildred Z. Solomon, Lydia O'Donnell, and Bruce Jennings, et al., "Decisions Near the End of Life: Professional Views on Life-Sustaining Treatments." *American Journal of Public Health* 83 [1992]: 14–23). The conclusions of this study are discussed and amplified by Nancy Neveloff Dubler.

---

## DOCUMENT 71: "Commentary: Balancing Life and Death— Proceed with Caution," Nancy Neveloff Dubler (1993)

---

In this Public Health Policy Forum, Solomon et al. present compelling data that indicate that a patient's last days may not be as comfortable and pain-free as good medicine and humane care should demand. My observations certainly support such an assertion. Nonetheless, I suspect that the authors' conclusion—that national recommendations are insufficiently respected as guidelines for care—fails to take into account the huge chasm that separates abstract principles from the messy reality of patient care.

Conceptual language is best suited to the presentation of principles and the analysis of concepts. Case material best illuminates anguish and explains ambivalence. Consider the following case, in which all identifying elements have been changed to shield the identity and protect the privacy of the patient and family:

Mr. B. was an 83-year-old White male who had taught piano for most of his adult life. In his late 70s he had developed diabetes, complications of which had led to one below-the-knee amputation and blindness in one eye and impaired vision in the other. He had also developed severe arthritis that prevented him from playing the piano pieces he had committed to memory over a lifetime. At the time of his hospital admission, he was homebound and confined to a wheelchair with a 24-hour home attendant and visiting nurse services. The patient's grandson had married recently, an event that Mr. B. had awaited eagerly. Shortly after the wedding he experienced difficulty breathing and was admitted to the hospital, where he was transferred almost immediately to the intensive care unit.

After 4 weeks of intensive care the patient had deteriorated rapidly. He was on a ventilator with a tracheostomy and on vasopressors, livophed, and dialysis. He drifted in and out of consciousness. The physician presented Mr. B.'s prognosis to the family. On the basis of the patient's septic shock, multiple organ failure, and progressive downward course, the physician concluded that there was less than a 1% chance that the patient would recover to leave the intensive care unit, let alone leave the hospital. In response to this statement, Mr. B.'s daughter, who visited him at the beginning and end of every day, stated that she possessed her father's living will, executed in the year before his admission, and that she thought that the time had come to follow its directives.

The nurses caring for Mr. B. stated that they thought that, despite his disabilities, he was capable of making the decision to terminate care. They reported that whenever he was at all lucid he mouthed "enough," "I want to die." These statements were confirmed by the daughter. However, on the day all of the staff and the family gathered to make the decision, Mr. B. was unable to focus and respond to questions.

The decision was made to use the living will, rather than contemporaneous patient refusal, as the basis for discontinuing care. Nonetheless, Mr. B.'s statements, documented by the nurses over time, were noted in the chart. The office of hospital counsel, the office of risk management, the members of the administration, liaison psychiatry, and the ethics consult team were all involved in the decision.

The nurses were horrified by the prospect of terminating ventilatory support and suggested instead that dialysis be terminated. Withholding dialysis seemed more compassionate to them. The expectation was that the patient would slip into uremic coma and die quietly and without discomfort.

Dialysis was terminated and Mr. B was discharged from the intensive care unit and moved to an unmonitored bed.

One week later, his kidney failure having largely abated, Mr. B. was conscious and alert and absolutely adamant that he no longer wanted to continue to receive medical care under these conditions. He communicated this wish to all of his medical and family visitors by mouthing the words "I want to die" and by writing them on a pad.

The chief physician in the intensive care unit, who had remained involved with the case, reconvened all of the parties. He agreed in advance to be the physician responsible for managing the death. The son and grandson gathered at the bedside with the family doctor, who had cared for the patient for over 30 years. After all were agreed, the family physician blurted out, "and Mr. B., when you are gasping for breath should I reconnect your tube?" At that, the intensive care unit physician pushed forward and assured Mr. B. that he would be fully sedated and would experience no discomfort. "Valium?," the patient mouthed. "No, morphine," the physician answered.

In a discussion with the nurses shortly after it had been decided to disconnect the ventilator that evening, the supervising nurse insisted that nursing responsibility still required turning the patient and monitoring his care. Ultimately the nurses agreed that their real concern was to not abandon the patient; they agreed to station a nurse at his bedside during the dying process as a reflection of their caring function and as a sign of respect. The patient was heavily sedated with morphine and died 8 hours after the ventilator was disconnected.

Removing life supports and permitting death is traumatic for some caregivers and alien to all. It demands a reexamination of the goals of care, an admission of the failure of medical science to forestall mortality, and an elevation of the patient's autonomy and legal right to refuse treatment over caregivers' notions of beneficence. Yet, as Solomon et al. correctly point out, the law often permits or even demands this outcome and national ethical guidelines support it. What they have not adequately addressed, in my opinion, is the complexity of medical culture and context, the lack of medical/administrative leadership in most hospitals, the peculiarly pernicious role of lawyers—as opposed to legal principles and developed case law—and the unsupported authority of the guidelines to which the authors regularly appeal.

Medical socialization begins before medical school and continues through postgraduate training. Most of that education, with the exception of some ethics classes, focuses on the use of medical technology and scientific knowledge to preserve life. Nursing education concentrates more on issues of patient comfort and patient choice, but nurses rarely call the shots in the acute care setting. Techniques of hospice care, including proper pain control and support for patient and family, are rarely, if ever, addressed in medical curricula. How can we expect staff to be comfortable with a process for which they have little or no training and which seems fraught with moral, legal, and regulatory dangers? Indeed, the complexity of these issues for most hospital administration is demonstrated by the number of professionals gathered at the bedside to make the decision. Note that the patient's lack of kidney function, that aspect of the clinical picture that was assumed stable and was expected to be the cause of death, reversed itself. Uncertainty is the ever-present and little-acknowledged companion of medical advice.

The miseducation of young professionals is subsequently reinforced by messages from hospital administrators. These professionals function in an era of increasing market competition for patient dollars, in which a lower than projected patient census may push the hospital into the red. Hospitals' publicity and public relations offices, strategic planners, and development staff would, I suspect, be horrified by a campaign that said, "We will respect your rights and let you die . . . come to us." This reluctance to highlight support for a patient's right to terminate care and accept death probably reflects the uncertainty of not only the physician, but also the patient and the family, about the right moment to accept death. No one is unambivalent about the process of dying, and respect for choices to die must coexist with robust determinations to preserve life. Indeed, patients and families might be willing to trade in some of their recognition of the right to terminate care for a determined care team doggedly pursuing recovery. Furthermore, although it is not central to the arguments of Solomon et al., my experience indicates that many people are suspicious about, or afraid of, these newly articulated rights.

I first encountered this phenomenon some years ago, in a project that offered patients with acquired immunodeficiency syndrome the opportunity to execute advance directives. Most of the patients were poor intravenous drug users and persons of color. Many had had very little access to care until their acute illness. They were not interested in living wills and durable powers of attorney limiting care—they were interested in access to care! Many feared that advance directives were part of an ongoing and unarticulated societal plan to cut costs and deprive them of care. They feared that if they issued directions to limit care under certain circumstances they would be interpreted, wrongly, as expressing a lack of desire for life.

Many older patients, too, fear that a living will, combined with their age and frailty, could be used to deprive them of care that they might want before the trigger event stipulated as the sign to withhold care. Indeed, some of these fears are probably justified. It is still common for many house staff and attending physicians to create a penumbra of nontreatment around orders not to resuscitate. Many still think these orders are incompatible with aggressive care. Some interpret the do-not-resuscitate provisions of a living will similarly. Concerns about the negative medical consequences of exercising one's rights as a patient may not be unfounded.

Some lawyers have also played a particularly troubling role in the limitation of patients' rights to refuse care. Whether as part of the office of hospital counsel or as outside experts, some lawyers acting as risk management consultants have argued for a pragmatic, rather than a principled, resolution of doubt about decisions to terminate care. The conflict between upholding the law and protecting the hospital from possible future liability has often relegated patients' rights to refuse life-sustaining treatment to a secondary status.

Many lawyer/risk managers have tipped the scale to override a patient's rights if any potential conflict exists. For example, if a daughter objects to a living will, her opposition may be dispositive. If someone contests the patient's choice, that disagreement may move the decision to a court despite the lack of a clear justiciable issue. This timidity and hesitation to honor patients' choices and advance directives is communicated clearly to staff. The message is: This is scary business; proceed with caution. The aura created, one of suspicion and possible future liability, is not conducive to advocacy for the patient's right to refuse care. This excessive caution is the rule in some institutions despite the paucity of case law. Granted, it is difficult or impossible to prove a negative proposition. Nonetheless, in an era in which many deaths are negotiated, it must reflect some developing societal agreement and norm of practice that almost never is such a decision contested later in court. The fact that family members or others have not sued in the past does not mean that they might not in the future—virtually anyone can sue for anything at any time and lots of people in this society choose to—but the reality is that risk management's fears in this area belie reality.

Finally, Solomon et al. assume that there is some necessary relationship between the decisionally capable patient's legal right to refuse life-sustaining care—both in the present and for the future—and "national recommendations" that propose supportive ethical analyses and commentary.

Bringing a patient's preferences and rights, family concerns, legal rules, and ethical principles into harmony is the task of the 1990s. All related professionals should be struggling toward a consolidation of existing wisdom and an implementation of existing rights as new areas are explored.

Mr. B. died a few weeks after he had apparently chosen that course, but only 1 week after his daughter, his protector and advocate, had raised the issue of his advance directives that were documented in a living will. Note that at least part of the prognosis—permanent kidney failure—offered by a skilled and experienced team in an intensive care unit proved to be incorrect. He died with his family there, with adequate sedation and enhanced nursing attention. It was a learning experience for all on the staff and will become part of the common ethic of how the institution implements decisions to withdraw care.

Both medical culture and the context of medical care decisions are changing, although the demands to support and preserve life will always exist in a somewhat uneasy alliance with the obligation to respect patients' and families' wishes and terminate care. Balancing life and death is an awesomely difficult task and should always be approached with caution and respect. And given the basis in reality of the fears of some patients that they will be ignored or abandoned, and given the fact that many in this society have limited or no access to care, caution is justified.

*Source*: Nancy Neveloff Dubler, "Commentary Balancing Life and Death—Proceed with Caution," *American Journal of Public Health* 83 (1993): 23–25 (references omitted).

* * *

The study of Solomon et al. was also the subject of a column in the *New York Times*.

---

## DOCUMENT 72: "Doctors Admit Ignoring Dying Patients' Wishes," Jane E. Brody (1993)

---

In a large new survey, doctors and nurses say they often violate their own personal beliefs and ignore requests from patients to withhold life support in cases of terminal illness.

They also say they often fail to provide adequate pain relief for dying patients in hospitals, despite the patients' expressed wishes to be spared severe pain. The lack of relief and the unwanted treatment occur even though laws, courts and hospitals support carrying out such requests, the study noted.

These findings, from a detailed survey of medical practitioners released yesterday, point to a wide gulf between rapidly changing societal beliefs about appropriate treatment and the actual practice of medicine on the firing line.

The survey was conducted through a 123-item questionnaire completed by 1,400 doctors and nurses at five major hospitals in different parts of the country. Its findings, collated by Dr. Mildred Solomon of the Education Development Center Inc., in Newton, Mass., were published yesterday in the January issue of the American Journal of Public Health.

### Regret About Overtreatment

Nearly half the attending physicians and nurses and fully 70 percent of resident physicians reported acting against their conscience in overtreating terminally ill patients, even when there is no chance for recovery and death is considered imminent. And four times as many of those surveyed were concerned about burdensome overtreatment as were concerned about undertreatment of dying patients.

The results suggest not only that patients' desires are often ignored but that in ignoring them, medical personnel may also be substantially contributing to the uncontrolled escalation of health care costs. In the final stages of a terminal illness, hospital care can cost $100,000 a month or more and divert scarce medical attention and costly resources from patients who have a chance to improve or recover.

In a commentary accompanying the report, Nancy Neveloff Dubler, a lawyer and bioethicist at Montefiore Medical Center in the Bronx, said the survey indicated "that a patient's last days may not be as comfortable and pain-free as good medicine and humane care should demand." She added that a "huge chasm" continued to separate "abstract principles from the messy reality of patient care."

For example, the researchers found that medical personnel were often unaware of national directives and hospital policies that sanction decisions to withhold or withdraw aids like respirators and kidney machines and other treatments, including feeding patients by tube or vein, that can prolong life in the terminally ill.

Since the landmark court decision in 1976 that allowed the removal of life support from Karen Ann Quinlan, who spent the last years of her life in a coma, there has been a wave of directives defining what is legally and ethically appropriate in caring for dying patients. The recommendations and rulings have come from a Presidential commission, major professional organizations in medicine, law and ethics, state and Congressional laws and numerous court decisions.

Despite some differences in details, in all cases the directives endorse the rights of doctors and nurses to respect the wishes of dying patients to withhold treatments that might prolong their lives and hence their suffering. The directives also call for the administration of adequate pain relief, without fear of causing addiction or hastening death, so that patients can die with dignity.

Yet, according to Dr. Solomon and her co-authors, two-thirds of the health professionals surveyed said they were dissatisfied with the way patients were involved in treatment decisions, and 81 percent of respondents agreed that "the most common form of narcotic abuse in caring for dying patients is undertreatment of pain."

## Changing Institutional Policy

In an editorial accompanying the report, Dr. Bruce C. Vladeck, president of the United Hospital Fund of New York, noted that "actual clinical behavior continues to diverge from the consensus about what is appropriate, but not because clinicians disagree with that consensus." Changing organizational behavior is far harder than changing individual attitudes, he said.

Accordingly, the Education Development Center, in conjunction with The Hastings Center, a bioethics institute in Briarcliff Manor, N.Y., has developed a program called Decisions Near the End of Life that is now in use at more than 50 hospitals and nursing homes around the country. The program first assesses prevailing views of the hospital staff, then provides education and training to improve the care of terminally ill patients.

Dr. Solomon said indications from a preliminary analysis of the results of the program in various institutions "are very encouraging." She said it is making a difference in changing institutional policies and in reducing the anxieties of medical personnel and the suffering of patients and their families.

Source: Jane E. Brody, "Doctors Admit Ignoring Dying Patients' Wishes," *New York Times*, January 27, 1993, C16.

\* \* \*

## COST SAVINGS

One might suspect that the use of advance directives would result in cost savings at the end of life. Considerable evidence, summarized by Ezekiel J. Emanuel and Linda L. Emanuel ("The Economics of Dying: The Illusion of Cost Savings at the End of Life," *New England Journal of Medicine* 330 [1994]: 540–544), indicates that this is not the case. "The amount that might be saved by reducing the use of aggressive life-sustaining interventions for dying patients is at most 3.3% of total national health care expenditures. In 1993, with $900 billion going to health care, this savings would amount to $29.7 billion."

## DO NOT RESUSCITATE (DNR) ORDERS

Before the development of technical means for extending life, death was signalled by cessation of breathing or of the heartbeat. In the late 1960s and early 1970s, remarkably effective measures were devised for resuscitating an individual whose heartbeat or respiration had ceased. Resuscitation was initially provided by professionals, but members of the general public received training in cardiopulmonary resuscitation (CPR) soon thereafter. Of apparently healthy ambulatory individuals who suffered cardiopulmonary arrest and received bystander-initiated CPR, 43 percent were subsequently discharged from the hospital (Robert G. Thompson, Alfred P. Hallstrom, and Leonard A. Cobb, "Bystander-Initiated Cardiopulmonary Resuscitation in the Management of Ventricular Fibrillation," *Annals of Internal Medicine* 90 [1979]: 737–740). The outlook was much less optimistic when the patient was elderly. According to four surveys cited by Donald J. Murphy, David Burrows, and Sara Santilli ("The Influence of the Probability of Survival on Patients' Preferences Regarding Cardiopulmonary Resuscitation," *New England Journal of Medicine* 330 [1994]: 545–549), elderly ambulatory patients had only a 10 percent chance of surviving to discharge when they were brought to the hospital after suffering cardiac arrest and resuscitation.

CPR then began to be used in hospitalized individuals who were very ill and often elderly. Under these circumstances, patients have a less than 5 percent chance of surviving to discharge. The article by Murphy and his coworkers summarized the literature indicating that most hospitalized elderly patients wished to undergo CPR if they suffered cardiac or respiratory failure. Health care personnel in hospitals unfortunately often make little effort to explain the likely outcome of

CPR, so that few of these patients understood its high failure rate and the poor chance of their leaving the hospital. To determine patients' choices before and after learning the chances of survival, Murphy and his colleagues interviewed 287 ambulatory patients in a geriatrics practice. When patients learned the true probability of survival to discharge, only half as many patients said that they would choose to have CPR if they suffered cardiopulmonary arrest during hospitalization.

To prevent the often futile use of psychologically and physically painful CPR in extremely ill or dying patients, the do-not-resuscitate (DNR) order was devised. Obviously, DNR orders are only issued when it is clear that the patient is unlikely to survive for very long.

Laws about executing a DNR order differ between states. In New York State, a patient with decisional capacity makes the decision regarding a DNR order. If a patient lacks decisional capacity, a DNR order can be made by the patient's agent, or if there is no agent or surrogate, the decision can be made by the treating physician in concurrence with a second physician.

**DOCUMENT 73: New York State DNR Order Form (1995)**

# State of New York
# Department of Health

# Nonhospital Order Not to Resuscitate
# (DNR Order)

Person's Name    _____

Date of Birth __ / __ / __

Do not resuscitate the person named above.

Physician's Signature    _____

Print Name _____

License Number _____

Date __ / __ / __

It is the responsibility of the physician to determine, at least every 90 days, whether this order continues to be appropriate, and to indicate this by a note in the person's medical chart. The issuance of a new form is NOT required, and under the law this order should be considered valid unless it is known that it has been revoked. This order remains valid and must be followed, even if it has not been reviewed within the 90-day period.

*Source*: New York State Department of Health.

* * *

If a patient is dying at home and suffers cardiopulmonary arrest, he or she may not want to be resuscitated. To prevent resuscitation if the emergency medical service (EMS) has been called, many states permit the patient to execute a nonhospital DNR order. Such an order usually must be prepared on a special form, signed by a physician, and renewed periodically. It directs EMS personnel or anyone else who is presented with such an order to refrain from attempting to resuscitate the patient.

## DOCUMENT 74: Typical Nonhospital DNR Form (1995)

## EMERGENCY MEDICAL SERVICES (EMS)
## DO NOT RESUSCITATE (DNR) FORM

### AN ADVANCE DIRECTIVE TO LIMIT THE SCOPE OF EMS CARE

*NOTE: THIS ORDER TAKES PRECEDENCE OVER A DURABLE HEALTH CARE POWER OF ATTORNEY FOR EMS TREATMENT ONLY*

I, _____, request limited EMS care as described in this document. If my heart stops beating or if I stop breathing, no medical procedure to restore breathing or heart functioning will be instituted, by any health care provider, including but not limited to EMS personnel.

I understand that this decision will not prevent me from receiving other EMS care, such as oxygen and other comfort care measures.

I understand that I may revoke this Order at any time.

I give permission for this information to be given to EMS personnel, doctors, nurses and other health care professionals. I hereby agree to this DNR Order.

_____    OR    _____
Signature                                    Signature/Authorized
                                             Health Care Decision Maker

                                             _____
                                             Relationship

I affirm that this patient/authorized health care decision maker is making an informed decision and that this is the expressed directive of the patient. I hereby certify that I or my designee have explained to the patient the full meaning of the Order, available alternatives, and how the Order may be revoked. I or my designee have provided an opportunity for the patient/authorized health care decision maker to ask and have answered any questions regarding the execution of this form. A copy of this Order has been placed in the medical record. In the event of cardiopulmonary arrest, no chest compressions, artificial ventilations, intubation, defibrillation, or cardiac medications are to be initiated.

_____        _____
Physician's Signature / Date              Physician's Name - PRINT

_____
Physician's Address / Phone

White Copy: To be kept by patient in white envelope and immediately available to Emergency Responders
Yellow Copy: To be kept in patient's permanent medical record
Pink Copy: If DNR Bracelet/Medallion is desired send to MedicAlert with enrollment form.

*Source*: New Mexico Department of Health.

## FURTHER READING

Annas, George, J. *The Rights of Patients: The Basic ACLU Guide to Patient Rights.* 2d ed. Carbondale, IL: Southern Illinois University Press, 1989.

Cantor, Normal L. *Advance Directives and the Pursuit of Death with Dignity.* Bloomington, IN: Indiana University Press, 1993.

Collins, Evan R., with Doron Weber. *The Complete Guide to Living Wills.* New York: Bantam Books, 1991.

Hill, T. Patrick, and David Shirley. *A Good Death: Taking More Control at the End of Your Life.* Reading, MA: Addison-Wesley, 1992.

Meisel, Alan. *The Right to Die.* 2d ed. 2 vols. New York: John Wiley and Sons, 1995.

# Part V

# The Role of the Courts in End-of-Life Decision Making

In our society, the courts play a vital role in establishing the rules of conduct in the absence of relevant legislation and are essential in interpreting legislation since statutes cannot be sufficiently explicit to cover every contingency. The state courts, as well as the U.S. Supreme Court, have played a crucial role in defining treatment options at the end of life and determining whether or not treatment may be withheld or withdrawn from a patient who is thought to be hopelessly ill and not able to make his or her own decisions. Generally speaking, the courts have addressed the following questions:

1. Does the request impinge upon the four state interests that should be considered before withdrawing life support? These interests are clearly set forth in a number of court decisions. They are the following:

   a) The interest of the state in the preservation of life

   b) The need to protect innocent third parties

   c) The duty to prevent suicide

   d) The requirement that the state help maintain the ethical integrity of the medical community

2. What is the mental status of the patient?

   (a) Does the patient presently have decisional capacity? Decisional capacity is a clinical designation referring to a person's ability to understand and appreciate the nature and consequences of the decision being made. Capacity is not absolute but is decision specific. This means that even persons with cognitive impairment such as early dementia may be capable of making certain medical decisions and appointing a health care agent. Technically, capacity differs from competence, which must be determined in a court of law.

(b) Has the patient lost capacity that he or she formerly had (e.g., is the patient in a persistent vegetative state)?

(c) Has the patient never had adequate capacity?

(d) Is the patient a minor?

3. What right does the patient or surrogate have to terminate life support?
4. What is the obligation of the health care facility to follow the patient's wishes?
5. What is the obligation of the responsible survivor to pay the cost of unwanted medical care?

We will present excerpts from a number of court decisions that deal with these and other critical topics.

## THE RIGHT TO DIE OF PATIENTS WITH CAPACITY

### Case of Abe Perlmutter

Florida was one of the first states in which a court addressed the right of a competent person to refuse life-sustaining medical treatment. Abe Perlmutter, a competent individual, suffered from a terminal illness and wished to end his life support (artificial ventilation). After reviewing the four state interests in preserving life that have been described earlier, the court concluded that life support could be withdrawn. The court limited its holding to the withdrawal of life support (here, a ventilator) from a competent, terminally ill adult with no minor dependents and the agreement of surviving children. In this decision, the Florida Supreme Court urged that guidelines for terminating life support be legally established, and the Florida legislature passed the Life-Prolonging Procedure Act in 1984.

---

**DOCUMENT 75:** *Satz, State Attorney for Broward County, Florida, Appellant v. Perlmutter,* **Florida (1980)**

---

The State here appeals a trial court order permitting the removal of an artificial life sustaining device from a competent, but terminally ill adult. We affirm.

Seventy-three year old Abe Perlmutter lies mortally sick in a hospital, suffering from amyotrophic lateral sclerosis (Lou Gehrig's disease) diagnosed in January 1977. There is no cure and normal life expectancy, from time of diagnosis, is but two years. In Mr. Perlmutter, the affliction has progressed to the point of virtual incapability of movement, inability to breathe without a mechanical respirator and his very speech is an extreme effort. Even with the respirator, the prognosis is death within a short time. Notwithstanding, he remains in command of his mental faculties and legally competent. He seeks, with full approval of his adult family, to have the respirator removed from his trachea, which act, according to his physician, based upon medical probability, would result in "a reasonable life expectancy of less than one hour." . . .

Pursuant to all of the foregoing, and upon the petition of Mr. Perlmutter himself, the trial judge entered a detailed and thoughtful final judgment which included the following language:

ORDERED AND ADJUDGED that Abe Perlmutter, in the exercise of his right of privacy, may remain in defendant hospital or leave said hospital, free of the mechanical respirator now attached to his body and all defendants and their staffs are restrained from interfering with Plaintiff's decision.

We agree with the trial judge.

The State's position is that it (1) has an overriding duty to preserve life, and (2) that termination of supportive care, whether it be by the patient, his family or medical personnel, is an unlawful killing of a human being under the Florida Murder Statute Section 782.04, Florida Statutes (1977) or Manslaughter under Section 782.08. . . .

[1] The pros and cons involved in such tragedies which bedevil contemporary society, mainly because of incredible advancement in scientific medicine, are all exhaustively discussed in *Superintentent [sic] of Belchertown v. Saikewicz*, Mass., 370 N.E.2d 417 (1977). As *Saikewicz* points out, the right of an individual to refuse medical treatment is tempered by the State's:

1. Interest in the preservation of life.
2. Need to protect innocent third parties.
3. Duty to prevent suicide.
4. Requirement that it help maintain the ethical integrity of medical practice.

[2] In the case at bar, none of these four considerations surmount the individual wishes of Abe Perlmutter. Thus we adopt the view of the line of cases discussed in *Saikewicz* which would allow Abe Perlmutter the right to refuse or discontinue treatment based upon "the constitutional right to privacy . . . an expression of the sanctity of individual free choice and self-determination." (*Id.* 426). We would stress that this adoption is limited to the specific facts now before us, involving a competent adult

patient. The problem is less easy of solution when the patient is incapable of understanding and we, therefore, postpone a crossing of that more complex bridge until such time as we are required to do so. . . .

It is all very convenient to insist on continuing Mr. Perlmutter's life so that there can be no question of foul play, no resulting civil liability and no possible trespass on medical ethics. However, it is quite another matter to do so at the patient's sole expense and against his competent will, thus inflicting never ending physical torture on his body until the inevitable, but artificially suspended, moment of death. Such a course of conduct invades the patient's constitutional right of privacy, removes his freedom of choice and invades his right to self-determine.

*Source: Satz v. Perlmutter* 362 So. 2d 160 (Fla. Dist. Ct. App. 1978), affirmed 379 So. 2d 359 (Fla. 1980).

* * *

### Case of Elizabeth Bouvia

The right of a competent individual to refuse tube feeding was also addressed in the *Bouvia* case. In this case, the trial court in 1983 rejected Ms. Elizabeth Bouvia's request to have her feeding tube removed. The trial court's decision was overturned in 1986 by the California Court of Appeals for the Second District.

---

## DOCUMENT 76: *Elizabeth Bouvia v. County of Riverside: Riverside General Hospital,* California (1983)

---

From the evidence presented, the Court finds that the following facts, among others, have been established: that the Plaintiff, Elizabeth Bouvia, has since birth suffered from cerebral palsy. This has left her with virtually no motor function in any of her limbs or other skeletal muscles; that she retains some slight control of her right hand sufficient to operate the mechanical control of an electrically powered wheelchair; that she maintains enough voluntary control of the muscles of her mouth, face and throat structures so that she can eat a normal diet when essentially fed by someone else; and that she can talk with only a very slight speech impediment.

The Court further finds that cerebral palsy which afflicts Plaintiff has left, in fact, her sensory nerves so that she experiences a fairly constant degree of pain and discomfort from her inability to change her own position, from the muscle contractures and increased spasticity that affects her limbs and from the arthritis which her bodily distortions have caused.

The Court further finds that Plaintiff is physically unable to take her own life; further, that though afflicted in her body, Plaintiff's mind and intellect are totally unaffected and are quite normal; that plaintiff has been able to live independently with constant attendants and has even earned a Bachelor of Science Degree in social work from San Diego State University; that Plaintiff was married in San Diego to Richard Bouvia . . . that [in] mid-August 1983 Plaintiff's husband left her. . . .

The Court is convinced that Plaintiff has made her own decision to forego further feedings and will vigorously resist any feedings forced upon her. This decision was made by her after careful and mature deliberation of the alternatives, consequences and irreversibility of her decision.

The Court further finds that her decision was rational and that Plaintiff is mentally competent to make decisions affecting her life; that her decision was primarily reached because of the nature and extent of her physical disability and that her dependence on others to maintain her person in all areas of physical activity and not from other experiences, such as a failed marriage, non-employment, failure to procreate or termination of her education.

The Court is convinced that the Plaintiff is sincere in her desire to terminate her life and that she no longer desires to live.

The Court is also convinced that all counsel want her to live, and they hope that she might change her mind. . . .

Despite displaying certain effects of depression, she has, rather she was at the time she filed this action on November 1st, 1983, free from any acute mental or physical disorder which would require care or treatment. . . .

During the hearing, Plaintiff's decision to end her life has been called various things: the right of self-determination, the right of privacy, the right to determine the quality of one's life, the right to control one's own life and own body, the right to be let alone, the right to determine one's own future, the right to be protected from force feeding, the right to escape a useless body, freedom of choice, the acceptance of death, self-starvation, self-destruction, suicide, voluntary euthanasia and, finally, the right to die with dignity.

All of the terms have some significance.

The Court has determined that the ultimate issue is whether or not a severely handicapped, mentally competent person who is otherwise physically healthy and not terminally ill has the right to end her life with the assistance of society.

The Court concludes that she does not. . . .

Self-starvation by the Plaintiff who is competent would constitute suicide. By not issuing the requested order, the State will be protecting the Plaintiff from suicide.

*Source: Elizabeth Bouvia, Plaintiff v. County of Riverside: Riverside General Hospital,* No. 159780 (Cal. Super. Ct. Riverside Co. Dec. 16, 1983).

\* \* \*

By 1986, Elizabeth Bouvia could no longer sit in a wheelchair and was in constant pain that could only be relieved by constant infusion of morphine. She had also had difficulty finding a permanent place to live. The facility that was caring for her inserted a feeding tube against her will and contrary to her express written instructions. (Her instructions were dictated to her lawyers, written by them, and signed by her by means of her making a feeble *X* on the paper with a pen that she held in her mouth.) She returned to court to ask that the forced feeding be stopped.

## DOCUMENT 77: *Bouvia v. Superior Court of Los Angeles County (Glenchur)*, **California (1986)**

OPINION AND ORDER FOR A PEREMPTORY WRIT OF MANDATE
BEACH, Associate Justice.

Petitioner, Elizabeth Bouvia, a patient in a public hospital seeks the removal from her body of a nasogastric tube inserted and maintained against her will and without her consent by physicians who so placed it for the purpose of keeping her alive through involuntary forced feeding.

Petitioner has here filed a petition for writ of mandamus and other extraordinary relief after the trial court denied her a preliminary injunction requiring that the tube be removed and that the hospital and doctors be prohibited from using any other similar procedures. We issued an alternative writ. We have heard oral argument from the parties and now order issuance of a peremptory writ, granting petitioner, Elizabeth Bouvia, the relief for which she prayed.

DISCUSSION.

*1. Availability of Immediate Relief Here.*

. . . The trial court denied petitioner's request for the immediate relief she sought. It concluded that leaving the tube in place was necessary to prolong petitioner's life, and that it would, in fact, do so. With the tube in place petitioner probably will survive the time required to prepare for trial, a trial itself and an appeal, if one proved necessary. The real party-physicians also assert, and the trial court agreed, that physically petitioner tolerates the tube reasonably well and thus is not in great physical discomfort.

Real parties' counsel therefore argue that the normal course of trial and appeal provide a sufficient remedy. But petitioner's ability to tolerate physical discomfort does not diminish her right to immediate relief. Her mental and emotional feelings are equally entitled to respect. She has been subjected to the forced intrusion of an artificial mechanism into her body against her will. She has a right to refuse the increased dehumanizing aspects of her condition created by the insertion of a permanent tube through her nose and into her stomach.

To petitioner it is a dismal prospect to live with this hated and unwanted device attached to her, through perhaps years of the law's slow process. She has the right to have it removed immediately. This matter constitutes a perfect paradigm of the axiom: "Justice delayed is justice denied."

By refusing petitioner the relief which she sought, the trial court, with the most noble intentions, attempted to exercise its discretion by issuing a ruling which would uphold what it considered a lawful object, i.e., keeping Elizabeth Bouvia alive by a means which it considered ethical. Nonetheless, it erred for it had no discretion to exercise. Petitioner sought to enforce only a right which was exclusively hers and over which neither the medical profession nor the judiciary have any veto power. The trial court could but recognize and protect her exercise of that right. . . .

It Is Ordered

Let a peremptory writ of mandate issue commanding the Los Angeles Superior Court immediately upon receipt thereof, to make and enter a new and different order granting Elizabeth Bouvia's request for a preliminary injunction, and the relief prayed for therein; in particular to make an order (1) protecting real parties in interest forthwith to remove the nasogastric tube from petitioner Elizabeth Bouvia's body, and (2) prohibiting any and all of the real parties in interest from replacing or aiding in replacing said tube or any other or similar device in or on petitioner without her consent. Pursuant to Rule 246, California Rules of Court, this Order is final as to this court upon filing.

*Source: Bouvia v. Superior Court (Glenchur) 179 (Cal.) App. 3d 1127, 225 Cal. Rptr 297 (Ct. App. 1986), review denied.*

* * *

## THE RIGHT TO DIE OF PATIENTS WHO HAVE LOST CAPACITY

### The Persistent Vegetative State

While various court decisions clarified the rights of competent patients to make their own decisions regarding medical treatment, decision making for patients without capacity has been a cause of considerable conflict and confusion. Many of the cases that have dealt with this issue have involved patients in a persistent vegetative state (PVS). This condition is described in a position paper from the Executive Board of the American Academy of Neurology.

---

## DOCUMENT 78: Position of the American Academy of Neurology (1988)

---

1. The persistent vegetative state is a form of eyes-open permanent unconsciousness in which the patient has periods of wakefulness and physiologic sleep/wake cycles, but at no time is the patient aware of himself or his environment. Neurologically, being awake but unaware is the result of a functioning brainstem, and the total loss of cerebral cortical functioning.

A. No voluntary action or behavior of any kind is present. Primitive reflexes and vegetative functions which may be present are either controlled by the brainstem or are so elemental that they require no brain regulation at all.

Although the PVS patient generally is able to breathe spontaneously because of the intact brainstem, the capacity to chew and swallow in a normal manner is lost because these functions are voluntary, requiring intact cerebral hemispheres.

*Source*: Position of the American Academy of Neurology on Certain Aspects of the Care and Management of the Persistent Vegetative State Patient. *Neurology* 39 (1989): 125–126.

* * *

A task force on the persistent vegetative state concluded that one year after injury, only 7 percent of 434 patients showed a good recovery of function, 17 percent had moderate disability, 28 percent had severe disability, 15 percent remained in a persistent vegetative state, and the remaining 33 percent had died (Multi-Society Task Force on PVS, "Medical Aspects of the Persistent Vegetative State" [second of two parts], *New England Journal of Medicine* 330 [1994]: 1572–1579).

### The Landmark Case of Karen Ann Quinlan

The case of Karen Ann Quinlan was the first court case that addressed decision making for a patient without capacity and that heavily influenced many courts that dealt with these issues. The case came before the New Jersey Superior Court on October 20, 1975. All of the lawyers represented in the case made summary statements. The conclusion of all but Paul Armstrong, Joseph Quinlan's lawyer, was that Karen Quinlan's life should be maintained as long as possible by continuing respiratory support, since she was not dead. In contrast, Armstrong argued that "Karen Ann Quinlan could lawfully take the action which is proposed to this Honorable Court, and that the Court may therefore in appropriate circumstances authorize such action on her behalf." The action, of course, was withdrawal of the respirator.

Judge Muir's opinion stressed that there was no precedent for a decision regarding withdrawal of life-sustaining treatment in an incompetent adult. He therefore appointed Joseph Quinlan as guardian ad litem only of his daughter's property and appointed Daniel Coburn as guardian of her person so that life support would continue.

---

## DOCUMENT 79: *In the Matter of Karen Quinlan, an Alleged Incompetent*, Superior Court of New Jersey (1975)

The court's findings of fact relating to Karen Quinlan's illness were as follows:

Karen Ann Quinlan, one of three children of Joseph and Julia Quinlan, was born April 24, 1954. She was baptized and raised a Roman Catholic. She attended Roman Catholic Church affiliated elementary and secondary schools. She is a member of her parents' local Roman Catholic Church in Mount Arlington, New Jersey. The parish priest is Father Thomas A. Trapasso.

Sometime in late 1974 or early 1975, Karen Quinlan moved from her parents' home. Thereafter, she had at least two subsequent residences, with the last being a lake cottage in Sussex County, New Jersey.

On the night of April 15, 1975, friends of Karen summoned the local police and emergency rescue squad, and she was taken to Newton Memorial Hospital. The precise events leading up to her admission to Newton Memorial Hospital are unclear. She apparently ceased breathing for at least two fifteen minute periods. Mouth to mouth resuscitation was applied by her friends the first time and by a police respirator the second time. The exact amount of time she was without spontaneous respiration is unknown.

Upon her admission to Newton Memorial, urine and blood tests were administered, which indicated the presence of quinine, aspirin, barbituates [sic] in normal range, and traces of valium and librium. The drugs found present were indicated by Dr. Robert Morse, the neurologist in charge of her care at St. Clare's, to be in the therapeutic range and the quinine consistent with mixing in drinks like soda water.

The cause of the unconsciousness and periodic cessations of respiration is undetermined. The interruption in respiration apparently caused anoxia—insufficient supply of oxygen in the blood—resulting in her present condition.

Hospital records at the time of admission reflected Karen's vital signs to be normal, a temperature of 100, pupils unreactive, unresponsivity to deep pain, legs rigid and curled up with decorticate brain activity. Her blood oxygen level was low at the time. She was placed upon a respirator at Newton Hospital.

At 10 p.m. on April 16, 1975, Dr. Morse examined Karen at the request of her then attending physician. He found her in a state of coma with evidence of decortication indicating altered level of consciousness. She required the respirator for assistance. She did not trigger the respirator, which means she did not breathe spontaneously nor independently of it at any time during the examination. . . .

Dr. Morse could not obtain any initial history (i.e., the circumstances and events occurring prior to Karen's becoming unconscious). There was no information available from her friends. He speculated at the outset on the possibility of an overdose of drugs, past history of lead poisoning, foul play, or head injury due to a fall. He indicated that the lack of an initial history seriously inhibits a diagnosis.

Karen was transferred to the Intensive Care Unit (I.C.U.) of St. Clare's Hospital, under the care of Dr. Morse. At the time of her transfer, she was still unconscious, still on a respirator, a catheter was inserted into her bladder and a tracheostomy had been performed.

Upon entry to the St. Clare's I.C.U. she was placed on a MA-1 Respirator, which provides air to her lungs on a controlled volume basis. . . .

The machine takes over completely the breathing function when the patient does not breathe spontaneously. . . .

In an effort to ascertain the cause of the coma, Dr. Morse conducted a brain scan, an angiogram, an electroencephalogram (EEG), a lumbar tap and several other tests. . . . All indicated brain rhythm or activity.

Subsequent tests and examinations did not further the establishment of the precise location and cause of Karen's comatose condition.

Dr. Morse testified concerning the treatment of Karen at St. Clare's. He averred she receives oral feedings since intravenous feeding is insufficient to sustain her. . . .

There is constant threat of infection, according to Dr. Morse. Antibiotics are administered to thwart potential infection with tests constantly being made to keep a check on this threat. . . .

The day-by-day charts entitled "Vital Signs", kept by nurses who give her 24-hour care indicate, in part, the following:

1. Her color was generally pale, her skin warm, she was almost constantly suffering from diaphoresis (sweating), many times profusely but occasionally moderately or not at all;
2. there was always a reaction to painful stimuli, she responded decerebrately to pain, she sometimes would grimace as if in pain, which would be followed by increased rigidity of her arms and legs;
3. there would be periodic contractions and spasms, periodic yawning, periodic movements of spastic nature;
4. pupils were sometimes dilated, sometimes normal but almost always sluggish to light;
5. body waste disposal through the urethral catheter and the bowel was indicated to occur;
6. feedings of Vivinex were given alternately with water on various nurses shifts;
7. the nurses were constantly moving, positioning, and bathing her;
8. body rashes occurred at times; decubiti were treated with heat lamps on occasions;
9. sometimes she would trigger and assist the respirator; other times she would go for periods without triggering it at all;
10. her extremities remained rigid with contraction of them being described as severe at times;
11. on May 7th, nurses indicated she blinked her eyes two times when asked to and appeared responsive by moving her eyes when talked to but there is no further evidence of this type [of] reaction thereafter.

Dr. Javed indicated efforts were made to wean or remove Karen from the respirator. The hospital records support this. Dr. Javed testified for weaning to be successful, the patient must have a stable respiratory pattern. Karen was taken off the respirator for short periods of time. Each time, her respiratory rate, rate of breathing, went up and the volume of air intake would decrease. He indicated her breathing rate would more than double in intensity while her "tidal volume" or air intake would drop 50 percent. The longest period of time she was off the respirator was one-half hour. . . .

Dr. Morse's hospital notes indicate there is no neurological improvement from the time of her admission to St. Clare's to date. . . .

In Dr. Morse's opinion, the cause of Karen's condition is a lesion on the cerebral hemispheres and a lesion in the brain stem. . . .

In absence of a clear history, Dr. Morse relied basically upon the decorticate posturing of Karen Quinlan and the respiratory difficulty for reaching his conclusion as to the brain lesion locations. He contrasted the decorticate posture to decerebrate posture of a patient for drawing his conclusions.

He asserted with medical certainty that Karen Quinlan is not brain dead. He identified the Ad Hoc Committee of Harvard Medical School Criteria as the ordinary medical standard for determining brain death and that Karen satisfied none of the criteria. . . .

Dr. Morse states Karen Quinlan will not return to a level of cognitive function (i.e., that she will be able to say "Mr. Coburn I'm glad you are my guardian.") What level or plateau she will reach is unknown. He does not know of any course of treatment that can be given and cannot see how her condition can be reversed but is unwilling to say she is in an irreversible state or condition. He indicated there is a possibility of recovery but that level is unknown particularly due to the absence of pre-hospital history.

Karen Ann Quinlan was examined by several experts for the various parties. All were neurologists with extensive experience and backgrounds. Some had done research in the area of brain injury, conscious and comatose behavior. . . .

Their testimonies did not vary significantly. . . .

All agree she is in a persistent vegetative state. She is described as having irreversible brain damage; no cognitive or cerebral functioning; chances for useful sapient life or return of discriminative functioning are remote. The absence of knowledge on the events precipitating the condition, the fact that other patients have been comatose for longer periods of time and recovered to function as a human made Dr. Cook qualify his statement as to the return to discriminative functioning. All agreed she is not brain dead by present known medical criteria and that her continued existence away from the respirator is a determination for a pulmonary internist.

On September 10, 1975, the plaintiff, Karen's father, Joseph Thomas Quinlan, entered a civil complaint through his attorney, Paul W. Armstrong. Portions of the complaint follow.

VI. The said KAREN ANN QUINLAN is an incompetent as a result of unsoundness of mind, as appears from the Affidavits of the Physicians annexed hereto. She is unable to govern herself and manage her affairs and has been in this state for approximately six months.

VII. On April 15, 1975, the said KAREN ANN QUINLAN was admitted to the Intensive Care Unit of the Newton Memorial Hospital, 75 High Street, Newton, New Jersey, in a coma of unknown etiology. A Tracheostomy was performed and she was transferred to the Intensive Care Unit of Saint Clare's Hospital on April 24, 1975, where her vital processes are artificially sustained via the extraordinary means of a mechanical MA-1 Respirator.

VIII. After consultation with his Religious, Medical and Legal counsellors, with the support of his wife, JULIA, his son, JOHN, and his daughter, MARY ELLEN, and in concert with the tenets and teachings of their shared Catholic faith and the expressed desires of his daughter, KAREN ANN QUINLAN, the Plaintiff, JOSEPH THOMAS QUINLAN therefore, with awe, sets before the Court the following prayer:

WHEREFORE, the Plaintiff, JOSEPH THOMAS QUINLAN, respectfully prays that this Honorable Court enter a Judgment adjudicating KAREN ANN QUINLAN to be mentally incompetent as a result of unsoundness of mind and granting to the Plaintiff letters of guardianship with the express power of authorizing the discontinuance of all extraordinary means of sustaining the vital processes of his daughter, KAREN ANN QUINLAN.

On September 15, Judge Robert Muir appointed Daniel R. Coburn, an attorney, as Karen's guardian ad litem (i.e., someone to represent a person who cannot speak for himself or herself). Portions of his affidavit follow.

... [D]ue to the immediacy of the situation, the extraordinary relief requested and the irreversible result of granting such extraordinary relief, it is my opinion at the present time that Karen Quinlan is not "brain dead" and until further medical proofs are elicited by all parties concerned, the existence of that fact should not be accepted by this Court; ... I have obtained or read every available piece of legal literature which I have been able to obtain concerning this subject and have explored various statutes and case law for some legal precedent in this matter. Briefly stated, the results of my research indicate that no court has authorized the cessation of supportive mechanical devices necessary to sustain life such as the respirator in the present case regardless of whether "brain death" has occurred or not. Insofar as the question of "brain death" is concerned, this particular case would appear to be one of first impression. The argument pro and con concerning such an extraordinary situation involve theological, ethical, medical, practical, and most important to me as Karen's guardian, legal considerations. ...

12. Assuming that the allegations in the Order to Show Cause are not meant to indicate that Karen has suffered "brain death," then the only other interpretation that I can give to the request is that her life be terminated because her medical condition is hopeless, based on the words of Dr. Arshad Javed as set forth in his Affidavit supporting this application: "There is no hope of improvement in patient's condition." Without debating the moral, theological or practical considerations in such an

application, it is absolutely certain in my mind that such a request is, in effect, asking that this Court authorize a "mercy killing." Without in any way intending to impugn the intentions or attitudes of any other party to this matter, it is my considered opinion as Karen's guardian and as an attorney-at-law of the State of New Jersey that such action is totally without precedent in the law and at this point would constitute a homicide.

13. Quite obviously, a great many other factors will undoubtedly come to light between today and the ultimate disposition of this matter. In light of my experiences during the last three days, I feel it would be naive to state what my ultimate opinion will be as Karen's guardian in this matter. I merely have set forth my views in response to this Court's Order dated September 17, 1975, requiring that my position be set forth in affidavit form on or before September 19, 1975.

The pretrial order issued by Judge Muir stated the nature of the action as follows:

1. Petition by parent to be appointed guardian of his adult daughter on grounds of the latter's incompetency with request for judicial order to authorize discontinuance of mechanical (cardiorespiratory) supportive measures allegedly sustaining continuance of her body functions and her life; counts to enjoin County Prosecutor, treating physicians and the hospital from interfering with the discontinuance of the supportive measures if Court authorization is given; count to enjoin Prosecutor from commencing criminal proceedings in the event authorization is given.

Judge Muir stated the legal and factual issues as follows:

A. What is or should be the legal definition of death; if the present definition is inadequate, to what extent and specificity should it be defined; applicability of a standard or norm to govern the medical determination, i.e., reasonable medical certainty, absolute certainty, ordinary medical practice;

B. Deleted.

C. Does this Court have the power, the authority and the jurisdiction generally respecting the life-death issue raised in this case. Secondly, does this Court have the power, authority and jurisdiction to direct the commission of an act in order to determine in advance that that act is not a violation of the prevailing criminal law in the State of New Jersey.

D. Constitutionally what is the effect of prior expressions of Karen Quinlan regarding cessation of maintenance of terminal care; The constitutionally protected religious rights with respect to the determination sought as it applies to both Karen Quinlan and her parents.

E. Does the medical evidence, background, history, diagnosis and prognosis, gathered from the medical experts, and the treating physicians, from other witnesses, from the surrounding circumstances and from other proofs justify the conclusion that Karen Quinlan is today legally dead, and therefore supportive devices and extraordinary supportive and resuscitative measures may be legally removed, abandoned or discontinued in the course of her medical care;

F. Should this Court place its stamp of approval to medical procedures that may result in the termination of the life of Karen Quinlan, or may result in the death or damage to some of her vital organs that may place her life beyond redemption;

G. Should this Court, in the absence of applicable statutes in New Jersey, leave the determination of death to the treating, attending and consulting physicians or alternatively to the parents or alternatively the parents and the physicians together;

Should this Court take cognizance of existing judicial determinations in New Jersey declaring that modern medicine is not an exact science, and therefore a definition of death formula to be applied here would be unjustified and a pre hoc life-death judgment in this case would be unwarranted, invalid and illegal;

H. Does the present condition of Karen Quinlan, in the light of presently acceptable medical criteria, qualify her for the extraordinary action sought in her name by the petitioner to this Court;

I. What should the burden of proof be on the petitioner;

J. Karen Quinlan's constitutional right to live;

K. Assuming the proof shows Karen Quinlan is legally dead, is the only relief cessation of the extraordinary devices;

L. In the event the Court rules against the cessation of the extraordinary devices should the petitioner be appointed the guardian of the person of Karen Quinlan.

A portion of the statement of facts to be proven in the trial was presented in the plaintiff's brief prepared by his lawyers.

Karen Ann Quinlan is presently confined to the Intensive Care Unit at Saint Clare's Hospital where her bodily condition continues to deteriorate due to the artificial maintenance of life functions through the extraordinary means of a mechanical MA-1 respirator used neither at the request, nor with the consent of Karen Ann Quinlan or her family.

The Quinlan family, including Karen Ann Quinlan, are members of the Roman Catholic Church and they believe as part of their Roman Catholic faith:

(i) that earthly existence is but one phase of a continuing life which reaches its perfection after death;

(ii) that death changes life but does not end it; and

(iii) that earthly life need not be clung to by the futile use of extraordinary medical measures.

They believe further that life-influencing decisions are to be left to the individual and the family, counseled and supported by the community of the Church; and that such life-influencing decisions are to be based on the spiritual best interests of the persons affected.

They do not allege that continuation of the medical treatment now being administered to Karen is in any way sinful or expressly forbidden by their religion, nor that there is any positive religious duty to discontinue such treatment; rather, they believe that the earthly phase of Karen's life has drawn to a close, that the time of striving and trial is over, and that further treatment merely holds her back from the realization and enjoyment of a better, more perfect life.

Karen Ann Quinlan has previously expressed her wishes with regard to the proposed action:

(1) In February of 1974, the father of a friend of Karen Ann Quinlan was dying of cancer. Karen, in discussions with her mother, Julia Quinlan, her sister, Mary Ellen, and her friend, Laurie Gaffney, made statements to the effect that if she were suffering from a terminal illness, she would not wish her life to be prolonged through the futile use of extraordinary medical measures.

(2) In March of 1975, a friend of the family died of cancer. His wish before dying was to return to his own home and die there. In discussions with her mother, Julia Quinlan, and her sister, Mary Ellen, Karen made statements to the effect that if she were in similar circumstances, she would not want anyone to prolong her illness and suffering through the futile use of extraordinary medical measures.

Pursuant to their religiously held beliefs, and taking into account the prior expressions of their daughter, Karen Ann Quinlan, the Quinlan family, Joseph and Julia, Mary Ellen and John, have requested the treating physician, Dr. Robert Morse, and the officials at Saint Clare's Hospital to discontinue the use of the MA-1 respirator and let Karen depart in peace and dignity.

On July 31, 1975, Joseph and Julia Quinlan executed a medical authorization and release from liability in favor of Dr. Robert Morse and Saint Clare's Hospital.

On September 12, 1975, a Complaint for the appointment of a Guardian for an Incompetent was filed in the Superior Court of New Jersey, Chancery Division, Morris County, pursuant to N.J. Court Rules, 1969, R4:83-1 through 4:83-8, by Joseph Quinlan, the father of the alleged incompetent, Karen Ann Quinlan.

On September 17, 1975, a Supplemental Complaint and Order to Show

Cause, pursuant to N.J. Court Rules, 1969, R4:67-2, was filed joining the defendants Donald G. Collester, Jr. Morris County Prosecutor, Dr. Robert Morse, Dr. Arshad Javed and Saint Clare's Hospital to this action.

On September 22, 1975, William F. Hyland, the Attorney General of the State of New Jersey, intervened as of right pursuant to N.J. Court Rules, 1969, R4:33-1.

Legal briefs were also presented by the guardian ad litem, the attorney general of New Jersey, Karen Quinlan's two physicians, the prosecutor of Morris County, and St. Clare's Hospital. We will indicate the points that were made in two of the briefs, but will not cite the legal precedents for the points that they made. In their brief for the plaintiff, Joseph Quinlan and his lawyers argued the following:

I. The court has jurisdiction to grant the relief sought by the petitioner; ... II. The court may properly grant the relief sought by petitioner without deciding the constitutional issues presented in this case ...; III. Denial of the relief sought by petitioner would violate the constitutionally protected rights of Karen Ann Quinlan and her family ...; IV. Plaintiff believes that Karen Ann Quinlan is not at present dead according to any legal standard recognized by the State of New Jersey ...; V. Plaintiff is required to adduce only a preponderance of the evidence in order to prevail in the matters at issue.

In his brief, Daniel R. Coburn, the appointed guardian ad litem, argued as follows:

I. This court has jurisdiction not only over the relief sought by the plaintiff but also to appoint a permanent guardian other than the plaintiff and to compel Karen's treating doctors at St. Clare's Hospital to make every possible effort to sustain Karen's life ...; II. The complaint in this case should be dismissed as a matter of law ...; III. The plaintiff must prove beyond a reasonable doubt that he is entitled to the relief requested ...; IV. The court should appoint someone other than the plaintiff as permanent guardian ad litem of the person of Karen Quinlan ...; V. Plaintiff's claim that the relief requested is constitutionally guarded as part of his religious beliefs is contrary to prevailing law ...; VI. Plaintiff's claim that the relief requested is constitutionally guarded as part of his right of privacy and personal autonomy is contrary to prevailing law. ...

During the trial, Karen Quinlan's physicians and other physicians were called as expert witnesses. Ultimately, all agreed that Karen Quinlan was not dead, as defined by the Harvard criteria of brain death, and that she was in a persistent vegetative state. The plaintiff, Joseph Quinlan, testified about how he came to the decision to request that Karen's artificial respiration be terminated.

MR. ARMSTRONG: ... Will you please explain how ... you and your family arrived at your decision to seek the aid of this Court to resolve the tragic plight of your daughter? ...

THE WITNESS: It took almost six months for me to personally arrive at that decision.

MR. ARMSTRONG: Q. When did you arrive at that decision?

A. I am terrible with dates.

Q. I am sorry. Go on.

A. I would say late August, early September, after the meetings that we had.

Q. What meetings were those?

A. With the doctors.

Q. What doctors?

A. Various medical meetings that we had with Dr. Javed and Dr. Morse.

Q. Could you explain to the Court what went on at these various medical meetings?

A. They would report to us Karen's medical condition, and they were very pessimistic, the reports that they had given us. I remember one time Dr. Morse, whom I love very much, and Dr. Javed both, I felt he didn't want me to get my hopes up, and at that time I had an awful lot of hope and I had an awful lot of faith, and I just felt this wasn't going to happen, but I wasn't ready for Dr. Morse at that time. But he had been telling me continuously not to get your hopes up, and at one time he had told me that, even if by some miracle Karen should survive, I would never take her home; she would spend the rest of her life in an institution. I thought on this and prayed on this all the way home in the car, and by the time I reached home, I had resolved my mind to the fact that, if this was God's will, I would accept it. I would take her under any conditions, as long as I had her.

Q. Mr. Quinlan, did you then seek the aid of your religion?

A. Not yet. I still wasn't convinced. As the reports got steadily worse, I was just told that there wasn't any hope, that Karen was going to die. It was just a matter of time. Dr. Morse couldn't tell me whether it would be six months, a year. The best estimate that he would give me is that he didnt [sic] think she would last a year. A year is a long time under those conditions.

   Gradually, after all of these meetings, I finally became convinced that this had to be the Lord's will, that he was going to take Karen.

Q. Who was present at these meetings, Mr. Quinlan?

A. There were a number of meetings all along, and towards the end, I guess they became like official meetings, where, you know, Dr. Javed and Dr. Morse and

Father Pat, a witness, in the room, and stuff like that; our whole family was there. These came pretty close to the end.

Q. Who is Father Pat?

A. Father Pat is the Chaplain at St. Clare's Hospital.

Q. Did you seek his aid and counsel at any time?

A. Yes, I did. I would say after I had arrived at my decision, and then, of course, I found out for the first time that my entire family had already arrived at this decision.

Q. Would you tell us about that, Mr. Quinlan?

MR. EINHORN: Can I have that last answer read?

THE COURT: Read it back, please.

[The Court Reporter reads the last answer.]

MR. COBURN: I object. In the next question he asks to have him tell us about that. Mr. Quinlan is telling about the decision being made by the family.

THE COURT: I will sustain the objection. You have the witnesses. They can testify to that.

Tell us what you said and what you did in response to what the others said, but don't tell us what they said.

MR. ARMSTRONG: Sequentially, I asked whether or not he was the last one to make the decision out of the members of his family.

BY MR. ARMSTRONG: (Resuming)

Q. Go ahead, Mr. Quinlan.

A. That's right. Of course, when I realized this, it made it even more difficult for me, because then I realized that my decision was final, and that is when I had to seek the counsel of Father Tom. I realized I would have problems with this decision that I knew I had to make.

Q. Was it Father Tom, did you say?

A. Father Tom first.

Q. Who is Father Tom?

A. Father Tom is my pastor, Father Thomas Trapasso. I am sorry.

Q. Of what church is he pastor?

A. Our Lady of the Lake.

Q. Would you tell us what advice he had given you?

MR. COBURN: I object. It is hearsay.

THE COURT: He can tell us what his reaction was to the Father's advice.

BY MR. ARMSTRONG: (Resuming)

Q. What was your reaction to Father Tom's advice?

A. Well, I hadn't thought about it too much at that time, because it just seemed like a natural follow-up, you know, the fact that we had done everything possible for Karen, and now we had reached this point where there wasn't any hope. It just seemed like the natural step to go into, to consider, and then the artificial means.

This I spoke to Father Tom about, and the fact that I had a problem with the decision, realizing that I was the holdout.

Can I mention what Father Tom said to me about that? He made me feel a lot better.

MR. COBURN: That's something he can testify to, but he can't say what the priest said to him. If he made him feel better, I don't object. If it is going to be something else, what the priest said to him, I object.

THE COURT: That is a valid objection.

BY MR. ARMSTRONG: (Resuming).

Q. Tell us how you felt after you received advice from Father Tom concerning this?

A. I felt a lot better, a lot better. He had enlightened me, helped me with my own conscience, and I felt a lot better about it.

Q. Were you able to make this decision?

A. Yes, I was. I think I had actually reached the decision before, but in talking with Father Tom, my pastor, it became definite.

Q. How did Doctors Morse and Javed advise you as to Karen's condition, Mr. Quinlan?

A. As to her condition, at that point they were both telling me that it was hopeless, and she just wouldn't survive.

Q. Did the physicians suggest to you that you remove the respirator from Karen?

MR. EINHORN: That is a leading question. Objection.

THE COURT: Sustain the objection.

BY MR. ARMSTRONG: (Resuming)

Q. What advice did you receive from the physicians concerning this condition?

A. One of them adviced [sic], the advice of one of the physicians, was that we terminate it, that we turn the machine off.

Q. Who was that?

A. Dr. Javed. Dr. Morse was the doctor in charge of the case, and Dr. Morse, at that time, didn't advise any way, one way or the other. He simply stated the medical facts and more or less left the decision up to us; but he didn't advise us as to the machine at that time. That was one of the meetings near the end. There were several near the end; I guess they were about a week apart, approximately.

Q. Did there subsequently come a time when you requested of both physicians to remove this treatment?

A. Yes. After I had spoken to Father Tom, Father Pat, the whole family was in agreement at that time, and we felt it was the right and proper and moral thing to do. Then we asked for a meeting with Dr. Javed and Dr. Morse, and we had this meeting, and at the meeting—first of all, Father Pat spoke on the Church, how our own Church felt about this. He was able to quote—I guess I shouldn't be commenting on what he said—but anyway, he was able to quote, going back as far as Piux [*sic*] XII in 1958—1957—when he not only said that in certain cases extraordinary means are not required of a Roman Catholic, but in certain cases it is preferable not to use them. I remember those words well.

I took it as applying to this particular case. Then he read some other letters from different, more or less, theologians. We went around the table. Each one gave their own opinion as to what should be done, and the whole family was in agreement that the machine should be turned off. What we asked the hospital and the doctors was that Karen be allowed to be brought back to a natural state. In my own mind, I had already resolved this spiritually through my prayers, that I had placed Karen's body and soul into the gentle, loving hands of the Lord, and this is what I explained I wanted to do physically, place her completely in the hands of the Lord and let His will be done. As we went around the table, Dr. Javed agreed; Dr. Morse still wouldn't advise us, but he did state that whatever we decided he would do. Of course, Father Pat agreed with us and that was it. It was resolved that we would turn the machine off.

Q. They have not done that, have they?

A. No, they haven't.

I think it was the next day, or the same night, we had a paper drawn up, and there was a couple [of] papers. I think the first one wasn't proper or something. And the hospital had another paper drawn up, a permission slip that my wife had to sign—

Q. A release?

A.—formally requesting the hospital and the doctors to turn the machine off, and releasing them of any and all responsibility. We signed the paper and we thought that was it. And that night we went home, and we were resolved that it was going to happen like the next day.

MR. ARMSTRONG: I have no further questions of this witness, Your Honor.

THE COURT: Mr. Coburn?

## CROSS-EXAMINATION

BY MR. COBURN:

Q. The question you can answer is: Did Karen ever tell you those were her religious beliefs?

A. No, not to my knowledge. No, sir.

Q. When were you first aware, if at all, of your ability to enforce Karen's right of self-determination? If you don't understand what that is—

A. As her parent, I felt I had that right. She was incompetent. She was dying, I felt, and she wasn't able to act for herself. And I simply wanted, since I felt so strongly that this was the Lord's will, to give her back to the Lord. That was my only reason for this whole thing.

Q. But for the Catholic Church's authorization of what you feel would be removal of extraordinary means, would you ask the doctors to do this?

A. If I felt it was morally wrong, I couldn't. I'd have to leave her on the machine no matter how many years it took. I couldn't do anything that I felt was morally wrong.

Q. When did you first conclude that it was not morally wrong to authorize the doctors to do this?

A. After I had made up my decision, and I talked it over with Father Tom and Father Pat. Then I realized that my decision was right in line with the Church's teachings and with moral law.

Q. Let me ask you this. At the time that you made the decision yourself, before you spoke to the priests, had you determined that it was not morally wrong to authorize this?

A. No, I just felt it was right. I felt it was the right thing to do. That was my own feelings.

Q. Was that regardless of what the Catholic Church position was?

A. You mean, would I have done it if the Catholic Church's position was against it?

Q. Yes.

A. I don't think so. I doubt that very much. That's my whole life.

Q. The Catholic Church?

A. Yes, sir.

Q. Or your religious beliefs?

A. Right.

Q. Now, are you aware of some of the other arguments that have been raised on your behalf, as the plaintiff in this case, concerning nonreligious aspects of Karen's right to die, or however we want to call it? I'm sure you're aware of what I'm talking about—the right of self-determination, that Karen could, as an individual, regardless of her religious beliefs; do you understand those arguments?

A. I think so, sir. I feel I had this right as her father, and I'm sure my wife felt the same way as her mother, that since she was imcompetent [sic] and wasn't able to act for herself, we could act on her behalf. Is that what you mean?

Q. In the event the Court said you could not act in that manner, how would you view your position as a parent?

A. In the event that the Court decided we couldn't turn the machine off?

Q. Yes, forgetting about the religious aspects now.

MR. ARMSTRONG: Objection; the question is too overly broad.

THE COURT: No, I'll allow it.

THE WITNESS: Well, I feel this is the right thing to do, and I'm hoping that the Court, I'm hoping and praying that the Court agrees with me. If the Court should decide against me, I don't know what I would do. I don't feel that I should do it on my own. This is a medical condition, and I think it should be done by medical people, with my priest and the family present.

If this isn't what you meant by your question, I'm sorry.

The position of the Catholic church regarding so-called extraordinary treatment was important in Joseph Quinlan's decision. This position is stated succinctly in the testimony of Father Pascal Caccavalle.

## PASCAL CACCAVAL[L]E,

called as a witness on behalf of the plaintiff, being duly sworn, testifies as follows:

### DIRECT EXAMINATION

BY MR. ARMSTRONG:

Q. . . . Father, as chaplain at St. Clare's, have the Quinlans had occasion to seek your advice concerning the plight of Karen?

A. Directed to that answer, Counsel, I would have to say no. They have not, they did not seek my advice directly. My advice came in on an occasion after all the events that have been described thus far, both by Mr. Quinlan and by Father Trapasso. I was summoned by Dr. Robert Morse to attend a special conference in the conference room, adjacent to the intensive care unit, and that was the first official time I had to officially counsel Mr. Quinlan.

Q. Will you tell the Court how you counselled Mr. Quinlan at the first time?

A. The circumstances to me were somewhat abrupt, and without any forewarning or foreknowledge, other than I was summoned by Dr. Morse to the effect that they were going to sit down with the Quinlans and with a nurse of the intensive care unit, because Mr. Quinlan, as Dr. Morse had indicated to me, had come to a resolution as to the condition and the state of his daughter, Karen. He had come to the—so during the course of that meeting, I was asked, "What is the Church's position in the specific case where, from all medical indications, Karen had reached an irreversible state? Is there, or is there not, the obligation to continue using extraordinary means—and, in this specific case, the artificial respirator?

Q. How did you so advise?

A. My advice at that particular occasion was quoting from the *allocutio* of Pope Pius XII in 1957. I also had a copy of the Medical Moral Ethics book, McFadden, which is in its sixth edition, and it is one of the official textbooks in our medical, Catholic medical schools; and there it specifically states, and I believe I'm not now quoting verbatim, but this is more or less the sentence: When a patient has reached an irreversible state, then the obligation to continue using extraordinary means ceases, obviously the determination of the irreversible state is to be made not by the Church but by the medical profession.

Now, when the Church or the theologian or the family is presented with this declaration that a patient has reached a point beyond medical knowledge to effectively help this person, or for any quality of human life, then to continue using extraordinary means—that is, the obligation to continue extraordinary means ceases, and that was my advice to Mr. Quinlan.

The following is testimony from Julia Quinlan about how the family arrived at a consensus.

Q. Mrs. Quinlan, do you support your husband in his decision to request of the Court this particular aid?

A. Yes, I do.

Q. And will you please explain when you arrived at your decision to seek the aid of the Court?

A. When I arrived at it personally?

Q. Yes.

A. You said to seek the aid of the Court.

Q. I'm sorry. When you arrived at your decision to have the extraordinary means removed from your daughter.

A. I don't know if I could pinpoint it to exactly one time—

THE COURT: Generally.

THE WITNESS: —you know, that I arrived at this. It was after talking to Dr. Morse on many occasions and to Dr. Javed on several occasions. The prognosis wasn't good. Dr. Morse continually told me that Karen was not improving, that the brain damage was irreversible. We discussed having another doctor come in for consultation, which we certainly agreed to, and we had Dr. Bender come in. And he concurred with Dr. Morse, what he had said.

And then, after discussing this also with Dr. Javed, that I felt that, and myself, seeing Karen daily, and I could see her getting worse each day, and different indications that I had—this is just my own personal feelings—different indications that I had, the different positions that her body was going into, that I felt that there was absolutely no hope.

I had discussed this with my other two children, Mary Ellen and John, and they didn't agree with me. And I knew that Joe didn't. So I felt—well, I was standing alone in it and I felt that I just had to accept this and to be patient with them. It was very difficult, because I really couldn't discuss it with them. But I did discuss it with Father Tom on many occasions. Nearly daily, I would speak to him about it. And he was a great consolation to me.

BY MR. ARMSTRONG: (Resuming)

Q. How did Father Tom advise you?

A. He just advised me also to be patient, you know, with Joe and with the children, until we all reached a decision together. Then, after Mary Ellen and John had reached this decision, I still felt that it would not be right for me to approach Joe, because it is something that you must reach this decision on your own. It isn't anything that you can actually talk someone into. So on many occasions I refrained from saying different things, that I felt Karen was going to die and she was not going to live, because Joe did not feel the same way as I did. It is enough of an emotional strain, so I tried to be very careful in what we discussed.

After we reached this plateau, it was much easier, because we could communicate and discuss this openly. I had discussed this also with Father Pat one evening as I was leaving the intensive care unit, crying as usual, and I met Father Pat in the hallway, and he sat and we went into a conference room, and he sat and he explained to me the moral issue and the Catholic stand on the issue, which Father Tom had also done. But again, I told him that my husband was not in agreement with me, and he also agreed that it would not be right for me to discuss it with him or for him to discuss it with Joe either.

Julia Quinlan's subsequent testimony related to discussions about life support that she had had with her daughter Karen.

BY MR. ARMSTRONG: (Resuming)

Q. Mrs. Quinlan, could you take us back to the circumstances of the first time that you had an opportunity to talk with Karen concerning the use of these extraordinary means?

A. Well, I'd like to say, first, that Karen had very definite ideas on many subjects. And the subject of "extraordinary means" was one of them. And when her Aunt Eleanor was dying, she had said that she would never, never want to be kept alive by any extraordinary means. She mentioned this on the other occasions, but she didn't only mention extraordinary means. Karen was very full of life, and she loved life; and she felt that if you're not able—I just don't know how to put it, really.

Q. Just try and relax, if you can.

A. Life was very important to her, and very dear to her; but the way that she could live her life was also very important to her. As I said, she was very full of life, a very active young girl, and she had always said that if she was dying: "Mommy, please don't ever let them keep me alive with any extraordinary means," or in any way that she could not really enjoy her life to the fullest. I cannot say that those were her exact words; and I don't know if I'm getting her true feeling across. But to her, her life was very dear and she wanted to enjoy life. And that's why, when I see her in this condition, I know in my heart as her mother that it is not the way that Karen would want to be.

Perhaps that's why it was easier for me to reach this decision, before anyone else, because Karen and I had discussed it on many occasions.

Q. Mrs. Quinlan, could you give us the circumstances of the second opportunity that you had to talk to Karen about this?

A. Well, I would say that each occurrence was similar, except that the last one in January of this year, which was only like two months before she became ill, and our friend, our very dear friend of the family for many years, Mr. Birch, had made the decision that he did not want to be kept alive by extraordinary means, and he had requested to be brought home from the hospital and to be just able to die at home. And Karen had felt that this is more or less what she would want to do, also, to be able to die in her own surroundings rather than to be just kept alive for X number of months or years.

Q. Was there anyone present at this last discussion, Mrs. Quinlan?

A. I think so. I couldn't say, clearly. It is very difficult for me, at this time, to think back to February of this year. I could not state that definitely. I am sorry. There might have been.

MR. ARMSTRONG: Thank you, Mrs. Quinlan. I have no further questions.

*Source: In the Matter of Karen Quinlan, an Alleged Incompetent,* Superior Court of New Jersey, Chancery Division, 1975. All relevant material is presented in *In the Matter of Karen Quinlan: The Complete Legal Briefs, Court Proceedings, and Decision in the Superior Court of New Jersey,* 2 vols. (Arlington, VA: University Publications of America, 1975 and 1976).

* * *

The case of Karen Quinlan was appealed to the Supreme Court of New Jersey. The New Jersey Catholic Conference filed an Amicus Curiae (friend of the court) brief. This brief clearly differentiates between allowing Karen Quinlan to die and euthanasia.

## DOCUMENT 80: Amicus Curiae Brief of the New Jersey Catholic Conference (1975 and 1976)

### STATEMENT OF BISHOP LAWRENCE B. CASEY CONCERNING KAREN ANN QUINLAN

The Position of the Bishop of Paterson on the Use of Extraordinary Means To Sustain the Life of Karen Ann Quinlan

3. What is being requested by Joseph and Julia Quinlan is not euthanasia.

Karen Ann Quinlan's parents have requested the termination of a medical procedure which is an extraordinary means of treatment. The Ethical and Religious Directives for Catholic Health Care Facilities, approved in November 1971 at the annual meeting of the National Conference of Catholic Bishops, states: "The failure to supply the ordinary means of preserving life is equivalent to euthanasia." It also states: "Neither the physician nor the patient is obliged to use extraordinary means." Since the Bishops in these directives forbid **all** forms of euthanasia, they thus teach that non-use of extraordinary means does not constitute euthanasia. Pope Pius XII in discussing the case of a patient in deep unconsciousness, a case, moreover, considered hopeless in the opinion of the competent doctor, said that the discontinuance of a respirator as an extraordinary means is not to be considered euthanasia in any way. "There is not involved here a case of direct disposal of the life of a patient, nor of euthanasia in any way; this would never be licit."

Euthanasia or "mercy killing" may be described as the deliberate and direct causing of the painless death of a human being who is helpless or who, for whatever reason, is deemed unable to live a so-called meaningful life. The Church teaches that: "Euthanasia is immoral and unlawful because it is intrinsically evil and entails a direct violation of man's right to life and of God's supreme dominion over His creatures." A person does have the ethical right to die peacefully and doctors and family do have the ethical right to allow such a death to happen in accord with the presumed will of the patient, when there is no reasonable hope for some recovery. However, there is never a right to take the life of a patient or to comply with a family or patient's request that the patient be allowed to take his own life. This would be contrary to divine law and contrary to the obligation of the state and society in general to uphold and defend the right to life from direct attack.

4. The possibility of God's intervention in the recovery of health is not and cannot be precluded.

God's intervention in human life takes many forms. He can do all things. He can and does work through His creation, and, in particular, through the knowledge and expertise of His people. These are interventions in accord with nature. For this reason we pray for those who undergo surgery and medical treatment. He can and does also work beyond the powers of nature, in which cases He does not need the intervention of man-made machines. He can restore life and health without them.

Lawrence B. Casey
Bishop of Paterson
November 1, 1975

## CONCLUSION

There are profound ethical considerations involved in the instant case.

The Bishop of Paterson has the authority and competence to present the Church's teaching in this matter, as a matter of faith and morals to be held and practiced by the people he serves.

All of the Catholic Bishops of New Jersey have adopted the position of Bishop Casey as contained in his Statement, as the uniform position of said Catholic Bishops in the State of New Jersey.

For these reasons, this *Amicus* respectfully urges this Court to accept the Statement of Bishop Casey as setting forth the application of the teaching of the Catholic Church to the request of the parents of Karen Ann Quinlan for permission to discontinue the use of a respirator as an extraordinary means of sustaining the life of Karen Ann Quinlan.

Respectfully submitted,
EDWARD J. LEADEM
*Attorney for New Jersey Catholic*
*Conference, Amicus Curiae*

Dated: January 12, 1976.

*Source*: Lawrence B. Casey, Bishop of Patterson and Edward J. Leadem, Attorney for New Jersey Catholic Conference, Amicus Curiae Brief of New Jersey Catholic Conference, Supreme Court of New Jersey, Docket No. A-116, 1975. Notes omitted.

* * *

In a landmark decision handed down on March 31, 1976, the Supreme Court of New Jersey reversed the lower court and granted the relief sought by Karen Quinlan's father. It upheld Karen Quinlan's constitutional right of privacy, citing her dim prognosis, and noted that "Ultimately there comes a point at which the individual's rights overcome the State interest." This was the first judicial decision that enunciated the constitutional right of privacy as the basis for withholding or withdrawing life support from a terminal patient without the need for automatic judicial review. The respirator was removed from Karen Quinlan. (The Quinlans did not seek to have the artificial nutrition and hydration stopped.) Ironically, she was able to breathe independently and survived for nine years in a persistent vegetative state, maintained by artificial nutrition and hydration.

## DOCUMENT 81: *In the Matter of Karen Quinlan,* Supreme Court of New Jersey (1976)

### DECLARATORY RELIEF

We thus arrive at the formulation of the declaratory relief which we have concluded is appropriate to this case. Some time has passed since Karen's physical and mental condition was described to the Court. At that time her continuing deterioration was plainly projected. Since the record has not been expanded we assume that she is now even more fragile and nearer to death than she was then. Since her present treating physicians may give reconsideration to her present posture in the light of this opinion, and since we are transferring to the plaintiff as guardian the choice of the attending physician and therefore other physicians may be in charge of the case who may take a different view from that of the present attending physicians, we herewith declare the following affirmative relief on behalf of the plaintiff. Upon the concurrence of the guardian and family of Karen, should the responsible attending physicians conclude that there is no reasonable possibility of Karen's ever emerging from her present comatose condition to a cognitive, sapient state and that the life-support apparatus now being administered to Karen should be discontinued, they shall consult with the hospital "Ethics Committee" or like body of the institution in which Karen is then hospitalized. If that consultative body agrees that there is no reasonable possibility of Karen's ever emerging from her present comatose condition to a cognitive, sapient state, the present life-support system may be withdrawn and said action shall be without any civil or criminal liability therefor on the part of any participant, whether guardian, physician, hospital or others. We herewith specifically so hold.

## CONCLUSION

We therefore remand this record to the trial court to implement (without further testimonial hearing) the following decisions:

1. To discharge, with the thanks of the Court for his service, the present guardian of the person of Karen Quinlan, Thomas R. Curtin, Esquire, a member of the Bar and an officer of the court.
2. To appoint Joseph Quinlan as guardian of the person of Karen Quinlan with full power to make decisions with regard to the identity of her treating physicians.

We repeat for the sake of emphasis and clarity that upon the concurrence of the guardian and family of Karen, should the responsible attending physicians conclude that there is no reasonable possibility of Karen's ever emerging from her present comatose condition to a cognitive, sapient state and that the life-support apparatus now being administered to Karen should be discontinued, they shall consult with the hospital "Ethics Committee" or like body of the institution in which Karen is then hospitalized. If that consultative body agrees that there is no reasonable possibility of Karen's ever emerging from her present comatose condition to a cognitive, sapient state, the present life-support system may be withdrawn and said action shall be without any civil or criminal liability therefor [sic], on the part of any participant, whether guardian, physician, hospital or others.

By the above ruling we do not intend to be understood as implying that a proceeding for judicial declaratory relief is necessarily required for the implementation of comparable decisions in the field of medical practice.

Modified and remanded.

Source: In the Matter of Karen Quinlan, an Alleged Incompetent, 355A. 2d 647 Supreme Court of New Jersey, 1976.

\* \* \*

The *Quinlan* decision received a great deal of comment in the press. An example follows.

## DOCUMENT 82: "Court Rules Karen Quinlan's Father Can Let Her Die," Joseph F. Sullivan, *New York Times* (April 1, 1976)

TRENTON, March 31—The New Jersey Supreme Court ruled today that the mechanical respirator that was keeping Karen Anne [sic] Quinlan alive might be disconnected if her attending physicians and a panel of hospital officials agreed that there was "no reasonable possibility" that she would recover.

The 7-to-0 decision, written by Chief Justice Richard J. Hughes, also ruled that there would be no civil or criminal liability if the mechanical device was removed following the guidelines laid down in the 59-page opinion.

The court appointed Miss Quinlan's father her guardian and empowered him to seek physicians and hospital officials who would agree to remove the respirator.

The 22-year-old woman has been in a coma for almost a year, and her parents petitioned last September for court approval for removal of "artificial" life-sustaining procedures so she might die "with grace and dignity." Their request was denied in a lower-court ruling.

Paul W. Armstrong, the attorney for the Quinlan family, said the young woman's parents "wept" when he informed them of today's opinion. He added: "The court has advanced a right of privacy on the part of the father to act in Karen Quinlan's best interests."

He said the opinion would allow the young woman's parents to "return their daughter to her natural life processes, and if those processes fail, she will die."

Medical experts who testified at the lower-court hearing in October said the young woman could not survive for very long without the mechanical respirator and other around-the-clock medical procedures.

When asked who would turn off the respirator if that decision was approved by the attending physicians and concurred in by the required medical panel, Mr. Armstrong said: "That decision will be a familial one, and any action will be taken in private."

Meeting with newsmen at Our Lady of the Lake Church in Mount

Arlington, Mr. and Mrs. Quinlan expressed joy and relief at the court decision and said they would begin consultations with doctors tomorrow as the first of a series of steps that could lead to the removal of their daughter's life-support system.

"This decision showed courage and the will of God," declared Mr. Quinlan, who said he had been "shocked and overwhelmed" by the ruling.

"This is the decision we've been praying for," said Mrs. Quinlan.

The high court quickly dispensed with Mr. Armstrong's novel constitutional arguments that Miss Quinlan's parents had a right to seek removal of the respirator under constitutional amendments that guarantee freedom of religion and ban cruel and unusual punishment.

But the court asserted a right of privacy for Miss Quinlan to make life-sustaining medical decisions and said that since the young woman was incompetent to make the decision herself, it belonged to her father, acting as her guardian.

"The magic of the common law has overcome the problems posed by technological advances in medicine," Mr. Armstrong said in commenting on the Supreme Court decision.

In ruling on the existence of Miss Quinlan's right of privacy, the court said: "We have no doubt, in these unhappy circumstances, that if Karen were herself miraculously lucid for an interval and perceptive of her irreversible condition, she could effectively decide on discontinuance of the life-support apparatus, even if it meant the prospect of natural death."

The court added: "If a putative decision by Karen to permit this noncognitive, vegetative existence to terminate by natural forces is regarded as a valuable incident of her right of privacy, as we believe it to be, then it should not be discarded solely on the basis that her condition prevents her conscious exercise of the choice.

"The only practical way to prevent destruction of the right is to permit the guardian and family of Karen to render their best judgment, subject to the qualifications here and after stated, as to whether she would exercise it in the circumstances.

"If their conclusion is in the affirmative, this decision should be accepted by a society, the overwhelming majority of whose members would, we think, in similar circumstances exercise such a choice in the same way for themselves or for those closest to them. It is for this reason that we determined that Karen's right of privacy may be asserted in her behalf, in this respect, by her guardian and family under the particular circumstances presented by this record."

William F. Hyland, the State Attorney General, who was one of the defendants in the case, said this evening that he agreed with many points of the ruling, especially the naming of Mr. Quinlan as guardian for his daughter, but he said no final decision on possible appeal had been made pending further review of the decision.

Mr. Armstrong said no final decision to remove the respirator would be sought until other parties to the case had an opportunity to file an appeal.

Near the end of its 59-page opinion, the court stated that "the exercise of a constitutional right, such as we here find, is protected from criminal prosecution."

"We do not question the state's undoubted power to punish the taking of human life," the ruling said, "but that power does not encompass individuals terminating medical treatment pursuant to their right of privacy."

In bolstering its recognition of an individual's right to privacy regarding life-sustaining medical decisions, the court referred to the United States Supreme Court decision in Griswold v. Connecticut, in which a woman's right to privacy in deciding whether to have an abortion was asserted.

"Presumably this right is broad enough to encompass a patient's decision to decline medical treatment under certain circumstances, in much the same way as it is broad enough to encompass a woman's decision to terminate pregnancy under certain conditions," the court said.

The high court also balanced the state's interest in preserving the sanctity of human life with the newly asserted right of privacy and found that in cases involving medical procedures, "the state's interest weakens and the individual's right to privacy grows as the degree of bodily invasion increases and the prognosis dims."

"Ultimately there comes a point at which the individual's rights overcome the state's interest," the court said.

The opinion also gave the guardian the stronger voice in deciding what constitutes the best interest of an incompetent, even in the face of an opposing opinion by attending physicians. In fact, the court authorized the Quinlans to change physicians, if they wished, in the event the present physicians failed to reconsider their opposition to the request to remove the respirator.

The court said, however, that Superior Court Judge Robert Muir Jr. was correct in denying the Quinlans' original request for removal of the respirator "under the law as it then stood," and it said the attending physicians, Dr. Robert Morse and Dr. Arshad Javed, were supported in their decision by proof offered at the trial "as to the then existing medical standards and practices."

But the court denied the existence of such uniform medical standards and put the blame for some of the reticence of physicians to give their best judgment in medical situations such as Miss Quinlan's on "the modern proliferation of substantial malpractice litigation and the less frequent, but even more unnerving possibility, of criminal sanctions."

The New Jersey Supreme Court sought to lay these fears to rest through its insertion of the protected right of privacy.

In its decision, which took the form of a declaratory judgment, the court said: "Upon the concurrence of the guardian and family of Karen, should the responsible attending physicians conclude that there is no reasonable possibility of Karen's ever emerging from her present comatose condition to a cognitive, sapient state and that the life-support apparatus now being administered to Karen should be discontinued, they shall consult with the hospital 'ethics committee,' or like body of the institution in which Karen is then hospitalized.

"If that consultant body agrees that there is no reasonable possibility of Karen's ever emerging from her present comatose condition to a cognitive, sapient state, the present life-support system may be withdrawn and said action shall be without any civil or criminal liability thereafter on the part of any participant, whether guardian, physician, hospital or others."

The Supreme Court invited the medical profession to use these guidelines without the necessity of seeking similar declaratory judgments from the courts in the future.

The high court also said its guidelines might be used in other types of terminal cases, without the necessity of applying the "hopeless loss of cognitive or sapient life" test as a prerequisite for action.

*Source*: Joseph F. Sullivan, "Court Rules Karen Quinlan's Father Can Let Her Die By Disconnecting Respirator If Doctors See No Hope," *New York Times*, April 1, 1976, 1, 23.

\* \* \*

## WHAT IS CLEAR AND CONVINCING EVIDENCE?

In the United States, each state has wide latitude to determine how certain aspects of community life will be conducted in that particular state. Consequently, a decision by a court in one state will not control decisions in another, although the reasoning may be influential. As a result, cases dealing with the same issues in different states may result in different outcomes or may arrive at the same outcome for different reasons. This has been true of end-of-life decision making for patients without capacity. Thus the Supreme Court of New Jersey based its 1976 finding in the Quinlan decision on the constitutional "right of privacy." This constitutional right is found in the Ninth and Fourteenth Amendments to the U.S. Constitution, although the former has not received definite interpretation by the Supreme Court. The landmark decision *Roe v. Wade* that covers a woman's right to choose abortion was based on the Fourteenth Amendment (see Document 132). In contrast, in 1981, after decisions by two lower courts, New York's highest court in the case *In the Matter of John Storar* permitted withdrawal of life support from Brother Joseph Charles Fox because it found "clear and convincing evidence" that the patient, Brother Fox, would not want to live in a persistent vegetative state. (The cases of John Storar and Brother Fox were reviewed together.) Although Brother Fox had already died, the New York Court of Appeals decided to hear the case.

---

## DOCUMENT 83: *In the Matter of John Storar*, New York Court of Appeals (1981)

---

The District Attorney's arguments [with regard to Brother Fox] underscore the very sensitive nature of the question as to whether, in case of incompetency, a decision to discontinue life sustaining medical treatment may be made by someone other than the patient. . . . However, that issue is not presented in this case because here Brother Fox made the decision for himself before he became incompetent. The Supreme Court [New York's lowest court] and the Appellate Division found that the evidence on this point, as well as proof of the patient's subsequent incompetency and chances of recovery was "clear and convincing." We agree that this is the appropriate burden of proof and that the evidence in the record satisfies this standard. . . . In sum, the evidence clearly and convincingly shows that Brother Fox did not want to be maintained in a vegetative coma by use of a respirator.

*Source: In the Matter of John Storar. . . . In the Matter of Philip K. Eichner, on Behalf of Joseph C. Fox, Respondent, v. Denis Dillon, as District Attorney of Nassau County, Appellant, Court of Appeals, New York, 420 N.E. 2d 64. 52 N.Y. 2d 363 (1981).*

\* \* \*

The decision with regard to Brother Fox did not answer the question of how decisions would be made for patients whose wishes were less clearly known or could never be known, but it became the precedent for another New York case with far-reaching consequences for medical decision making in New York State. In 1988, New York's highest court, the Court of Appeals, used the *Eichner* case as the basis of its decision in the case of Mary O'Connor, a former hospital employee, who was unresponsive and unable to swallow (*In re Westchester County Medical Center [O'Connor]* [1988]). O'Connor had repeatedly stated to her two daughters, both practical nurses, that she did not want her life prolonged by artificial means if she were unable to care for herself. She also said that it was "monstrous" to keep someone alive by using "machinery, things like that" when they were "not going to get better." The court overruled the lower courts and directed that a feeding tube be put in place, having concluded that O'Connor's expressed wishes did not constitute "clear and convincing evidence." The point at issue was not the means by which life was being sustained, but the standard for decision making. The result of this decision has been that individuals in New York State whose wishes are not known or can never be known (for example, a mentally retarded person) cannot have treatment stopped. The stringent "clear and convincing evidence" standard is also in effect in Delaware, Missouri, Michigan (under certain circumstances), and Wisconsin. In states that require clear and convincing evidence to stop treatment, an advance directive may be the only way to ensure that one's wishes are followed if one is unable to communicate them.

Other states have less stringent standards. For example, as illustrated in the following case, Pennsylvania law provides for the use of "substituted judgment," which permits someone close to a patient in a persistent vegetative state to request termination of life-sustaining treatment.

## DOCUMENT 84: *In re Daniel Joseph Fiori*, Supreme Court, Pennsylvania (1995)

Daniel Joseph Fiori, the nominal subject of this appeal, suffered severe head injuries in 1972 when he was approximately twenty years old. He regained consciousness after this injury, but his cognitive abilities were severely limited. In 1976, Fiori suffered a second head injury while being treated at a Veterans Administration hospital ("VA"). Fiori never regained consciousness after this second injury, and he was diagnosed as being in a persistent vegetative state ("PVS")....

After Fiori's second accident, his mother, Rosemarie Sherman, was appointed guardian of his person by court order entered in 1980. In February of 1992, Sherman requested that the Mayo Nursing Center, which was the nursing home caring for Fiori, remove his gastrostomy tube. The nursing home refused to comply with her request without a court order; Sherman thus filed a petition in the Court of Common Pleas for Bucks

County requesting an order directing the nursing home to terminate treatment. The Attorney General appeared in the proceedings and, pursuant to his request, an independent medical expert was appointed.

The opinions of two neurologists, one retained by Sherman and the other the court appointed independent expert, were entered into evidence. Both agreed that within a reasonable degree of medical certainty, Fiori's condition would not improve and he would remain in a PVS as he had done for the last seventeen years. They also stated that existing medical technology could continue to support Fiori's life functions so that his life span could extend for another ten or twenty years.

Sherman testified that her son had never spoken to her about his wishes should he ever lapse into a PVS. Nevertheless, based on her son's "love of life," Sherman was of the opinion that her son would wish the gastrostomy tube to be removed.

The trial court granted Sherman's motion, and the Attorney General appealed.

The Superior Court, sitting *en banc*, affirmed. The court determined that the decision to remove life sustaining treatment from an adult in a PVS who did not leave directions as to the maintenance of life support may be made by a close family member and two qualified physicians without court approval.

The Attorney General filed a petition for allowance of appeal on January 23, 1995. . . .

In this appeal, we must determine the procedures and guidelines for removal of life sustaining treatment from a PVS patient where the patient, prior to his incompetency, failed to express his desires on such treatment. Specifically, we must determine who may make the decision for the PVS patient, what standard the decision-maker should employ, and whether the court must approve that decision. . . .

The right to refuse medical treatment has deep roots in our common law. More than a century ago, the United States Supreme Court recognized that "[n]o right is held more sacred, or is more carefully guarded, by the common law, than the right of every individual to the possession and control of his own person" [cit.]

From this right to be free from bodily invasion developed the doctrine of informed consent [cit.] The doctrine of informed consent declares that absent an emergency situation, medical treatment may not be imposed without the patient's informed consent [cit.] A logical corollary to this doctrine is the patient's right, in general, "to refuse treatment and to withdraw consent to treatment once begun" [cit.] Courts have unanimously concluded that his right to self-determination does not cease upon the incapacitation of the individual [cit.]

This right, however, is not absolute. The right of the patient to abstain from medical treatment must be balanced against interests of the state. . . .

Having determined that a PVS patient's right to self-determination outweighs any interests the state may have in maintaining life-sustaining treatment for the patient, we must examine how that right may be exercised. Where a PVS patient created advance written directives prior to incapacitation, we have statutory provisions which provide for the implementation of the patient's wishes [cit.] Yet, the Act does not address the situation where no advance directives were left as to treatment.

Where a statute does not exist on the subject, there are various legal theories on which authorization to terminate life support may be predicated. The approach taken by many of our sister states [cit.], and by the Superior Court below, is to allow a close family member to exercise "substituted judgment" on behalf of the patient. . . .

The minority of states requires that there be "clear and convincing" evidence of the patient's intent to withdraw life support. This is the most stringent approach. . . .

The Attorney General argues that the clear and convincing evidence standard should be used. . . . We disagree. . . .

[W]e find the clear and convincing evidence test to be overly restrictive, one which would thwart the PVS patient's right to determine the medical care to be received. . . . [T]he "choice" would be dependent simply upon how far the frontiers of medical science had advanced; if the life sustaining procedures were available, they would be automatically administered. This we cannot tolerate.

Thus, we agree with the Superior Court below that the substituted judgment standard is the proper approach. . . . We also hold that a close family member is well-suited to the role of substitute decision maker. . . . Furthermore, concomitant with the substitute decision maker's exercise of the PVS patient's right to refuse treatment, the surrogate must also obtain written statements of two doctors qualified to evaluate the patient's condition. . . .

The final question for our review is what role the judiciary will play when situations such as Fiori's arise. We believe that where the physicians and the close family member are in agreement, and there is no dispute between "interested parties," [note] there is no need for court involvement.

*Source: In re Daniel Joseph Fiori, an Adjudged Incompetent*, 673 A.2d 905 (Pa. 1996) Supreme Court, Pennsylvania, 1996.

* * *

## ARTIFICIAL NUTRITION AND HYDRATION

Decisions about withdrawal of treatment can be a source of serious personal and interpersonal conflict. This is especially true of artificially supplied food and water, administered by a nasogastric tube or through a tube inserted through a gastrostomy (an artificial opening through the skin into the stomach). Many individuals make a strong emotional connection between "feeding" and "caring," so that failure to supply food and liquid may be viewed as causing starvation and dehydration, with attendant discomfort. However, observation of unconscious patients indicates that the process is peaceful, and conscious patients who are elderly or neurologically impaired usually suffer little or no discomfort (see Documents 88 and 89).

In 1982, a group of prestigious physicians met to discuss the physician's responsibility toward hopelessly ill patients. Their statements regarding artificial nutrition and hydration follow.

---

## DOCUMENT 85: "The Physician's Responsibility toward Hopelessly Ill Patients," Sidney H. Wanzer et al. (1984)

Naturally or artificially administered hydration and nutrition may be given or withheld, depending on the patient's comfort. If these supports are to be withheld or withdrawn, however, the physician must be sensitive to the symbolic meaning of this step. The provision of food and water is so important symbolically that family, friends, and staff need to understand that many patients in a terminal situation are not aware of thirst or hunger.

When [a persistent vegetative state] has been established with a high degree of medical certainty, and has been carefully documented, it is morally justifiable to withhold antibiotics and artificial nutrition and hydration, as well as other forms of life-sustaining treatment, allowing the patient to die. This obviously requires careful efforts to obtain knowledge of the patient's prior wishes and the understanding and agreement of the family. Family attitudes will clearly influence the type of care given in these cases.

*Source*: Sidney H. Wanzer, S. James Adelstein, Ronald E. Cranford et al., "The Physician's Responsibility toward Hopelessly Ill Patients," *New England Journal of Medicine* 310 (1984): 955–959.

* * *

This was a radical statement for its day, and the article was widely reported in the press.

## DOCUMENT 86: "Don't Force All to Live, Doctors Say," *Chicago Tribune* (April 13, 1984)

BOSTON (AP)—Doctors ethically need not force-feed severely demented, elderly people who have stopped eating on their own as long as the patients are kept comfortable, a group of prominent physicians said in guidelines published Thursday.

The nation's oldest congressman, Rep. Claude Pepper, 84, [D., Fla.], denounced the recommendations as "a sign of callousness" by doctors "taking advantage of [patients'] helplessness."

"If you're not going to do everything possible to save the lives of the ill, you might as well hit them over the head with a sledgehammer," Pepper said.

The Guidelines are not intended to "hasten" the deaths of elderly people, said Dr. Sidney H. Wanzer, who included them in a report in Thursday's New England Journal of Medicine.

The report said the rules are meant to help doctors decide how to treat "hopelessly ill" patients who can no longer express their feelings about their treatment. Elderly people make up the bulk of those in the "severely and irreversibly demented" category, the report said.

"These poor, pathetic beings just go on and on, and people have felt uncomfortable in the past about not giving intravenous fluids or antibiotics or nasogastric feeding if they quit desiring this spontaneously," Wanzer said. "And yet we feel that it is ethical not to push ahead with those things."

Such patients need not be given antibiotics if they get pneumonia or other disorders, although they must be kept comfortable while they die, the guidelines said.

But the report cautioned: "The provision of food and water is so important symbolically that family, friends and staff need to understand that many patients in a terminal situation are not aware of thirst or hunger."

Wanzer is on the staff of Emerson Hospital in Concord, Mass. The rules were created at a meeting at Harvard Medical School headed by Dr. Daniel D. Federman, former president of the American College of Physicians. Among those attending were doctors from Hennepin County Medical Center in Minneapolis, the University of Virginia Medical Center, the Mayo Clinic and the medical schools at Harvard, the University of Pittsburgh, Johns Hopkins and the University of Texas.

The guidelines say doctors must always obey the patients' wishes, but that aggressive treatment is wrong if it only prolongs a painful death. Such decisions are especially difficult for doctors when patients are too sick or demented to say how much care they want.

"Severely and irreversibly demented patients need only care given to make them comfortable," the guidelines say. "If a patient rejects food and water by mouth, it is ethically permissible to withhold nutrition and hydration [water] artificially administered by vein or gastric tube."

Barbara Meara, director of public relations for the Right to Life organization in New York, said her group agreed with most of the recommendations.

"But withholding food and water seems extreme," Meara said. "There are instances that a patient cannot ingest food and water, but a recommendation to withhold food and water seems inconsistent with offering them comfort."

Lillian Sarno, head of the Gray Panthers chapter in New York, said patients sometimes "make startling recoveries" from seemingly irreversible mental illness.

The doctors recommended that patients always be told the truth about their conditions when they have fatal illnesses. This way they can choose the level of care they want when death grows near.

If the patient requests general nursing care but rejects emergency resuscitation, intensive care or other medical treatment, everything should be done to keep him comfortable.

*Source*: "Don't Force All to Live, Doctors Say," *Chicago Tribune*, April 13, 1984, 12.

* * *

The Judicial Council of the American Medical Association issued a statement in 1986 that specifically included removal of artificial nutrition and hydration among the life-prolonging treatments that could be withdrawn from patients in irreversible coma. This conclusion is among those presented in the article "Decision Near the End of Life" (*Journal of the American Medical Association* 267 [1992]: 2229–2233).

In the mid-1980s, a number of state courts ruled on the legality of withdrawing artificial nutrition and hydration from patients with different degrees of mental incompetence.

### Patients in a Persistent Vegetative State

Helen Corbett was a seventy-three-year-old woman who was left in a persistent vegetative state following a stroke. Her life was maintained by use of a nasogastric tube. Because the Florida Life-prolonging Procedure Act was ambiguous, Thomas E. Corbett, her husband, asked the court to permit withdrawal of artificial nutrition and hydration. The lower court declined to authorize the withdrawal. Although Helen Corbett then died, Thomas Corbett appealed the case. The Florida District Court of Appeals (*Corbett v. D'Alessandro*, 487 So. 2d 368 [Fla. Dist. Ct. App.], review denied 1986) held that provision of artificial sustenance constitutes medical treatment and that the right to reject it is constitutionally protected as part of the constitutional right of privacy guaranteed by both the federal and the Florida constitutions and may not be abridged or limited by a state statute. The Florida Supreme Court declined to review the decision, thus agreeing with the lower court.

The medical issues regarding artificial nutrition and hydration were clearly addressed in the Massachusetts case of *Brophy v. New England Sinai Hospital, Inc.*, in 1986. In 1983, Paul Brophy suffered a brain hemorrhage and was determined to be in a persistent vegetative state. After lower-court decisions, the Massachusetts Supreme Judicial Court ruled that individuals in a persistent vegetative state do not feel pain, that a feeding tube can be "intrusive and extraordinary," and that when such artificial nutrition is removed, the cause of death is the underlying condition. This decision supported the following legal trends: (1) patients can refuse artificial nutrition and hydration like other treatments; (2) there is no legal or moral difference between withholding and withdrawing life support; (3) refusal of life-sustaining treatment is not suicide; and (4) the patient's substituted judgment, especially when there is no hope of recovery to sapient life, outweighs the state interest in preserving life, even if the patient is not "terminally ill." Three justices of the U.S. Supreme Court refused to block the ruling. Paul Brophy's feeding tube was removed on October 23, 1986, and he died peacefully eight days later of pneumonia. Patricia Brophy has described her husband's illness and her anguish.

---

## DOCUMENT 87: "Death with Dignity?" Patricia Brophy (1997)

---

I was told by two physicians in 1985 that there was no such thing as death with dignity. They were the then president of the Massachusetts Citizens for Life, Dr. Joseph Stanton, and the physician-in-chief of the New England Sinai Hospital, Dr. Richard Field. I vehemently disagreed with them. The following story explains my position.

Paul Brophy was the youngest of nine children in an Irish Catholic family. . . .

I knew Paul since we were children. We lived exactly a mile apart. . . .

We had been married nearly 25 years and Paul was 45 years old when tragedy struck. Paul came to bed the night of March 22, 1983, grabbed his head and said, "I have a splitting headache," and passed out. Our world ended in the twinkling of an eye.

I could not arouse him. . . . He was transported to the emergency room at Goddard Hospital, where it was determined that he had suffered a ruptured brain aneurysm. After transfer to the neurologic intensive care unit (ICU) of the New England Medical Center in Boston, he was kept in a stimulation-deprived environment for 10 days while the blood around his brain dissipated and the brain swelling subsided. This was to ensure the best conditions for operating and clipping the aneurysm. . . .

A craniotomy was performed on April 6, 1983. The surgery was successful, but vasospasms after the surgery caused a massive stroke, and Paul never regained consciousness. For the next three and a half years, he remained in a coma that evolved into a persistent vegetative state.

Following three months of acute care, Paul was transferred to New England Sinai Hospital, a chronic care facility, just 10 miles from our home. I chose this facility because of its location. I could go each day to help Paul in his rehabilitation. I could be involved in his care until I could bring him home. So I thought—and hoped.

When Paul arrived at Sinai, he was being nourished via a nasogastric tube. He also had a tracheostomy with oxygen mist to facilitate breathing. As time passed, Sinai asked my permission to insert a gastrostomy tube because the nasogastric tube was causing pneumonia and other respiratory problems. The doctor also stressed the possibility of permanent damage to the larynx from the nasogastric tube. I gave my permission for insertion of the gastrostomy tube, not having an inkling of what I was about to face.

Days passed; weeks turned into months. There were many hugs and tears, but more than anything else, still hope—hope that today would be the day Paul would wake up. People stopped asking, stopped visiting; it was as though he was gone. Well, he was, yet he lingered. His hands curled in, and his arms grew stiff. His legs that once were strong from running were now like twigs. They were curling up and contracting more each day. He wore sneakers to prevent footdrop. It was so sad, so very painful to watch this man who, a few months ago, had been vital, happy, and healthy.

He was such a strong person, with a strong heart, and he lingered on. For many frustrating months, I stood at the foot of his bed, watching him wither, wondering why. Why did this happen to Paul? Why did this happen to us—we are good people, faithful to each other and to our God. Why did the vasospasms occur after a fairly successful operation?

Why does he not respond—he was such a healthy person before the aneurysm burst. Why are my prayers not being answered? I discovered later that my prayers were being answered. They just were not answered in the way I had hoped. . . .

Nearly a year and a half into Paul's illness, the hospital inititated [sic] an eight-week program for families of head-injured patients. It was given by a retired psychologist, Dr. Yager, who had recently lost his wife to cancer. In the course of the program, he said he had not allowed the insertion of a feeding tube into his wife. He also very bluntly said, "Don't you realize your loved ones are going to die? They will never recover." This statement hit me like a ton of bricks. I had prayed and prayed for a miracle to happen. But the Lord did not change the situation I was in; He used the situation to change me!

The most unselfish act of love is the ability to let go of someone you love. Paul was a father, son, brother, husband, and friend to so many. We all loved him in our own very special way. He, in turn, enriched all our lives with his specialness—his strength and guidance, his ability to make tough decisions and stick to them. It might have been easier for me to allow things to continue as they were. Many families do. Yet the conflict inside me kept urging, prodding. "This isn't right." Days and months spread into years of grief that did not end.

New England Sinai Hospital never had what I would call a friendly atmosphere, even before I made my decision to let Paul die. The nurses and attendants were so constantly busy that it was impossible for them to spend quality time with families. I never had much contact with social workers or other hospital personnel and found the most comfort from meeting and talking with other families informally and attending the Tuesday afternoon Catholic Mass with Paul. After the first three weeks of Paul's internment, all rehabilitation programs were stopped, and he was on chronic maintenance care. The nursing care Paul received at Sinai was, for the most part, good. However, I believe this was so because I was so constantly there and never silent about care when it was lacking.

I began asking myself questions. What is the difference between being terminally ill and irreversibly ill—in this case, in a persistent vegetative state? A terminally ill person, in 1984, could legally, morally, and ethically have all treatment stopped or not started, whereas a person in a persistent vegetative state had to be nourished with artificial, chemical nutrition and hydration. What moral obligation did Paul have to live in this state? Why must his death be prolonged? When treatment received is not bringing about recovery, why can it not be stopped? Why is it more moral not to start a treatment than to stop ineffective therapy?

I reflected on Paul's life values. . . . I was completely convinced that Paul would never, never want to live like this.

I finally came to the conclusion that I had three choices: do nothing, walk away and forget that Paul existed, or step out in faith and do what I knew Paul would expect me to do as his wife—stop the tube feedings and allow him to die. Emotionally, all of Paul's family and friends were dying, a piece at a time. I approached my pastor and asked his guidance. He gave me not only guidance, but his blessing and support for a decision that I could be at peace with. This decision came through much counseling and prayer. One of the scripture verses that served as a guideline was *Micah*, Ch 6, V. 8. "This is what Yahweh expects of you, only this—to love tenderly, act justly, and walk humbly with your God."

The final decision came after we brought Paul home for Christmas in 1984. . . .

I found myself sharing funny memories with him. I shared them with other family members and close friends, and I could finally laugh at some without rushing from the room to catch my breath. Dreams of panic washed through me at night. I ran from the pain, the anger, the hurt. I had come to realize I could only run so far. The doctors at Sinai wished that I would run away forever and forget, move on, whatever, as long as I did not cause them any discomfort or disrupt their sterile world. But I could not run any more.

I finally opened my heart to a church friend. He, in turn, helped me to contact Father John Paris, who introduced me to attorney Frank Reardon and Dr. Ronald Cranford. These three people became the backbone of my case. I now realize that when I surrendered an impossible situation to the Lord, he began to open doors.

The decision was made to help Paul—to let him die. His life had been over for quite some time now. It was January 1985, and Paul's condition had not changed in almost two years. I searched my soul for the millionth time, looked for guidance from elders and support from family, friends, and church community. Confusion was constant, as many people just did not understand. My five children, Paul's entire family of seven brothers and sisters, and his 90-year-old mother gave me their undivided support. I asked Paul's doctor to stop tube feedings. He refused. Attorney Reardon contacted Dr. Field and asked for a meeting, which he flatly refused, stating there was nothing to talk about. He refused to communicate with us in any way. So, on February 6, 1985, we petitioned the Norfolk County Probate Court for declaratory relief to stop tube feedings. The doctor was furious that I had gone to court, and from that day forward, we received a cold shoulder from all but a few of the hospital staff.

In early May, we came before Judge Kopelman for a hearing. He was not satisfied with the setup, which included an attorney for the hospital, an attorney for me, and a guardian ad litem to research the facts of the case. The judge said that Paul also had a right to counsel, and an attorney was appointed. This pitted me against my husband. Wait! There is something wrong with this picture! I find myself in a triangle; everybody's fighting over him: the hospital, the court-appointed attorney who does not even know him, and me. And Paul lies there, unaware, lingering. I have lost him once before; I know how much it hurts. Why do they not see that I am doing this for Paul? They try to figure out what I have to gain, while I try to figure out how I am going to survive this experience. The ball is in my court, however, and I am taking my best shot. The ball has bounced into a court of law. . . .

We were persecuted by pro-life-backed testimony in the courtroom and in the media. They called us abusive, cruel, inhumane, and no better than Nazi murderers. They painted a picture of starvation: lips cracked, eyes sunken in the sockets, tongue swollen and stuck to the mouth. This nearly destroyed me. Pro-life forces did not seem to realize that I had opted for life all the way until we came to the end of the road. When the Lord showed me there was no life and no hope of recovery, I knew that I had to surrender Paul to his Creator. I had to stop pumping him full of artificial, chemical nutrition. I tried and tried to explain this. More than anything else in the world, I wanted him back—we all did—but it had been two years!

Prior to Paul's illness, we had discussed living wills. There was no legislation in place in Massachusetts at the time, but we had decided that when it became legal, we would each execute one. Until then, we knew what we each wanted, so there would be no problem. This was a grave mistake on our part. It was emphasized in the courtroom that something in writing might have been taken into consideration. Nevertheless, as the Bible states in *Romans* Ch. 8, V. 28, "We know that, in everything, God works for good with those who love Him, who are called according to His purpose."

One distressing thing in the courtroom was the fact that, after the family finished testifying, Paul Brophy was no longer considered. He was lost in a debate of two factions: the right to life and the right to die. At this point, I felt like a scapegoat, a pawn in a battle of ideologies.

Five months later, the lower court's ruling was handed down (*Brophy v. New England Sinai, Hospital, Inc.* 1985). The court agreed with the substituted judgment issue. Judge Kopelman ruled that Paul would not want to live in this condition, but the quality of treatment was more important than the quality of life. We were disappointed but not surprised. My attorney had prepared us for the denial. The important issue was the substituted judgment issue, and the judge had agreed to that. We, as a family, were more determined than ever to go on, and we filed an appeal.

The Supreme Judicial Court of Massachusetts heard oral arguments in March 1986. Its ruling came out in September (*Brophy v. New England Sinai Hospital, Inc.* 1986). We had now been in the court system for a year and a half, and Paul had been in a persistent vegetative state for three and a half years. Try to imagine yourself waking up every day for one and a half years, wondering, is this the day? In the meantime, trying to go on with life, working, visiting Paul, feeling, at times, a failure.

The lower court's decision was turned over by a 4–3 vote. Yes, we could discontinue feedings, but the hospital would not be forced to do so if it was against its policy. However, they were instructed to help us find a willing facility and transfer Paul there. As the hospital had not been cooperative in the past, neither were they now. This was a most horrendous experience. An irreversible comatose husband whom I loved dearly, one and a half years in courts, and a hospital that fought us every step of the way. . . .

Paul was transferred to Emerson Hospital on October 15, 1986. I had no idea what to expect after what I had been through at Sinai, but the staff actually talked to me as if I were a normal person. I was treated with compassion, emotional support, and, most of all, with respect for the agonizing decision that I had made. Going from Sinai to Emerson was like going to another planet. Everything that Sinai did wrong, Emerson did right. A cot was brought into Paul's room where I was allowed to stay 24 hours a day. I spent days watching the Red Sox playoffs on TV. The priests from my parish came in to support us. Friends sent cards. My five children were awesome. My brother and his wife even flew in from Texas to be near. The head nurse on Paul's team was hospice-trained. She realized the importance of family involvement. I was allowed to take part in both medical decision making and hands-on nursing care during the dying process.

This final phase of Paul's life was the most difficult yet the most rewarding eight days of my life. Paul died a peaceful death on October 23, 1986. . . .

As a result of this experience, my philosophy on the meaning of death emerged. It is different and probably a bit more liberal than some. I believe that a quality of life must be factored into the whole picture of life on earth . . . However, with the advent of technology, the body can be nourished for an unpredictable number of years while the cortex of the brain does not work. This is an unacceptable definition of life to me.

Death is not a failure. It is the fulfillment of life. It is an opening to a changed life. If I lose my ability to think, to respond to my environment inside or outside of my body, then I am not living. Body, mind, and spirit must be integrated. When the cerebral cortex dies, there will never again be integration of mind and body. I am not sure where the spirit fits into the picture. Perhaps, at this point it is straining to be freed.

Death is being medicalized and legalized in our society. The movement toward legalizing physician-assisted suicide has become a definite threat. Contrary to popular belief, much can be done for the dying. Physicians, patients, and families can continue to learn how and when to withhold or withdraw technical interventions that are burdensome and degrading to the sanctity of life. Stopping ineffective therapy and allowing death to occur naturally seems compatible with respect for life.

The Washington Catholic Bishops adopted arguments against euthanasia, adding the admonition of Father Richard McCormack that those who insist that life support systems must be used at all times, even though the patient will not benefit, could well be unwittingly contributing to public acceptance of active euthanasia. People cringe at the thought of dying a prolonged death. They are aware of the Karen Ann Quinlans, the Paul Brophys, and the Nancy Cruzans of this world, who lingered on hopelessly year after year.

Although much legislation is in place today to help people avoid the predicament of *Brophy*, society has a long way to go to provide a consensus of acceptable behavior about right-to-life/right-to-die issues.

I hope that my family's experience has helped society to move toward resolution of the ongoing struggle of families caught in the turmoil of life and death issues.

*Source*: Patricia Brophy, "Death with Dignity?" in *Medical Futility and the Evaluation of Life-Sustaining Interventions*, ed. Marjorie B. Zucker and Howard D. Zucker (Cambridge: Cambridge University Press, 1997), 15–23 (references and cases omitted).

* * *

### Withdrawal of Nutrition and Hydration from Incompetent Patients Who Are Not in a Persistent Vegetative State

The 1985 decision by the New Jersey Supreme Court in *In re Conroy* permitted withdrawal of artificial nutrition and hydration from elderly incompetent nursing-home patients, but only under very specific conditions: the patient would probably die within a year, the patient would have refused treatment under the existing conditions, the treatment would only prolong suffering, or the treatment "clearly and markedly outweighs the benefits the patient derives from life"; there must be a judicial determination that the patient is incompetent to make the decision; a guardian must be designated if the patient does not already have one; the court must determine whether the guardian is a suitable person to make this decision; the guardian must notify the state Office of the Ombudsman; and the ombudsman must treat each such notification as possible "abuse" and must therefore investigate the situation. A Florida decision, *In re Guardianship of Browning* (Florida Supreme Court, 1990), established the same right of a noncomatose patient to refuse treatment that had been recognized for patients in a persistent vegetative state in *Corbett v. Alessandro*.

## Withdrawal of Nutrition and Hydration from Competent Patients

A number of recent scientific articles have demonstrated that failure to provide nutrition and hydration to dying, mentally alert patients results in a peaceful death. The following is the abstract of one such article.

---

## DOCUMENT 88: "Comfort Care for Terminally Ill Patients," Robert M. McCann, William J. Hall, and Annmarie Groth-Juncker (1994)

---

**Objective.**—To determine the frequency of symptoms of hunger and thirst in a group of terminally ill patients and determine whether these symptoms could be palliated without forced feeding, forced hydration, or parenteral alimentation.

**Design.**—Prospective evaluation of consecutively admitted terminally ill patients treated in a comfort care unit.

**Setting.**—Ten-bed comfort care unit in a 471-bed long-term care facility.

**Participants.**—Mentally aware, competent patients with terminal illnesses monitored from time of admission to time of death while residing in the comfort care unit.

**Main Outcome Measures.**—Symptoms of hunger, thirst, and dry mouth were recorded, and the amounts and types of food and fluids necessary to relieve these symptoms were documented. The subjective level of comfort was assessed longitudinally in all patients.

**Results.**—Of the 32 patients monitored during the 12 months of study, 20 patients (63%) never experienced any hunger, while 11 patients (34%) had symptoms only initially. Similarly, 20 patients (62%) experienced either no thirst or thirst only initially during their terminal illness. In all patients, symptoms of hunger, thirst, and dry mouth could be alleviated, usually with small amounts of food, fluids, and/or by the application of ice chips and lubrication to the lips. Comfort care included use of narcotics for relief of pain or shortness of breath in 94% of patients.

**Conclusions.**—In this series, patients terminally ill with cancer generally did not experience hunger and those who did needed only small amounts of food for alleviation. Complaints of thirst and dry mouth were relieved with mouth care and sips of liquids far less than that needed to prevent dehydration. Food and fluid administration beyond the specific requests of patients may play a minimal role in providing comfort to terminally ill patients.

*Source*: Robert M. McCann, William J. Hall, and Annmarie Groth-Juncker, "Comfort Care for Terminally Ill Patients: The Appropriate Use of Nutrition and Hydration," *Journal of the American Medical Association* 272 (1994): 1263–1266. Abstract.

* * *

The following article describes the death of a seriously ill, mentally alert elderly woman who chose to refuse food and drink.

## DOCUMENT 89: "A Conversation with My Mother," David M. Eddy (1994)

You have already met my father. Now meet my mother. She died a few weeks ago. She wanted me to tell you how.

Her name was Virginia. Up until about 6 months ago, at age 84, she was the proverbial "little old lady in sneakers." After my father died of colon cancer several years ago, she lived by herself in one of those grand old Greek revival houses you see on postcards of small New England towns. Hers was in Middlebury, Vermont.

My mother was very independent, very self-sufficient, and very content. My brother and his family lived next door. Although she was quite close to them, she tried hard not to interfere in their lives. She spent most of her time reading large-print books, working word puzzles, and watching the news and professional sports on TV. She liked the house kept full of light. Every day she would take two outings, one in the morning to the small country store across the street to pick up the *Boston Globe*, and one in the afternoon to the Grand Union across town, to pick up some item she purposefully omitted from the previous day's shopping list. She did this in all but the worst weather. On icy days, she would wear golf shoes to keep from slipping and attach spikes to the tip of her cane. I think she was about 5 feet 2 and 120 pounds, but I am not certain. I know she started out at about 5 feet 4, but she seemed to shrink a little bit each year, getting cuter with time as many old people do. Her wrinkles matched her age, emphasizing a permanent thin-lipped smile that extended all the way to her little Kris Kringle eyes. The only thing that embarrassed her was her thinning gray hair, but she covered that up with a rather dashing tweed fedora that matched her Talbots outfits. She loved to tease people by wearing outrageous necklaces. The one made from the front teeth of camels was her favorite.

To be sure, she had had her share of problems in the past: diverticulitis and endometriosis when she was younger, more recently a broken hip, a bout with depression, some hearing loss, and cataracts. But she was a walking tribute to the best things in American medicine. Coming from a family of four generations of physicians, she was fond of bragging that, but for lens implants, hearing aids, hip surgery, and Elavil, she would be blind, deaf, bedridden, and depressed. At age 84, her only problems were a slight rectal prolapse, which she could reduce fairly easily, some urinary incontinence, and a fear that if her eyesight got much worse she would lose her main pleasures. But those things were easy to deal with and she was, to use her New England expression, "happy as a clam."

*"David, I can't tell you how content I am. Except for missing your father, these are the best years of my life."*

Yes, all was well with my mother, until about six months ago. That was when she developed acute cholelithiasis. From that point on, her health began to unravel with amazing speed. She recovered from the cholecystectomy on schedule and within a few weeks of leaving the hospital was resuming her walks downtown. But about six weeks after the surgery she was suddenly hit with a case of severe diarrhea, so severe that it extended her rectal prolapse to about 8 inches and dehydrated her to the point that she had to be readmitted. As soon as her physician got her rehydrated, other complications quickly set in. She developed oral thrush, apparently due to the antibiotic treatment for her diarrhea, and her antidepressants got out of balance. For some reason that was never fully determined, she also became anemic, which was treated with iron, which made her nauseated. She could not eat, she got weak, her skin itched, and her body ached. Oh yes, they also found a lump in her breast, the diagnosis of which was postponed, and atrial fibrillation. Needless to say, she was quite depressed.

Her depression was accentuated by the need to deal with her rectal prolapse. On the one hand, she really disliked the thought of more surgery. She especially hated the nasogastric tube and the intense postoperative fatigue. On the other hand, the prolapse was very painful. The least cough or strain would send it out to rub against the sheets, and she could not push it back the way she used to. She knew that she could not possibly walk to the Grand Union again unless it was fixed.

It was at that time that she first began to talk to me about how she could end her life gracefully. As a physician's wife, she was used to thinking about life and death and prided herself on being able to deal maturely with the idea of death. She had signed every living will and advance directive she could find, and carried a card that donated her organs. Even though she knew they would not do anyone much good (*"Can they recycle my artificial hip and lenses?"*), she liked the way the card announced her acceptance of the fact that all things must someday end. She dreaded the thought of being in a nursing home, unable to take care of herself, her body, mind, and interests progressively declining until she was little more than a blank stare, waiting for death to mercifully take her away.

*"I know they can keep me alive a long time, but what's the point? If the pleasure is gone and the direction is steadily down, why should I have to draw it out until I'm 'rescued' by cancer, a heart attack, or a stroke? That could take years. I understand that some people want to hang on until all the possible treatments have been tried to squeeze out the last drops of life. That's fine for them. But not for me."*

My own philosophy, undoubtedly influenced heavily by my parents, is that choosing the best way to end your life should be the ultimate individual right—a right to be exercised between oneself and one's beliefs, without intrusions from governments or the beliefs of others. On the other hand, I also believe that such decisions should be made only with an accurate understanding of one's prognosis and should never be made in the middle of a correctable depression or a temporary trough. So my brother, sister, and I coaxed her to see a rectal surgeon about having her prolapse repaired and to put off thoughts of suicide until her health problems were stabilized and her antidepressants were back in balance.

With the surgeon's help, we explored the possible outcomes of the available procedures for her prolapse. My mother did not mind the higher mortality rates of the more extensive operations—in fact, she wanted them. Her main concern was to avoid rectal incontinence, which she knew would dampen any hopes of returning to her former lifestyle.

Unfortunately, that was the outcome she got. By the time she had recovered from the rectal surgery, she was totally incontinent "at both ends," to use her words. She was bedridden, anemic, exhausted, nauseated, achy, and itchy. Furthermore, over the period of this illness her eyesight had begun to fail to the point she could no longer read. Because she was too sick to live at home, even with my brother's help, but not sick enough to be hospitalized, we had to move her to an intermediate care facility.

On the positive side, her antidepressants were working again and she had regained her clarity of mind, her spirit, and her humor. But she was very unhappy. She knew instinctively, and her physician confirmed, that after all the insults of the past few months it was very unlikely she would ever be able to take care of herself alone or walk to the Grand Union. That was when she began to press me harder about suicide.

"Let me put this in terms you should understand, David. My 'quality of life'—isn't that what you call it?—has dropped below zero. I know there is nothing fatally wrong with me and that I could live on for many more years. With a colostomy and some luck I might even be able to recover a bit of my former lifestyle, for a while. But do we have to do that just because it's possible? Is the meaning of life defined by its duration? Or does life have a purpose so large that it doesn't have to be prolonged at any cost to preserve its meaning?

"I've lived a wonderful life, but it has to end sometime and this is the right time for me. My decision is not about whether I'm going to die—we will all die sooner or later. My decision is about when and how. I don't want to spoil the wonder of my life by dragging it out in years of decay. I want to go now, while the good memories are still fresh. I have always known that eventually the right time would come, and now I know that this is it. Help me find a way."

I discussed her request with my brother and sister and with her nurses and physician. Although we all had different feelings about her request, we agreed that she satisfied our criteria of being well-informed, stable, and not depressed. For selfish reasons we wanted her to live as long as possible, but we realized that it was not our desires that mattered. . . .

I bought *Final Exit* for her, and we read it together. If she were to end her life, she would obviously have to do it with pills. But as anyone who has thought about this knows, accomplishing that is not easy. . . . The way she really wanted to die was to be given a morphine drip that she could control, to have her family around her holding her hands, and for her to turn up the drip.

As wonderful as that might sound, it is illegal. One problem was that my mother did not have a terminal condition or agonizing pain that might justify a morphine drip. Far from it. Her heart was strong enough to keep her alive for 10 more years, albeit as a frail, bedridden, partially blind, partially deaf, incontinent, and possibly stroked-out woman. But beyond that, no physician would dare give a patient access to a lethal medicine in a way that could be accused of assisting suicide. . . .

I had no difficulty finding a friend who could write a prescription for restricted drugs and who was willing to help us from a distance. In fact, I have yet to find anybody who agrees with the current laws. ("So why do they exist?") But before I actually had to resolve any lingering conflicts and obtain the drugs, my mother's course took an unexpected and strangely welcomed twist. I received a call that she had developed pneumonia and had to be readmitted to the hospital. By the time I made contact with her, she had already reminded her attendants that she did not want to be resuscitated if she should have a heart attack or stroke.

*"Is there anything more I can do?"*

Pneumonia, the old folks' friend, I thought to myself. I told her that although advance directives usually apply to refusing treatments for emergencies such as heart attacks, it was always legal for her to refuse any treatment. In particular, she could refuse the antibiotics for the pneumonia. Her physician and nurses would undoubtedly advise her against it, but if she signed enough papers they would have to honor her request.

*"What's it like to die of pneumonia? Will they keep me comfortable?"*

I knew that without any medicine for comfort, pneumonia was not a pleasant way to die. But I was also confident that her physician was compassionate and would keep her comfortable. So she asked that the antibiotics be stopped. Given the deep gurgling in her throat every time she breathed, we all expected the infection to spread rapidly. She took a perverse pleasure in that week's cover story of *Newsweek*, which described the spread of resistant strains.

*"Bring all the resistant strains in this hospital to me. That will be my present to the other patients."*

But that did not happen. Against the odds, her pneumonia regressed. This discouraged her greatly—to see the solution so close, just to watch it slip away.

*"What else can I do? Can I stop eating?"*

I told her she could, but that that approach could take a long time. I then told her that if she was really intent on dying, she could stop drinking. Without water, no one, even the healthiest, can live more than a few days.

*"Can they keep me comfortable?"*

I talked with her physician. Although it ran against his instincts, he respected the clarity and firmness of my mother's decision and agreed that her quality of life had sunk below what she was willing to bear. He also knew that what she was asking from him was legal. He took out the IV and wrote orders that she should receive adequate medications to control discomfort.

My mother was elated. The next day happened to be her 85th birthday, which we celebrated with a party, balloons and all. She was beaming from ear to ear. She had done it. She had found the way. She relished her last piece of chocolate, and then stopped eating and drinking.

Over the next four days, my mother greeted her visitors with the first smiles she had shown for months. She energetically reminisced about the great times she had had and about things she was proud of. (She especially hoped I would tell you about her traveling alone across Africa at the age of 70, and surviving a capsized raft on Wyoming's Snake River at 82.) She also found a calming self-acceptance in describing things of which she was not proud. She slept between visits but woke up brightly whenever we touched her to share more memories and say a few more things she wanted us to know. On the fifth day it was more difficult to wake her. When we would take her hand she would open her eyes and smile, but she was too drowsy and weak to talk very much. On the sixth day, we could not wake her. Her face was relaxed in her natural smile, she was breathing unevenly, but peacefully. We held her hands for another two hours, until she died.

I had always imagined that when I finally stood in the middle of my parents' empty house, surrounded by the old smells, by hundreds of objects that represent a time forever lost, and by the terminal silence, I would be overwhelmingly saddened. But I wasn't. This death was not a sad death; it was a happy death. It did not come after years of decline, lost vitality, and loneliness; it came at the right time. My mother was not clinging desperately to what no one can have. She knew that death was not a tragedy to be postponed at any cost, but that death is a part of life, to be embraced at the proper time. She had done just what she wanted to do, just the way she wanted to do it. Without hoarding pills, without making me a criminal, without putting a bag over her head, and without huddling in a van with a carbon monoxide machine, she had found a way to bring her life gracefully to a close. Of course we cried. But although we will miss her greatly, her ability to achieve her death at her "right time" and in her "right way" transformed for us what could have been a desolate and crushing loss into a time for joy. Because she was happy, we were happy.

*"Write about this, David. Tell others how well this worked for me. I'd like this to be my gift. Whether they are terminally ill, in intractable pain, or, like me, just know that the right time has come for them, more people might want to know that this way exists. And maybe more physicians will help them find it."*

Maybe they will. Rest in peace, Mom.

Source: David M. Eddy, "A Conversation with My Mother," *Journal of the American Medical Association* 272 (1994): 179–181 (notes omitted).

\* \* \*

The following excerpt expresses the reactions of a physician who is deeply committed to hospice care at the end of life.

## DOCUMENT 90: "Patient Refusal of Nutrition and Hydration: Walking the Ever-finer Line," Ira Byock (1995).

... In every circumstance—legal or not—acceding to a patient's request for a lethal prescription entails a complicity on the part of the clinician. In its meaning the act is a collusion in the patient's belief that their situation is hopeless and that their existence is beyond conceivable value.

In my own practice, while I steadfastly refuse to write a prescription with lethal intent or otherwise help the patient commit suicide, I can share with the patient information that he or she already has the ability to exert control over the timing of death. Virtually any patient with far-advanced illness can be assured of dying—comfortably, without any additional physical distress—within one or two weeks simply by refusing to eat or drink. This is less time than would be legally imposed by waiting periods of assisted suicide initiatives. The discussion and subsequent decision are wholly ethical and legal, requiring no mandated psychiatric evaluations, attorneys, court decisions, or legislation. . . .

Clinically, for a number of people at the very end of life, the decision to refuse food and fluid may not arise from depression or emotional denial as much as from a felt sense of "being done." Most such persons I have encountered one way or another expressed a sense that eating or drinking were no longer relevant to their situation. They were far along in a process of withdrawal, having turned their attention inward or "beyond." Even here the option of PRNH [Patient Refusal of Nutrition and Hydration] has important advantages over complying with a patient's request to be killed, for it allows the clinician's attention to remain focused on relief of suffering—physical, psychosocial, and spiritual. It requires—or frees—the clinician to remain vigilant for treatable depression and to remain, in humility, open to the possibility of unexpected opportunities for the person to again discover value in the life that is waning.

The powerful symbolism of nurturing associated with feeding and the notion of suffering associated with starvation and dehydration are deeply rooted. This is perhaps especially true for those of our patients who lived through world wars and the Great Depression of this century. While the topic of PRNH may no longer be taboo, it must be approached with extraordinary sensitivity. However, discussion of what we know can help reduce anxiety of what we fear. The more we know and the more confidently we know it, the better able we are to make sound decisions. My experience is that the information presented has been well received and resulted in noticeable allaying of fears. This has been the case in private discussions as well as in public and professional forums. The recognition that patients with far-advanced illness have always had control over the timing of their demise can enable the focus of discussion and intervention to remain fixed on the goals of comfort and quality of life.

*Source*: Ira Byock, "Patient Refusal of Nutrition and Hydration: Walking the Ever-finer Line," *The American Journal of Hospice and Palliative Care*, March/April 1995: 12–13.

* * *

## THE U.S. SUPREME COURT DECISION IN THE CASE OF NANCY CRUZAN

The landmark ruling by the U.S. Supreme Court in the case of Nancy Cruzan served to clarify and affirm certain principles formulated by various state courts. However, it failed to establish a national standard for decision making on behalf of incompetent patients.

In January 1983, Nancy Cruzan, then twenty-five, was found lying unconscious near her overturned car. After resuscitation efforts, cardiac function and spontaneous respiration recommenced eighteen minutes after the accident. Cruzan remained unconscious, and a gastrostomy tube was implanted several weeks later to facilitate nutrition and hydration.

Within a few weeks, Cruzan was declared to be in a persistent vegetative state. Her parents, as coguardians, asked the hospital to end the gastrostomy feedings. When the request was refused, the Cruzans filed a declaratory-judgment action seeking judicial sanction of their instructions. The trial court approved their request, finding that there was clear and convincing evidence that Nancy Cruzan "would not wish to continue with nutrition and hydration," that she had a "right to liberty," and that to deny her coguardians authority to act would deprive her of equal protection of the law.

The state and the guardian ad litem appealed the case to the Missouri Supreme Court. A guardian ad litem is an individual appointed by the court to represent the interests of the incompetent individual. After citing a number of relevant cases in other states, the majority concluded that Nancy's prognosis was hopeless. With regard to her artificial nutrition and hydration, they did not think that the question of its ability to cure was germane, but rather that the issue was whether it was a burden to her, and whether she would refuse the continuation of tubal feeding were she able to do so. The court found that the statement of Nancy's roommate about her wish to refuse treatment was inadequate to justify termination of treatment.

The court departed dramatically from the decisions unanimously reached by other courts given similar facts. This was the first case in which an appellate court declined to approve withdrawing artificial feeding from a permanently unconscious patient. It was also the first in which a court stated that tube feeding is not medical treatment. Despite this court's challenge to the constitutional basis for the right to refuse treatment, it accepted that at least in some cases the common-law right could be exercised after incompetence if clear and convincing evidence could be put forth that the patient would have chosen not to have this form of treatment.

## DOCUMENT 91: *Cruzan v. Harmon*, Missouri Supreme Court (1988)

As we said, this case presents a single issue for resolution: May a guardian order that food and water be withheld from an incompetent ward who is in a persistent vegetative state but who is otherwise alive . . . and not terminally ill? As the parties carefully pointed out in their thoughtful briefs, this issue is a broad one, invoking consideration of the authority of guardians of incompetent wards, the public policy of Missouri with regard to the termination of life-sustaining treatment and the amorphous mass of constitutional rights generally described as "the right to liberty," "the right to privacy," equal protection and due process. This is also a case in which euphemisms readily find their way to the fore, perhaps to soften the reality of what is really at stake. But this is not a case in which we are asked to let someone die. Nancy is not dead. Nor is she terminally ill. This is a case in which we are asked to allow the medical profession to make Nancy die by starvation and dehydration. The debate here is thus not between life and death; it is between quality of life and death. We are asked to hold that the cost of maintaining Nancy's present life is too great when weighed against the benefit that life conveys both to Nancy and her loved ones and that she must die.

To be sure, no one carries a malevolent motive to this litigation. Only the coldest heart could fail to feel the anguish of these parents who have suffered terribly these many years. They have exhausted any wellspring of hope which might have earlier accompanied their now interminable bedside vigil. And we understand, for these loving parents have seen only defeat through the memories they hold of a vibrant woman for whom the future held but promise.

. . . [T]he co-guardians do not have authority to order the withdrawal of hydration and nutrition to Nancy. We further hold that the evidence offered at trial as to Nancy's wishes is inherently unreliable and thus insufficient to support the co-guardians claim to exercise substituted judgment on Nancy's behalf. The burden of continuing the provision of food and water, while emotionally substantial for Nancy's loved ones, is not substantial for Nancy. The State's interest is in the preservation of life, not only Nancy's life, but also the lives of persons similarly situated yet without the support of a loving family. This interest outweighs any rights invoked on Nancy's behalf to terminate treatment in the face of the uncertainty of Nancy's wishes and her own right to life.

This State has expressed a strong policy favoring life. We believe that policy dictates that we err on the side of preserving life. If there is to be a change in that policy, it must come from the people through their elected representatives. Broad policy questions bearing on life and death issues are more properly addressed by representative assemblies. These have vast fact and opinion gathering and synthesizing powers unavailable to courts; the exercise of these powers is particularly appropriate where issues invoke the concerns of medicine, ethics, morality, philosophy, theology and law. Assuming change is appropriate, this issue demands a comprehensive resolution which courts cannot provide.

The efforts of courts to establish guidelines have been less than satisfactory. In *Quinlan*, the New Jersey Supreme Court attempted to establish guidelines for decisions concerning the termination of life support apparatus. More than ten years later, that same court wrote, "We recognize, . . . that given the fundamental societal questions that must be resolved, the Legislature is the proper branch of government to set guidelines in this area. . . ." *In re Farrell*, 529 A.2d at 407. *Quinlan* had failed to provide sufficient guidelines to meet the broad diversity of cases presenting termination of life-support issues.

To the extent that courts continue to invent guidelines on an *ad hoc*, piecemeal basis, legislatures, which have the ability to address the issue comprehensively, will feel no compulsion to act and will avoid making the potentially unpopular choices which issues of this magnitude present.

There is another compelling reason to leave changes in policy in this area to the legislature. Representative bodies generally move much more deliberately than do courts; they are a bit slow and ponderous. Courts, on the other hand, are facile and eager to find and impose a solution.

*Source: Cruzan v. Harmon, 760 S.W. 2d 408 (Mo. 1988).*

\* \* \*

In 1989, the U.S. Supreme Court accepted the case for review. In its decision, the Court upheld the right of the state of Missouri to insist on clear and convincing evidence as a standard for decision making for patients without decision-making capacity, but the decision also made clear that other states did not have to have such a strict standard. The Court also asserted that artificial nutrition and hydration were medical treatments and clearly affirmed that competent patients can refuse any treatment for any reason. The unusual number of written concurring and dissenting opinions demonstrates the complexity of the issues involved as well as the emotions that they generate.

## DOCUMENT 92: Chief Justice William Rehnquist, Majority Opinion, *Cruzan v. Director, Missouri Department of Health,* U.S. Supreme Court (1990)

. . . In this Court, the question is simply and starkly whether the United States Constitution prohibits Missouri from choosing the rule of decision which it did. This is the first case in which we have been squarely presented with the issue whether the United States Constitution grants what is in common parlance referred to as a "right to die." . . .

. . . The principle that a competent person has a constitutionally protected liberty interest in refusing unwanted medical treatment may be inferred from our prior decisions. . . .

. . . [F]or purposes of this case, we assume that the United States Constitution would grant a competent person a constitutionally protected right to refuse lifesaving hydration and nutrition.

Petitioners go on to assert that an incompetent person should possess the same right in this respect as is possessed by a competent person. . . .

. . . Missouri requires that evidence of the incompetent's wishes as to the withdrawal of treatment be proved by clear and convincing evidence. The question, then, is whether the United States Constitution forbids the establishment of this procedural requirement by the State. We hold that it does not. . . .

In sum, we conclude that a State may apply a clear and convincing evidence standard in proceedings where a guardian seeks to discontinue nutrition and hydration of a person diagnosed to be in a persistent vegetative state. . . .

. . . But we do not think the Due Process Clause requires the State to repose judgment on these matters with anyone but the patient herself.

*Source: Cruzan v. Director, Missouri Department of Health,* U.S. Supreme Court 497 U.S. 261 (1990).

\* \* \*

There were four separate opinions. Justices Sandra Day O'Connor, Antonin Scalia, Byron White, and Anthony Kennedy joined Justice Rehnquist in the majority opinion. O'Connor and Scalia filed separate concurring opinions. Justice William Brennan filed a dissenting opinion in which Justices Thurgood Marshall and Harry Blackmun joined, and Justice John Paul Stevens filed a separate dissenting opinion. . . . Justice Stevens's dissent moved away from the opinions of the rest of the Court. The eight other Justices had, in one way or another, looked to subjective individual choice as the guiding principle. Stevens instead questioned seriously whether the mere persistence of the bodies of patients like Nancy Cruzan is "life" as the word is commonly understood. To Stevens, the critical question was not how to prove the controlling facts, but rather what proven facts should be controlling. Excerpts from these concurring and dissenting opinions follow.

---

## DOCUMENT 93: Concurring and Dissenting Opinions, *Cruzan v. Director, Missouri Department of Health*, U.S. Supreme Court (1990)

Justice O'Connor, concurring.

. . .

Today's decision, holding only that the Constitution permits a State to require clear and convincing evidence of Nancy Cruzan's desire to have artificial hydration and nutrition withdrawn, does not preclude a future determination that the Constitution requires the States to implement the decisions of a patient's duly appointed surrogate. . . . Today we decide only that one State's practice does not violate the Constitution; the more challenging task of crafting appropriate procedures for safeguarding incompetents' liberty interests is entrusted to the "laboratory" of the States. . . .

Justice Scalia, concurring.

. . .

. . . I would have preferred that we announce, clearly and promptly, that the federal courts have no business in this field; that American law has always accorded the State the power to prevent, by force if necessary, suicide—including suicide by refusing to take appropriate measures necessary to preserve one's life; that the point at which life becomes "worthless," and the point at which the means necessary to preserve it become "extraordinary" or "inappropriate," are neither set forth in the Constitution nor known to the nine Justices of this Court any better than they are known to nine people picked at random from the Kansas City telephone directory; and hence, that even when it *is* demonstrated by clear and convincing evidence that a patient no longer wishes certain measures to be taken to preserve his or her life, it is up to the citizens of Missouri to decide, through their elected representatives, whether that wish will be honored. . . .

What I have said above is not meant to suggest that I would think it desirable, if we were sure that Nancy Cruzan wanted to die, to keep her alive by the means at issue here. I assert only that the Constitution has nothing to say about the subject. . . .

Justice Brennan, with whom Justice Marshall and Justice Blackmun
join, dissenting.

. . .

A grown woman at the time of the accident, Nancy had previously expressed her wish to forgo continuing medical care under circumstances such as these. Her family and her friends are convinced that this is what she would want. . . . A guardian ad litem appointed by the trial court is also convinced that this is what Nancy would want. . . . Yet the Missouri Supreme Court, alone among state courts deciding such a question, has determined that an irreversibly vegetative patient will remain a passive prisoner of medical technology—for Nancy, perhaps for the next 30 years. . . .

Today the Court, while tentatively accepting that there is some degree of constitutionally protected liberty interest in avoiding unwanted medical treatment, . . . affirms the decision of the Missouri Supreme Court. . . . Because I believe that Nancy Cruzan has a fundamental right to be free of unwanted artificial nutrition and hydration, which right is not outweighed by any interests of the State, and because I find that the improperly biased procedural obstacles imposed by the Missouri Supreme Court impermissibly burden that right, I respectfully dissent. Nancy Cruzan is entitled to choose to die with dignity.

Justice Stevens, dissenting.

. . .

. . . Missouri insists, without regard to Nancy Cruzan's own interests, upon equating her life with the biological persistence of her bodily functions. . . .

It seems to me that the Court errs insofar as it characterizes this case as involving "judgments about the 'quality' of life that a particular individual may enjoy." . . . Nancy Cruzan is obviously "*alive*" in a physiological sense. But for patients like Nancy Cruzan, who have no consciousness and no chance of recovery, there is a serious question as to whether the mere persistence of their bodies is "*life*" as that word is commonly understood, or as it is used in both the Constitution and the Declaration of Independence. The State's unflagging determination to perpetuate Nancy Cruzan's physical existence is comprehensible only as an effort to define life's meaning, not as an attempt to preserve its sanctity.

This much should be clear from the oddity of Missouri's definition alone. Life, particularly human life, is not commonly thought of as a merely physiological condition or function. Its sanctity is often thought to derive from the impossibility of any such reduction. When people speak of life, they often mean to describe the experiences that comprise a person's history, as when it is said that somebody "led a good life." They may also mean to refer to the practical manifestation of the human spirit, a meaning captured by the familiar observation that somebody "added life" to an assembly. If there is a shared thread among the various opinions on this subject, it may be that life is an activity which is at once the matrix for, and an integration of, a person's interests. In any event, absent some theological abstraction, the idea of life is not conceived separately from the idea of a living person. Yet, it is by precisely such a separation that Missouri asserts an interest in Nancy Cruzan's life in opposition to Nancy Cruzan's own interests. The resulting definition is uncommon indeed.

*Source*: *Cruzan v. Director, Missouri Department of Health*, U.S. Supreme Court 497 U.S. 261, 110 S. Ct 2841 (1990) (notes omitted).

* * *

On November 1, 1990, the Cruzans returned to the trial court with additional evidence from three new witnesses concerning Nancy's previously expressed wishes. In those discussions Nancy had indicated that she did not want to be force-fed or machine dependent "like a vegetable." The attorney general's office no longer opposed the request of the family to terminate treatment, asserting that the state's interest in clarifying the law had been satisfied. On December 14, 1990, the circuit-court judge found clear and convincing evidence that Nancy Cruzan, if mentally able, would terminate her nutrition and hydration, and authorized removal of the feeding tube. Nancy died peacefully on December 26, 1990.

The *Cruzan* decision elicited editorial comment from virtually every newspaper in the country. Two, from different sections of the country, and a magazine column are reproduced here.

## DOCUMENT 94: "A Right to Let Die?" *The Virginian-Pilot and Ledger-Star*, Norfolk, Virginia (July 1, 1990)

In the case of Nancy Cruzan, the Supreme Court has, correctly, confirmed a right to refuse medical treatment when that refusal would likely result in death.

But who has the right to refuse treatment on behalf of a patient unable to speak for herself? The court answered—incorrectly, we think—that absent "clear and convincing" evidence of a patient's wishes, states may intervene to mandate continued treatment, to prevent a family or guardian from discontinuing treatment.

Nancy Beth Cruzan, now 32, has been in an unconscious state for seven years. Unable to swallow on her own, she is administered food and fluids through a tube surgically implanted when her family held out hope of her recovery. With this nutrition-and-hydration device, she could remain in her current state for another 30 years. Without it, she will die. Her family, finally facing no hope of her recovery and citing Nancy's aversion, expressed in casual conversation, to lingering helplessly, asked to withdraw the tube.

A trial court, weighing medical testimony as to Nancy's state and anecdotal evidence as to her wishes, found them both sufficient to consent to withdrawal. But the state of Missouri, citing its "interest in life," appealed to the Missouri Supreme Court. That court found the evidence of Nancy's wishes insufficient and the quality of her life irrelevant.

The U.S. Supreme Court has now ruled that the quality of life may be relevant but only when supported by "clear and convincing" evidence as to a patient's view of when life may no longer be worth living.

Precisely what the court means by "clear and convincing" is unclear. The dropped remark, the casually expressed wish does not meet the court's standard. If, however, the court, as seems implied, is requiring written evidence prior to incompetency, then its standard of evidence is far too stringent.

The court has not said, though it has implied, that a Living Will, designating a person's preferences while competent, should suffice. Very few 25-year-olds—few people of any age—have engraved their wishes. Virginians now moved to do so may obtain the form and helpful information from the Medical Society of Virginia (4205 Dover Road, Richmond 23221), the Norfolk Academy of Medicine (229 W. Bute Rd., Suite 600, Norfolk 23510) or other local medical society.

Certainly everyone wants to prevent the abuse of any procedure that may result in death. And certainly every decision to withdraw life-support machinery should be subject to a judicial test to determine that it is a decision informed by medical advice, made without malice.

But most cases involve families who are acting on the advice of medical, psychological and often spiritual counselors, who are making an agonizing decision concerning much-loved ones. To disregard available evidence as to the wishes of their family member, to dismiss a family's wishes and its familiarity with the patient make no sense. Those families, not "the state," should have the last word.

The Supreme Court has not said that a state must intervene in cases such as the Cruzans', only that it may. Some states will do so. Others will not. And not just the Cruzans will have to decide whether to move to a jurisdiction which allows them to do what knowledge of their loved one, competent physicians and common sense tell them is right.

*Source*: Law column, "A Right to Let Die?" *The Virginian-Pilot and Ledger-Star*, Norfolk, VA, July 1, 1990.

---

## DOCUMENT 95: "For Family, a Cruel Decision; for the Rest of Us, a Warning," *Press-Telegram*, Long Beach, California (June 26, 1990)

---

Nancy Cruzan, in a deep vegetative coma since a 1983 car wreck, is likely now to "live" another 30 years, her only connection to the world the tubes that feed water and artificial food into her already devastated body. That's the way the state of Missouri wants her to exist because it will not accept her parents' word that Nancy, if she were conscious of her condition, would want to die. And the United States Supreme Court, in its unwillingness to stand between government and the individual, has come down on Missouri's side.

The decision, which was based on the fact that Cruzan did not leave behind clear documentation on her desires for medical treatment if she became incapacitated, is a disaster for the Cruzans and for countless other families forced now to watch loved ones live as mindless shells sustained only by feeding tubes cut into their stomachs. The decision must also be counted as a damaging blow against the role of surrogates without well-defined legal standing—even loving, dedicated and selfless surrogates—in medical matters that revolve around life and death.

At the same time, there are reasons to glean some solace from the court's action. The effort to allow deeply comatose people to die with dignity has been crippled, often severely, by arguments that providing them with water and artificial food is nothing more than a humane act. In the Cruzan decision, the court correctly recognizes that artificial feeding and hydration therapy are medical treatments subject to the same judgments as respirators. If you can pull a plug you can pull a feeding tube. If you can refuse a semipermanent connection to an artificial machine, you can refuse connection to a bag full of calories and protein.

Just as important, the court's Cruzan decision accepts as legitimate another anathema to the right-to-life absolutists—the legal documents that allow patients to delineate precisely what medical care should be withheld in case they can no longer make their wishes known. Even states like Missouri, where the Legislature seems to feel that it is a crime to die of natural causes, will have to accept the validity of living wills and durable powers of attorney for health care.

Pity the Cruzans. They and their unfortunate daughter are the vehicle by which this warning has been issued to you: See to it that your folder of personal papers includes a statement of your medical treatment expectations. Otherwise you may share Nancy Cruzan's fate.

*Source*: Editorial, "For Family, a Cruel Decision; for the Rest of Us, a Warning," *Press-Telegram*, Long Beach, CA, June 26, 1990.

## DOCUMENT 96: "The Right to Die in Dignity," Marcia Angell (July 23, 1990)

Americans are confused by the Supreme Court's decision that Nancy Cruzan, a 32-year-old Missouri woman who has been in a coma since a car accident seven years ago, must remain tethered to a feeding tube indefinitely. You might assume that the decision was based on a slim chance that she would one day recover, but it wasn't. Everyone agrees that she will never wake up. Instead, the court denied Nancy's parents the right to remove the feeding tube because Nancy failed to leave clear instructions that this is what she would want. Careless of her. Without such instructions the court saw no reason to override the Missouri court's presumption that people would prefer being vegetables to being dead, although it's hard to find anyone who would.

We can imagine what this decision means for Nancy's parents, who fought intelligently and valiantly through the courts to end their nightmare and their daughter's indignity. But what does it mean for the rest of us? Here is where the Supreme Court has created consternation. It seems that our right to refuse medical treatment is hedged by all sorts of unknowable and shifting conditions that vary from state to state. In Missouri, for example, you must foresee what calamities might befall you, what kinds of technologies might be available to keep you going after you can no longer think, and you must express your views about all this in the right way.

If we don't guess right about our state's requirements, we may end up like Nancy Cruzan: subject to the mindless application of whatever technologies can extend our lives. For those of you who think a living will is the answer, think again. In most states the laws recognizing living wills limit their use to those who are terminally ill, which Nancy Cruzan is not, and many do not permit withholding tube feeding even for those who are. Missouri is one of the states with such restrictions. Thus, a living will might not help someone like Nancy Cruzan in Missouri; it would merely be a nonbinding expression of wishes, which the courts might or might not choose to honor.

A tragedy of the Cruzan decision is that it undermines a consensus, building slowly since the case of Karen Ann Quinlan, on the right to refuse life-sustaining treatment. According to this consensus, a rational adult has the right to refuse any medical treatment whatsoever; fortunately, the Supreme Court affirmed this. To force treatment on someone is to commit a battery. For those unable to make their own choices, like Nancy Cruzan, a growing body of case law and expert opinion held that decisions should be made by families with the advice of doctors. The entirely reasonable presumption was that these are usually the people who know and love the patient best and that doctors are in the best position to advise them. The courts were to be reserved for settling disputes. For example, a doctor who believed that a family's decision to withhold treatment was hasty or unreasonable could go to court. In only a few states did higher courts depart from this general understanding of how these decisions should be made.

Now, with the Cruzan decision, this hard-won consensus is undone. In New York as well as Missouri, all life-sustaining treatment will be given to anyone unable to refuse it, except in the unlikely event that the patient has left specific instructions to the contrary. Other states may establish different rules. Families seem to have no standing whatsoever, and doctors are no longer trusted advisers, but instead may be reluctant adversaries forced to impose treatment against the wishes of their patients' families and their own best judgment.

**Living wills**: As Justice Stevens pointed out in his dissent, there is no room for such common-sense concerns as the best interests of the patient. Yet this is, after all, what lies at the heart of the problem. Who among us—indeed, which Supreme Court Justice—would *really* prefer the life of Nancy Cruzan over death? A CBS News poll last spring showed that the overwhelming majority of Americans would want the tube feeding stopped if they were in Nancy Cruzan's situation. For the court to assume otherwise, which it seems to be doing by requiring detailed advance instructions for stopping tube feeding but not for continuing it, is to be out of touch with the widespread recognition that it is cruel and senseless to keep comatose people alive indefinitely. To see the court's decision as erring on the side of life is not to understand fully that for such patients life in any meaningful sense is already over.

So where does this leave us? What can we do to protect ourselves from ending up like Nancy Cruzan? Everyone, even young people, should make their wishes known to their families, friends and doctors—preferably in writing and in as much detail as possible. It is not enough to say that you would not want "heroic treatment"; you must specify that you would not want "artificial feeding." Living wills, while extremely limited in their legal scope, are nevertheless useful in indicating your position. A legal document designating someone else to make decisions for you if you are unable to do so (termed a durable power of attorney for health care) is much better, because its scope is not as limited. Most important, people should discuss this issue with their doctors. In this new, more uncertain climate in a litigious society, many doctors will find it safer to treat everyone aggressively, rather than to act on the wishes of their patients' families and their own best judgment. Thus, it is important to ascertain that your doctor is courageous as well as competent and compassionate.

Unfortunately, the Cruzan decision means that all of this may not be enough—depending on which state you live in. What we need are legislative remedies much broader than the laws recognizing living wills and perhaps at the federal level, that will restore the rights of families and doctors to act in our best interests when we no longer can.

*Source*: Marcia Angell, "The Right to Die in Dignity," *Newsweek*, July 23, 1990, 9.

* * *

## THE RIGHT TO DIE OF PATIENTS WHO WERE NEVER COMPETENT

The preceding discussion applies to persons who were once competent and who therefore could have expressed their wishes orally or in writing. The situation is more complex when the patient has never been competent, for example, for infants or for adults who are seriously mentally deficient.

In general, the state's interest in the life of a terminally or incurably ill child does not override parental authority. For example, in 1984, the Georgia Supreme Court ruled that an infant in whom 85–90 percent of brain tissue was destroyed could be allowed to die if the family or legal guardians and the treating physician and two other physicians agreed (*In re L.H.R.*, 1984). The case is important because it establishes that there is no legal difference between infants and incompetent adults without advance directives.

What about adults who were never competent? The *Saikewicz* decision (*Superintendent of Belchertown State School v. Saikewicz*, Massachusetts, 1977) reiterates that the constitutional right of privacy is a basis for a patient's right to refuse treatment. The court recognized that the right of privacy protects the always-incompetent person as well as the competent or once-competent. In this, Massachusetts is different from New York, where the highest state court reversed the decision of the lower court, holding that the mother of a mentally retarded person could not authorize cessation of treatment because as a matter of law the patient had never been able to make a valid decision (*In re Storar*, New York, *cert. denied*, 1981). The Massachusetts court in *Saikewicz* rejected the reasoning of the New Jersey Supreme Court in *Quinlan* (1976) and declined to hold that a person's right to refuse treatment was best exercised in the traditional patient/family/physician relationship. Instead, it called for recourse to the courts and a resulting adversary process that can be time-consuming and burdensome. The decision created confusion and consternation in medical circles.

A later interpretation by the Massachusetts Appeals Court in *In re Dinnerstein* (1978) narrowed the need for court intervention. The Spring case (*In re Spring*, Massachusetts, 1980) led to further clarification of *Saikewicz* by the Massachusetts Supreme Judicial Court, including recognition of problems inherent in a lengthy judicial process.

In recent years, decisions in several states have indicated that to speak of "substituted judgment" for patients who were never competent makes no sense. For example, the Wisconsin Supreme Court (*In re Guardianship of L. W.*, 1992) rejected the standard of "clear and convincing evidence" of the patient's medical treatment wishes, stating that to adopt such a standard "would doom many individuals to a prolonged vegetative state," and concluded that when it is in "the best interests" of the ward, "the guardian has not only the authority but a duty to consent to the withholding or withdrawal of treatment." A meaningful substituted judgment analysis was impossible. Finally, the court held that judicial approval of the guardian's decision was not required, but that court review could be initiated by any "interested party" who objected to the guardian's decision.

## MEDICAL FUTILITY

The preceding legal cases have dealt with permitting the death of a person who was hopelessly ill. What happens when the family of a person who is hopelessly ill and can no longer speak for himself or herself refuses to permit the physicians to remove life support? This was the case in 1991 with Helga Wanglie, an eighty-seven-year-old woman who was permanently unconscious and ventilator dependent. The medical staff believed that because of her age and medical condition, Wanglie would not benefit from continuing medical support. However, her husband, daughter, and son insisted that all medical treatment be continued, a decision that they made based on Wanglie's religious and personal beliefs. The hospital ethics committee recommended that the hospital staff should follow the wishes of the family. However, the hospital indicated that it did not believe that it was obliged to provide "inappropriate medical treatment that [could not] advance a patient's personal interest," and filed papers in the county court, seeking the appointment of a conservator for Wanglie to decide whether continued treatment was appropriate. The decision is important because the court was unwilling to have treatment discontinued over the objections of the family, concluding that a competent family member is in the best position to make medical treatment decisions for an incompetent patient.

## DOCUMENT 97: *In re Conservatorship of Wanglie*, District Court, Hennepin County, Minnesota (1991)

Findings of Fact with Regard to Helga Wanglie

1. The proposed Conservatee/Ward, Helga Wanglie, is 87 years old. She has been married to Oliver Wanglie for 53 years and is the mother of two adult children, David Wanglie and Ruth Wanglie. . . .

7. Helga Wanglie is incapable of interacting with other people at this time. She is unable to establish new relationships.

8. Helga Wanglie does not have a living will. She no longer has the capacity to express a preference for one person or another to become her Conservator. . . .

Findings of Fact with Regard to Petitioner Steven H. Miles, MD.

1. Steven H. Miles, M.D., (Miles) is a physician licensed to practice medicine in the State of Minnesota. He is a board certified internist and a geriontologist [*sic*]. He is a member of the Hennepin County Medical Center Ethics Committee.

2. He has been a consultant to the physicians treating Helga Wanglie on issues of medical ethics since October, 1990. He was also an ethical consultant to physicians caring for her in June, 1990, when the feasibility of cardiopulmonary resuscitation for Helga Wanglie was discussed. Other medical ethicists have also consulted with the treating physicians during Helga Wanglie's extensive hospitalization.

3. At no time when Helga Wanglie was conscious and able to express her own wishes did any physician or staff member at the Hennepin County Medical Center discuss her treatment preferences with her.

4. Other than proving that Oliver Wanglie does not accept the advice and counsel of the physicians treating Helga Wanglie and refuses to consent to remove the ventilator which breathes for her, Miles has offered no evidence that Oliver Wanglie is incompetent to discharge the trust as Conservator of the Person of his wife.

5. Miles has petitioned the Court to appoint an independent conservator to make medical care and abode choices for Helga Wanglie. . . .

### Findings of Fact with Regard to Oliver Wanglie

1. Oliver Wanglie is the closest person to Helga Wanglie, and he knows her conscientious, religious and moral beliefs intimately. . . .

3. Oliver Wanglie is fully able to maintain a current understanding of Helga Wanglie's mental and physical needs.

4. Oliver Wanglie is dedicated to promoting his wife's welfare. . . .

5. Oliver Wanglie's children are in agreement that he should be the person to make decisions for their mother's medical care. . . .

### CONCLUSIONS OF LAW

1. Helga Wanglie is an incapacitated person as defined by Minn. Stat. 525.54, Subd. 2 and Subd 3.

2. No protective arrangement or other transaction as described in Minn. Stat. 525.54, Subd. 7, nor other alternative to guardianship would provide adequate protection for Helga Wanglie.

3. Helga Wanglie requires the continuing protection of a guardian of her person and estate, which guardian would have all the powers described in Minn. Stat. 525.56, Subd 3 and 4.

4. It is in Helga Wanglie's best interest that Oliver Wanglie, her husband, be appointed as the guardian of her person and estate.

5. Oliver Wanglie is the most suitable and best qualified person among those nominees who are now available.

### ORDER

. . .

3. Oliver Wanglie be and hereby is appointed Guardian of the Person and Estate of Helga Wanglie. . . .

### MEMORANDUM

The Court is asked whether it is in the best interest of an elderly woman who is comatose, gravely ill, and ventilator-dependent to have decisions about her medical care made by her husband of 53 years or by a stranger.

Minnesota guardianship law requires the guardian to be the individual whose appointment is in the best interest of the incapacitated person. . . .

Petitioner Miles does not contest that Oliver Wanglie is a suitable person to be the guardian of Helga Wanglie's estate. Similarly, Miles does not dispute that Oliver Wanglie is qualified to be guardian with regard to providing food and clothing, fulfilling her social and emotional requirements, and arranging training, education and rehabilitation. Miles believes that Oliver Wanglie is not competent to be Helga Wanglie's conservator with regard to making decisions about her shelter, medical care, and religious requirements. . . .

Oliver Wanglie has shown himself to be dedicated to his wife's proper medical care. He visits her regularly, although the frequency is in dispute. He expresses the belief that the nurses caring for his wife are skilled professionals and compassionate people. Except with regard to the issue of removing the ventilator, he has thoughtfully agreed with the treating physicians about every major decision in his wife's care. He is in the best position to investigate and act upon Helga Wanglie's conscientious, religious and moral beliefs and he has indicated that he will do so....

No Court order to continue or stop any medical treatment for Helga Wanglie has been made or requested at this time. Whether such a request will be made, or such an order is proper, or this Court would make such an order, and whether Oliver Wanglie would execute such an order are speculative matters not now before the Court.

Oliver Wanglie believes that he is the best person to be the guardian for his wife. Their children agree with him. The evidence clearly and convincingly supports their position.

*Source: In re Conservatorship of Wanglie*, No. PX-91-283 (Minn. Dist. Ct. Hennepin Co., July 1991).

\* \* \*

The "Baby K" case dealt with a hospital's request to withdraw treatment from an anencephalic baby against the wishes of the family. (This term denotes congenital absence of much of the brain.)

According to George J. Annas ("Asking the Courts to Set the Standard of Emergency Care—The Case of Baby K," *New England Journal of Medicine* 330 [1994]: 1542–1545), "many misjudgments were made in this case, but all relate to the failure to distinguish among medical standards, ethical precepts, and legal requirements." Annas faults the physicians for not resolving the issue of mechanical ventilation before birth; the ethics subcommittee for not making enough effort to resolve the issue; the hospital's administration and attorney, who regarded the problem as legal rather than as an issue of medical practice or ethics; and the trial judge, who did not recognize the unusual character of anencephalic infants.

---

## DOCUMENT 98: *In re Baby "K,"* U.S. District Court, Eastern Division, Virginia (1993)

### Findings of Fact

1. Plaintiff Hospital is a general acute care hospital located in Virginia that is licensed to provide diagnosis, treatment, and medical and nursing services to the public as provided by Virginia law. Among other facili-

ties, the Hospital has a Pediatric Intensive Care Department and an Emergency Department.

2. The Hospital is a recipient of federal and state funds including those from Medicare and Medicaid and is a "participating hospital" pursuant to 42 U.S.C. § 1395cc.

3. The Hospital and its staff (including emergency doctors, pediatricians, neonatologists and pediatric intensivists) treat sick children on a daily basis.

4. Defendant Ms. H, a citizen of the Commonwealth of Virginia, is the biological mother of Baby K, an infant girl born by Caesarean section at the Hospital on October 13, 1992. Baby K was born with anencephaly.

5. Anencephaly is a congenital defect in which the brain stem is present but the cerebral cortex is rudimentary or absent. There is no treatment that will cure, correct, or ameliorate anencephaly. Baby K is permanently unconscious and cannot hear or see. Lacking a cerebral function, Baby K does not feel pain. . . .

6. Baby K was diagnosed prenatally as being anencephalic. Despite the counselling of her obstetrician and neonatologist that she terminate her pregnancy, Ms. H refused to have her unborn child aborted.

7. A Virginia court of competent jurisdiction has found defendant Mr. K, a citizen of the Commonwealth of Virginia, to be Baby K's biological father.

8. Ms. H and Mr. K have never been married.

9. Since Baby K's birth, Mr. K has, at most, been only distantly involved in matters relating to the infant. Neither the Hospital nor Ms. H ever sought Mr. K's opinion or consent in providing medical treatment to Baby K.

10. Because Baby K had difficulty breathing immediately upon birth, Hospital physicians provided her with mechanical ventilator treatment to allow her to breathe.

11. Within days of Baby K's birth, Hospital medical personnel urged Ms. H to permit a "Do Not Resuscitate Order" for Baby K that would discontinue ventilator treatment. Her physicians told her that no treatment existed for Baby K's anencephalic condition, no therapeutic or palliative purpose was served by the treatment, and that ventilator care was medically unnecessary and inappropriate. Despite this pressure, Ms. H continued to request ventilator treatment for her child.

12. Because of Ms. H's continued insistence that Baby K receive ventilator treatment, her treating physicians requested the assistance of the Hospital's "Ethics Committee" in overriding the mother's wishes.

13. A three person Ethics Committee subcommittee, composed of a family practitioner, a psychiatrist, and a minister, met with physicians providing care to Baby K. On October 22, 1992, the group concluded that Baby K's ventilator treatment should end because "such care is futile" and decided to "wait a reasonable time for the family to help the care-

giver terminate aggressive therapy." If the family refused to follow this advice, the committee recommended that the Hospital should "attempt to resolve this through our legal system."

14. Ms. H subsequently rejected the committee's recommendation. Before pursuing legal action to override Ms. H's position, the Hospital decided to transfer the infant to another health care facility. . . .

20. Baby K will almost certainly continue to have episodes of respiratory distress in the future. In the absence of ventilator treatment during these episodes, she would suffer serious impairment of her bodily functions and soon die.

21. Ms. H visits Baby K daily. The mother opposes the discontinuation of ventilator treatment when Baby K experiences respiratory distress because she believes that all human life has value, including her anencephalic daughter's life. Ms. H has a firm Christian faith that all life should be protected. She believes that God will work a miracle if that is his will. Otherwise, Ms. H believes, God, and not other humans, should decide the moment of her daughter's death. As Baby K's mother and as the only parent who has participated in the infant's care, Ms. H believes that she has the right to decide what is in her child's best interests.

22. On the Hospital's motion, a guardian *ad litem* purporting to represent Baby K was appointed pursuant to Virginia Code § 8.01–9.

23. Both the guardian *ad litem* and Mr. K share the Hospital's position that ventilator treatment should be withheld from Baby K when she experiences respiratory distress.

24. The Hospital has stipulated that it is not proposing to deny ventilator treatment to Baby K because of any lack of adequate resources or any inability of Ms. H to pay for the treatment.

. . .

## VI. Constitutional and Common Law Issues

Baby K's parents disagree over whether or not to continue medical treatment for her. Mr. K and Baby K's guardian *ad litem* join the Hospital in seeking the right to override the wishes of Ms. H, Baby K's mother. Regardless of the questions of statutory interpretation presented in this case, Ms. H retains significant legal rights regarding her insistence that her daughter be kept alive with ventilator treatment. A parent has a constitutionally protected right to "bring up children" grounded in the Fourteenth Amendment's due process clause. . . . Parents have the "primary role" in the "nurture and upbringing of their children." . . . Decisions for children can be based in the parent's free exercise of religion, protected by the First Amendment. . . .

These constitutional principles extend to the right of parents to make medical treatment decisions for their minor children. Absent a finding of neglect or abuse, parents retain plenary authority to seek medical care for their children, even when the decision might impinge on a liberty interest of the child. . . . Indeed, there is a "presumption that the parents act in the best interests of their child" because the "natural bonds of affection lead parents to act in the best interests of their children." . . .

State law rights to make medical and surgical treatment decisions for a minor child are grounded in the common law and can also be inferred from state statutes. . . .

Based on Ms. H's "natural bonds of affection," . . . and the relative noninvolvement of Baby K's biological father, the constitutional and common law presumption must be that Ms. H. is the appropriate decision maker. "[W]hen parents do not agree on the issue of termination of life support . . . this Court must yield to the presumption in favor of life." . . . This presumption arises from the explicit guarantees of a right to life in the United States Constitution, Amendments V and XIV, and the Virginia Constitution, Article 1, Sections 1 and 11.

The presumption in favor of life in this case is also based on Ms. H's religious conviction that all life is sacred and must be protected, thus implicating her First Amendment rights. When an individual asserts "the Free Exercise Clause in conjunction with other constitutional protections, such as . . . the right of parents," only a clear and compelling governmental interest can justify a statute that interferes with the person's religious convictions. . . .

The Hospital cannot establish any "clear and compelling" interest in this case. The Supreme Court has not decided whether the right to liberty encompasses a right to refuse medical treatment, often called a "right to die." *Cruzan v. Director, Missouri Dept. of Health* . . . (refusing to decide this question). Parents have standing to assert the constitutional rights of their minor children. . . . When one parent asserts the child's explicit constitutional right to life as the basis for continuing medical treatment and the other is asserting the nebulous liberty interest in refusing life-saving treatment on behalf of a minor child, the explicit right to life must prevail. . . .

Reflecting the constitutional principles of family autonomy and the presumption in favor of life, courts have generally scrutinized a family's decision only where the family has sought to terminate or withhold medical treatment for an incompetent minor or incompetent adult. *See, e.g., Cruzan* . . . (and cases cited therein). In a recent case in which a hospital sought to terminate life-supporting ventilation over the objections of the patient's husband, a Minnesota state court refused to remove decision-making authority from the husband. *In re Wanglie.* . . . Likewise, where parents disagreed over whether to continue life-supporting mechanical ventilation, nutrition, and hydration for a minor child in an irreversible stupor or coma, a Georgia state court gave effect to the decision of the parent opting in favor of life support. . . .

At the very least, the Hospital must establish by clear and convincing evidence that Ms. H's treatment decision should not be respected because it would constitute abuse or neglect of Baby K. This clear and convincing evidence standard has been adopted by numerous courts and was upheld by the Supreme Court in *Cruzan* in authorizing the withdrawal of life-supporting treatment from an incompetent patient. . . . In this case, where the choice essentially devolves to a subjective determination as to the quality of Baby's K's life, it cannot be said that the continuation of Baby K's life is so unreasonably harmful as to constitute child abuse or neglect.

For the foregoing reasons, the Hospital's request for a declaratory judgment that the withholding of ventilator treatment from Baby K would not violate the Emergency Medical Treatment and Active Labor Act, the Rehabilitation Act of 1973, the Americans with Disabilities Act, the Child Abuse Amendments of 1984, and the Virginia Medical Malpractice Act should be DENIED. Under the Emergency Medical Treatment and Active Labor Act, the Rehabilitation Act of 1973, and the Americans with Disabilities Act, the Hospital is legally obligated to provide ventilator treatment to Baby K. The court makes no ruling as to any rights or obligations under the Child Abuse Amendments of 1984 and under the Virginia Medical Malpractice Act.

An appropriate order shall issue.

*Source: In re Baby "K,"* U.S. District Court, Eastern Division, Virginia, *Health Law News* (see also [832 F. Supp. 1022] E.D. Va. 1993) (notes omitted).

\* \* \*

The hospital appealed the decision. A U.S. court of appeals upheld the decision, using essentially the same arguments as the lower court. Portions of the dissenting opinion of Senior Circuit Judge Sprouse are quoted.

---

## DOCUMENT 99: Judge Sprouse, Dissenting Opinion, *In re Baby "K"* (1994)

---

I have no quarrel with the majority's conclusion that the duty imposed on hospitals by EMTALA [Emergency Medical Treatment and Active Labor Act] to provide stabilizing treatment for an emergency condition is different from its duty to provide "appropriate medical screening." There is no question that once a medical condition is characterized as an "emergency medical condition" contemplated by EMTALA, the patient must be stabilized to prevent material deterioration of the condition. . . .

I simply do not believe, however, that Congress, in enacting EMTALA, meant for the judiciary to superintend the sensitive decision-making process between family and physicians at the bedside of a helpless and terminally ill patient under the circumstances of this case. Tragic end-of-life hospital dramas such as this one do not represent phenomena susceptible of uniform legal control. . . .

The tragic phenomenon Baby K represents exemplifies the need to take a case-by-case approach to determine if an emergency episode is governed by EMTALA. Baby K's condition presents her parents and doctors with decision-making choices that are different even from the difficult choices presented by other terminal diseases. Specifically, as an anencephalic infant, Baby K is permanently unconscious. She cannot hear, cannot see, and has no cognitive abilities. She has no awareness of and cannot interact with her environment in any way. Since there is no medical treatment that can improve her condition, she will be in this state for as long as she lives. Given this unique medical condition, whatever treatment appropriate for her unspeakably tragic illness should be regarded as a continuum, not as a series of discrete emergency medical conditions to be considered in isolation. Humanitarian concerns dictate appropriate care. However, if resort must be had to our courts to test the appropriateness of the care, the legal vehicle should be state malpractice law.

In my view, considering the discrete factual circumstances of Baby K's condition and previous treatment, if she is transferred again from the nursing home to the hospital in respiratory distress, that condition should be considered integral to the anencephalic condition, and I would hold that there has been no violation of EMTALA. I emphasize that this view contemplates a case-by-case determination. Individual cases involving victims of trauma, cancer, heart attack, or other catastrophic illness, who are denied potentially life-saving treatments, may well require different analyses.

*Source: In re Baby "K,"* Dissenting opinion of Judge Sprouse, U.S. Court of Appeals, 16 F. 3d 590 (4th Cir.), *cert. denied,* 115 S. Ct. 91 (1994).

* * *

Marcia Angell, associate editor of the *The New England Journal of Medicine*, put forth an interesting suggestion about decision making for individuals who could not speak for themselves, including Helga Wanglie and Baby K.

---

## DOCUMENT 100: "After Quinlan: The Dilemma of the Persistent Vegetative State," Marcia Angell (1994)

In 1968 an ad hoc committe of Harvard Medical School recommended that death be defined as cessation of all brain function.[1] Before that time, a patient was not pronounced dead until heart and lung function had ceased. One by one, the states accepted brain death as the legal definition of death—a movement that was accelerated when the President's Commission formulated the Uniform Determination of Death Act in 1981.[2] All 50 states and the District of Columbia now accept this standard.[3] It is remarkable how rapidly the concept of brain death attracted an ethical, social, and legal consensus, as well as medical endorsement. There is no longer any requirement to continue cardiopulmonary support for someone who is brain-dead.

But this important change in the definition of death did not speak to the problem of the many patients in a persistent vegetative state. This condition is characterized by the loss of all higher brain functions, including awareness, feelings, and the capacity to suffer. However, the brain-stem and hypothalamic activity necessary for prolonged survival continues, so that such patients may survive for years or even decades with artificial feeding and, when necessary, cardiopulmonary support. In contrast, brain-dead patients cannot survive for long, even with maximal support, since the brain stem does not function.

When a persistent vegetative state is deemed to be irreversible, it is termed a permanent vegetative state, as explained elsewhere in this issue of the *Journal* by the Multi-Society Task Force on PVS.[4] For many families, the possibility of sustaining the life of a patient in a permanent vegetative state means that the tragedy of losing a loved one is compounded by the anguish of the daily physical reminder of what that person once was.

Beginning with the case of Karen Ann Quinlan in 1975,[5] family members began to assert a right to discontinue life support for patients in a permanent vegetative state. These efforts have slowly led to an ethical and legal consensus that families or other proxies may authorize the discontinuation of life-sustaining treatment, including artificial feeding, for such patients.[6,7] We owe Joseph and Julia Quinlan, Karen's parents, our gratitude for turning their personal calamity into a public benefit by launching the right-to-die movement.[8,9] Without this movement we would not have our present right to prepare advance directives or living wills that permit us to name a proxy decision maker and to authorize discontinuation of treatment under specified circumstances. In this issue of the *Journal*, the Quinlans, with their characteristic openness and courage, close the chapter on their daughter's death by permitting the publication of the findings of the postmortem examination of her brain.[10]

But what about the reverse situation? Suppose a family wishes to keep a patient who is in a permanent vegetative state alive as long as possible? Do care givers—demoralized by providing limitless, expensive care in a hopeless case—have the right to stop treatment anyway, so that the patient will die? We are beginning to see such cases reach the courts. Instead of families like the Quinlans asking to stop life-sustaining treatment over the objections of doctors or hospitals, we are seeing doctors who wish to stop treatment over the objections of the family. The case of Helga Wanglie was the first such instance to be widely publicized.[11] The courts upheld her husband's insistence on continued treatment. We now have an analogous situation in the case of Baby K, discussed elsewhere in this issue.[12] Baby K is an infant with anencephaly, a condition comparable to a permanent vegetative state, in that higher brain function is absent but at least some brain-stem activity is preserved. So far the courts are upholding the mother's right to insist on continued treatment.[13]

Here I review the debate on this reverse situation and suggest possible solutions. I also argue that any solution must be a principled one that applies generally and is established by consensus, in the same way that death was redefined as brain death. A general solution is much needed because our current method of dealing with the problem on a case-by-case basis is cruel and capricious.

Those like Annas who favor the right of doctors and hospitals to stop treatment over the objection of families often see the issue as one of medical judgment. In their view, if doctors believe a treatment is futile or inappropriate, it should not be provided.[12] No one, after all, should have the right to demand any treatment they choose, even though we all have the right to refuse any recommended treatment. This argument is sharpened by the increasing concern about cost containment in our health care system. The continued support of patients in a permanent vegetative state is said to be not only demoralizing for care givers, but wasteful of valuable resources.

Those who believe the family's wishes should be decisive see the issue as one of autonomy.[14] To them, a family's right to discontinue treatment implies an analogous right to have it continued. Decision-making authority means nothing unless the decision can go either way. Furthermore, they maintain that such treatment is not futile, since it maintains life. Whether to do so is in their view not a medical judgment but a personal one.

I argued earlier in regard to the Wanglie case that although most people would not want life-sustaining treatment for themselves or their loved ones in a permanent vegetative state, some would, and we should not override their wishes on an ad hoc basis.[15] If we do, a family can easily construe this not as a judgment about a category of patients but as a judgment about their particular relative. To such families, the doctors are saying, in effect, that a loved one's life is not worth the expense or effort of maintaining it. This can seem particularly heartless if the patient is very old, as in the case of Helga Wanglie, or "handicapped," as in the case of Baby K, not to mention poor or of a minority group. It also smacks of a return to paternalism, a discredited mode of medical care. After all, the judgment about whether to keep such patients alive, once the medical facts are established, requires no medical expertise.

So what is to be done? There are three alternatives to having to make difficult ad hoc decisions. One approach is to redefine death to include a permanent vegetative state, as argued by Veatch,[16] and anencephaly. Those who advocate this approach point to the earlier success of redefining death as cessation of all brain function. Although brain function is a continuum from the lower brain stem to the upper cortex, most experts would agree that a critical level of brain function can be defined without which sentient human existence is impossible.

One reason for a reluctance to redefine death to include a permanent vegetative state is the possibility of an incorrect diagnosis. There have been anecdotes of sudden, unexpected recovery in patients who had been in a persistent vegetative state for many years. The Multi-Society Task Force on PVS explains the criteria for the diagnosis of a persistent vegetative state, as well as the conditions with which it might be confused.[4] They also discuss the duration of a persistent vegetative state necessary to establish its irreversibility. According to this authoritative group, if reasonable care is taken, a permanent vegetative state can be diagnosed with virtual certainty.

A more telling objection to including a permanent vegetative state in the definition of brain death is the fact that cardiopulmonary function may continue indefinitely, as may reflexes and periods of wakefulness. These patients just do not "look dead." In contrast, patients with total brain death have no signs of life, and they can be supported for only a relatively short time before circulatory function also ceases. Thus, even if a permanent vegetative state were redefined as death, it would, paradoxically, be necessary to withdraw life-sustaining treatment, including artificial feeding, to stop cardiopulmonary function.

A second approach might be to leave the neurologic definition of death unchanged, but establish criteria for treatment based on the extent of neurologic damage and duration. We might reach a broad consensus, similar to the consensus on brain death, that would permit treatment to be discontinued in all anencephalic infants and patients in a permanent vegetative state after a certain specified time, depending on the category of brain damage. If that were done and incorporated into law, we would not have these matters being settled in a series of heart-wrenching cases, in which families may see themselves as protecting the life of a loved one. The decision would be made before the fact and it would be general, not particular.

A third and less sweeping approach—and the one that I favor—would be simply to shift the burden from those who want to discontinue treatment to those who want to continue it. At present it is presumed that patients in a permanent vegetative state would want to be kept alive. Families who wish to discontinue life-sustaining treatment must therefore argue their case, usually asserting that they are acting in accord with what they know would be the wishes of the patient. Certain states require clear and convincing evidence that the patient would want treatment discontinued.

In my view we should instead presume that patients in a persistent vegetative state would *not* want to be kept alive indefinitely—a presumption buttressed by public opinion polls.[17] On this basis we could establish a standard of care that included routinely stopping treatment after a specified time in a persistent vegetative state. This time would vary with the medical circumstances, but would be sufficiently long to establish irreversibility with virtual certainty. If particular families objected to discontinuing treatment at that time, they would have to justify their position, perhaps by documenting the wishes of the patient as expressed earlier. The crucial points are that the matter be dealt with in a principled and general way, and that the burden be shifted to those holding the idiosyncratic view. Before such a solution can be widely accepted, however, we will need more debate and a better public understanding of the issues. This is not just a medical matter. Like the redefinition of death, it is also an ethical, social, and legal matter.

MARCIA ANGELL, MD

## References

1. A definition of irreversible coma: report of the Ad-Hoc Committee of the Harvard Medical School to Examine the Definition of Brain Death. JAMA 1968; 205:337–40.

2. President's Commission for the Study of Ethical Problems in Medicine and Biomedical and Behavioral Research. Defining death: a report on the medical, legal and ethical issues in the determination of death. Washington, D.C.: Government Printing Office, 1981.

3. Brain death. In: Meisel A. The right to die. 1993 Cumulative supplement no. 2. New York: John Wiley, 1993:123–8.

4. The Multi-Society Task Force on PVS. Medical aspects of the persistent vegetative state. N Engl J Med 1994;330:1499–508.

5. In re Quinlan, 70 N.J. 10, 355 A.2d 647, cert. denied sub nom. Garger v. New Jersey, 429 U.S. 922 (1976).

6. President's Commission for the Study of Ethical Problems in Medicine and Biomedical and Behavioral Research. Deciding to forego life-sustaining treatment: a report on the ethical, medical, and legal issues in treatment decisions. Washington, D.C.: Government Printing Office, 1983.

7. Cruzan v. Harmon, 760 S.W. 2d 408 (1988).

8. Angell M. The legacy of Karen Ann Quinlan. Trends Health Care Law Ethics 1993;8(1):17–9.

9. Quinlan J. Karen Ann Quinlan. Trends Health Care Law Ethics 1993;8(1):65–8.

10. Kinney HC, Korein J, Panigrahy A, Dikkes P, Goode R. Neuropathological findings in the brain of Karen Ann Quinlan—the role of the thalamus in the persistent vegetative state. N Engl J Med 1994;330:1469–75.

11. In re Helga Wanglie, Fourth Judicial District (Dist. Ct., Probate Ct. Div.) PX-91-283. Minnesota, Hennepin County.

12. Annas GJ. Asking the courts to set the standard of emergency care—the case of Baby K. N Engl J Med 1994;330:1542–5.

13. In the matter of Baby K, 1994 U.S. App. Lexis 2215 (4th Cir.).

14. Veatch RM, Spicer CM. Medically futile care: the role of the physician in setting limits. Am J Law Med 1992;18(1–2):15–36.

15. Angell M. The case of Helga Wanglie—a new kind of "right to die" case. N Engl J Med 1991;325:511–2.

16. Veatch RM. Brain death and slippery slopes. J Clin Ethics 1992;3:181–7.

17. Blendon RJ, Szalay US, Knox RA. Should physicians aid their patients in dying? The public perspective. JAMA 1992;267:2658–62.

\* \* \*


## WHAT IF THE HEALTH CARE FACILITY DOES NOT FOLLOW THE PATIENT'S WISHES TO TERMINATE CARE?

There have been numerous instances in which a health care facility has been accused of treating a patient even though a valid advance directive or do-not-resuscitate order was in place. Documents from two legal cases concerning such treatment are presented here. In the first case, the legal issue was payment for the care rendered against the patient's alleged wishes. In the second case, a physician and health care facility were sued for failing to honor advance directives of a patient, resulting in a battery.

## DOCUMENT 101: *First Healthcare Corporation v. Rettinger,* North Carolina Court of Appeals (1995)

Lawrence Rettinger (hereinafter Mr. Rettinger) cared for his first wife during her prolonged illness and eventual death from cancer. Mr. Rettinger married his second wife, Nell Rettinger (hereinafter Mrs. Rettinger), in November 1985. Prior to marrying Mrs. Rettinger, Mr. Rettinger was diagnosed with Parkinson's Disease. On 18 August 1983, Mr. Rettinger executed a "Declaration Of A Desire For A Natural Death" pursuant to G.S. 90-321. In that document, Mr. Rettinger stated that he did not wish his life to be prolonged by "extraordinary means if [his] condition [was] determined to be terminal and incurable."

Mr. Rettinger was placed in the Winston-Salem Convalescent Center (hereinafter Hillhaven) on 11 January 1990. Mrs. Rettinger signed a document entitled "Standard Nursing Facility Services Agreement" in which she agreed to be financially responsible for services provided by Hillhaven to her husband. Hillhaven was aware that Mr. Rettinger had executed a living will and retained a copy of it in Mr. Rettinger's medical file at Hillhaven.

On 4 February 1991, Dr. Fredric J. Romm, Mr. Rettinger's attending physician, transferred Mr. Rettinger to North Carolina Baptist Hospital for treatment of pneumonia. Dr. Mark Knudson, Mr. Rettinger's primary physician at Baptist Hospital, inserted a nasogastric tube to facilitate administration of his pneumonia medications. On 4 March 1991, Mr. Rettinger was returned to Hillhaven. Mrs. Rettinger stated in her affidavit that when Mr. Rettinger was returned to Hillhaven, he was "bedridden, lying in a fetal position, unable to move and unable to communicate." She further stated that the family was informed that "he had little mental functioning, suffered from dementia, was in the late stages of irreversible Parkinson's Disease, and would die." Mrs. Rettinger alleged that Dr. Knudson had assured her that the tube would be removed within ten days of her husband's return to Hillhaven. The tube was not removed.

Mrs. Rettinger prepared a "No Code Blue" form for Mr. Rettinger in March 1991, requesting that the staff not resuscitate her husband. Because she amended the form to request that no nasogastric tube be used, Hillhaven returned the form as invalid. Mrs. Rettinger then attempted to move her husband to another facility, but could not find another facility. She stated that she wanted to take him home but the Hillhaven staff told her she could not, "apparently because they felt [she] was not able to care for him." In March 1991, Dr. Romm informed Mrs. Rettinger that Hillhaven had a policy of not removing nasogastric tubes "if to do so would likely cause a patient to starve or dehydrate to death." In a letter dated 20 June 1991, Hillhaven informed Mr. Rettinger's attorney, Norman L. Sloan, that Hillhaven would not remove the nasogastric tube unless the requirements of G.S. 90-321 were satisfied or Mrs. Rettinger obtained a court order for the removal of the tube. Mrs. Rettinger then filed suit against Hillhaven on 27 June 1991 for a declaratory judgment requiring removal of the nasogastric tube. On 12 September 1991, Judge William B. Reingold ordered that the tube be removed. There was no appeal from Judge Reingold's order. The tube was removed on 5 October 1991 and Mr. Rettinger died on 22 October 1991.

On 4 May 1993, Hillhaven filed a complaint against Mrs. Rettinger, individually and as personal representative of Mr. Rettinger's estate, for $14,458.43 for services rendered to Mr. Rettinger from 26 June 1991 to 22 October 1991. On 21 May 1993, Kenneth P. Carlson, Jr. was appointed as Guardian Ad Litem for Mrs. Rettinger to represent her in the action filed by Hillhaven. An answer was filed on Mrs. Rettinger's behalf on 23 June 1993 denying any indebtedness to Hillhaven based in part on the assertion that the services for which Hillhaven sought payment had been expressly rejected by Mr. Rettinger through his living will and by Mrs. Rettinger. Hillhaven made a motion for summary judgment on 4 January 1994 which was granted by Judge C. Preston Cornelius on 19 January 1994. Subsequently, Mrs. Rettinger died. Ashlyn H. Chadwick, the personal representative of Mrs. Rettinger's estate and the substituted personal representative of Mr. Rettinger's estate, appeals. . . .

Mrs. Rettinger also argues that summary judgment was not appropriate because she is not obligated to pay for medical services rendered by Hillhaven after 26 June 1991. Mrs. Rettinger argues that she had previously requested removal of the nasogastric tube and if her late husband's declaration and her expressed wishes for the nasogastric tube to be removed had been honored, no other medical services would have been necessary. The plain language of the "Standard Nursing Facility Services Agreement" that Mrs. Rettinger signed when Mr. Rettinger was admitted to Hillhaven provided that Mrs. Rettinger agreed to pay for all services rendered to her husband. The agreement contains no language stating that Mrs. Rettinger would only pay for services she authorized. However, we have concluded above that there are genuine issues of material fact as to whether and when the requirements of G.S. 90-321(b), the living will statute, were met. If a jury determines that the requirements of the living will statute were complied with in July 1991, then the nasogastric tube should have been removed at that time. If the nasogastric tube had been removed in July 1991, it is likely that Mr. Rettinger would not have survived until 22 October 1991 and Mrs. Rettinger's alleged financial obligation to Hillhaven would have been substantially less.

Accordingly, we reverse the summary judgment order and remand for trial to determine whether the requirements of G.S. 90-321(b) were satisfied in July 1991. If so, the factfinder will then need to determine how long after the nasogastric tube was removed would Mr. Rettinger have likely survived. If the requirements of G.S. 90-321(b) are found by the factfinder to have been met, Mrs. Rettinger will be responsible for paying for services rendered between 26 June 1991 and the date the factfinder determines Mr. Rettinger would have died if the tube had been removed in July 1991, but not for any costs incurred thereafter.

Hillhaven argues in their brief that Mrs. Rettinger guaranteed payment of the services rendered from 26 June 1991 until 22 October 1991. We have reviewed the agreement which Mrs. Rettinger signed and conclude that Mrs. Rettinger did not sign as a guarantor. Under the terms of the agreement, Mrs. Rettinger was a joint obligor. Accordingly, Hillhaven's argument based on Mrs. Rettinger's purported status as a guarantor fails.

Hillhaven also argues that Mrs. Rettinger is liable for the services rendered under the doctrine of necessaries. We do not address this argument because we have already concluded that Mrs. Rettinger will be obligated to pay for the entire amount of medical services rendered by Hillhaven pursuant to the plain language of the agreement she signed unless the factfinder determines that the requirements of G.S. 90-321(b) were met in July 1991.

In sum, we reverse the entry of summary judgment and remand for trial.

Reversed and remanded.

*Source: First Healthcare Corp. v. Rettinger,* North Carolina Court of Appeals, *Health Law News,* 1995.

\* \* \*

The North Carolina Court of Appeals decided 2 to 1 in favor of Rettinger. First Healthcare Corporation appealed the decision.

Choice In Dying, a nonprofit organization dedicated to fostering communication about complex end-of-life decisions among individuals, their loved ones, and health care professionals, filed an amicus curiae (friend of the court) brief. Its argument and conclusion are presented here. Both stress the importance of honoring a patient's wishes.

## DOCUMENT 102: Amicus Curiae Brief of Choice In Dying, *First Healthcare Corporation v. Rettinger*, North Carolina Supreme Court (1996)

### ARGUMENT

I. MR. RETTINGER'S RIGHT TO REFUSE LIFE-SUSTAINING TREATMENT WAS WELL-ESTABLISHED AS A MATTER OF LAW AND MEDICAL PRAC-TICE IN 1991

II. THE CENTER DID NOT ACT IN ACCORDANCE WITH EITHER THE LAW OR PREVAILING MEDICAL OPINION WHEN IT REFUSED TO HONOR MR. RETTINGER'S LIVING WILL AND MRS. RETTINGER'S REQUEST TO STOP ARTIFICIAL NUTRITION AND HYDRATION

A. IN 1991, ARTIFICIAL NUTRITION AND HYDRATION WAS CONSID-ERED LIFE-SUSTAINING TREATMENT BY THE LAW AND PREVAILING MEDICAL OPINION

B. MRS. RETTINGER'S REPEATED PLEAS TO STOP ARTIFICIAL NUTRI-TION AND HYDRATION SHOULD HAVE BEEN HONORED WITHOUT COURT INTERVENTION

III. THE PREVAILING PRACTICE OF NONCOMPLIANCE WITH THE ESTAB-LISHED RIGHT TO PATIENT SELF-DETERMINATION CAN BE REMEDIED BY THIS COURT

A. THERE WAS NO REASONABLE FEAR OF LIABILITY FOR HONORING A PATIENT'S WISH TO REFUSE TREATMENT

B. REFUSAL OF COMPENSATION FOR THE PROVISION OF UNWANTED MEDICAL TREATMENT IS A REASONABLE REMEDY FOR THIS COURT TO RECOMMEND

### CONCLUSION

Choice In Dying respectfully urges this Court to minimize the possi-bility of this kind of conflict in the future by declaring that there is no risk of liability in following a patient's known wishes; declaring that courts may provide a remedy for instances in which a individual's right to refuse unwanted treatment is clearly violated; and remanding the case to the trial court with an instruction that it rule in favor of Mrs. Rettin-ger's estate in this matter if the trial court finds that Mr. Rettinger's living will should have been honored as early as March 1991.

*Source*: Argument and Conclusion from the amicus curiae brief of Choice In Dying (Washington, DC) to the Supreme Court of North Carolina, May 2, 1995.

* * *

The North Carolina Supreme Court reversed the decision of the North Carolina Court of Appeals, based on the dissenting opinion of that court, which essentially held that the legal requirements relating to withdrawal of the nasogastric tube were not met until after the tube had been removed, and therefore the Rettinger estate was responsible for the charges.

The second case dealt with the issue of medical battery. The patient, Brenda Young, had a history of brain hemorrhages and seizures. Upon the recommendation of the hospital doctor and nurse, Young executed a durable medical power of attorney for health care, appointing her mother, Ramona Osgood, as her advocate. She also orally stated to the hospital nurse and her attorney that she preferred death to life support.

In February 1992, Young suffered another seizure that resulted in coma and severe shock. It was undisputed that Osgood handed the durable power of attorney for health care to the attending physician and nurse and stated that if her daughter would not have a "meaningful life," no life support should be administered. Despite these statements, life support was instituted. Young eventually came out of the coma with irreversible brain damage and her mother continued her care at home.

A jury awarded Brenda Young, her mother, and her daughter over $16 million for physical pain and suffering, mental anguish, and past and future expenses for medical treatment. The hospital filed several postjudgment motions. The court reduced the amount of the award considerably, and eventually, the parties reached a settlement for an undisclosed amount.

For the past twenty years, proponents of the right to die have focused on establishing a legal right to patient self-determination, believing that health care providers will follow a patient's wishes when they are assured that the law permits them to do so. Unfortunately, most advance-directive laws impose no adverse consequences on health care providers who refuse to follow the instructions of advance directives and may foster a belief among some that noncompliance is legally acceptable. The Osgood decision is the beginning of a trend where there has been a failure to follow advance directives. The courts are becoming more willing to find that a battery has occurred when health care providers fail to honor the directions of a health care agent and/or an advance directive.

## DOCUMENT 103: *Osgood v. Genesys Regional Medical Center,* Michigan Circuit Court, Genessee Co. (1997)

Defendant hospital has not convinced the court in its motion that a palpable error was committed which misled the court and the parties. Defendant hospital's motion merely presents the same issue as decided by the court previously, namely that somehow this is a malpractice action that warrants imposition of the statutory caps on the non-economic damage awards. The court previously ruled that this was an intentional tort case and defendant hospital's motion should be denied, as it merely raises the same issue previously decided.

### A. Battery Theory of Liability

The battery theory of liability for providing unwanted treatment was reflected in *Cruzan v Director, Missouri Department of Health,* 110 S Ct 2841, 2846 (1990), in which the plurality opinion noted that the common law basis for informed consent is that treatment without such consent can constitute a battery. Well known Justice Cardozo in the case of *Schloendorff v Society of New York Hospital,* 211 NY 125, 129–30, 105 NE 92, 93 (1914) wrote, "Every human being of adult years and sound mind has a right to determine what shall be done with his own body; and a surgeon who performs an operation without his patient's consent commits an assault, for which he is liable in damages." . . .

### B. Evidence Presented

The court is satisfied from a full review of the trial transcript that defendant hospital committed a battery when it misrepresented the nature of the medical procedures it performed, in direct contravention of the patient advocate's directions and the directions of the durable power of attorney for health care. The following trial testimony of Ramona Osgood from Transcript IV supports this position:

She always told me that—you know, if she ever got real bad where she couldn't, you know, live a normal life, like take care of herself and bath [sic] herself, and, you know, as she called it, "[do] her own thing," why, she never wanted me— she said, "I do not want you ever to have to take care of me and bath [sic] me," she said. "I do not want that," she said, "and I want you to promise me that you will never, ever let them put a life support on me." (p 165) . . .

Ramona Osgood further testified as to each and every consent form she signed, that not one of the nurses who procured the consent forms ever told her that the proposed procedures were life supporting in nature. . . . The defendant hospital did not call any witnesses to rebut this testimony which shows the hospital staff rendered life support treatments to Brenda Young in direct contravention of her wishes. . . .

Motion for reconsideration is DENIED.

*Source*: *Osgood v. Genesys Regional Medical Center*, no. 94-26731-NH (Mich. Cir. Ct. Genesee Co., March 7, 1997).

## FURTHER READING

Choice In Dying. *Right-to-Die Law Digest: A Quarterly Review of Legislative Activity and Case Law*. Washington, DC, and New York: annual supplement.

*In the Matter of Karen Quinlan*. 2 vols. Arlington, VA: University Publications of America, 1975.

Meisel, Alan. *The Right to Die*. 2nd ed. 2 vols. New York: John Wiley and Sons, 1995.

Zucker, Marjorie B., and Howard D. Zucker, eds. *Medical Futility and the Evaluation of Life-Sustaining Interventions*. Cambridge, England: Cambridge University Press, 1997.

# Part VI

# Suicide, Assisted Suicide, and Euthanasia

Suicide, assisted suicide, and euthanasia denote different actions, but the definitions as well as the acts themselves cannot always be clearly separated. Suicide is generally defined as the intentional taking of one's own life. Assisted suicide means suicide with the assistance of another person. The assistance often takes the form of providing a lethal drug. When a physician has provided the means by which a person (usually a patient) can end his or her life, such as prescribing a lethal dose of medication, it is called physician-assisted suicide. Euthanasia etymologically means a good death and usually describes an act that hastens a suffering person's death. It may be voluntary, that is, with the consent of the patient, or involuntary, without the patient's full consent, as in the case of adults who lack the mental capacity to understand the situation or in the case of infants. Early attempts to promote euthanasia have been discussed in previous parts.

Assisted suicide must be distinguished from the concept of the double effect, in which large amounts of medication are prescribed with the clear intention of controlling pain even though they may unintentionally shorten the patient's life. This is considered ethically and legally acceptable since the intention is to relieve suffering, not to cause death. Such an action has been accepted by the pope (see Document 38). Withholding or withdrawing treatment also must be distinguished from assisted suicide because the action is based on the right to be free of unwanted treatment even if this results in death.

We will review some of the historical and contemporary attitudes of medical and legal professionals and the general public as well as the status of the law about these controversial subjects. The subject is of particular interest today when Americans are debating the morality and practicality of legalizing physician-assisted suicide.

## SUICIDE

Many individuals consider that the ability to commit suicide is an important right. *Final Exit*, a book written by Derek Humphry in 1991, provides specific instructions about how to commit suicide while urging very serious consideration before undertaking such an act. The book was on the best-seller list of the *New York Times* for eighteen weeks; by 1998 it had sold over one million copies in North America and is still selling strongly.

It is not possible to review here the abundant scholarly literature about the attitudes of earlier Western cultures on suicide. The reader is referred to *Suicide and Euthanasia*, edited by Baruch Brody, and *The Least Worst Death*, by Margaret Pabst Battin. Excerpts from the latter very briefly summarize the early views of the Christian and Jewish religions.

---

## DOCUMENT 104: *The Least Worst Death*, Margaret Pabst Battin (1994)

---

It is one of the more prevalent assumptions of Western religious culture that the Bible prohibits suicide; inspection of the biblical texts, however, shows that this is by no means clearly the case. To begin with, there is no explicit prohibition of suicide in the Bible. There is no word anywhere in the Bible, either in Aramaic, Hebrew, or Greek, that is equivalent to the English term suicide, either in its nominal or verbal form, nor is there any idiomatic way of referring to this act that suggests that it is a distinct type of death. Nor is there any passage in either the Old or New Testament that can be directly understood as an explicit prohibition of suicide; those passages that are often taken to support such a prohibition require, as we shall see, a considerable amount of interpretation and qualification.

However, the biblical texts do describe a number of cases—eight in the Old Testament, two of which are in the Apocrypha, and one in the New Testament—of the phenomenon most contemporary English-speakers would call suicide. None of these passages offers explicit comment on the morality of suicide, nor is there anywhere in the Bible an explicit discussion of the ethical issues. Nevertheless, these passages are of considerable importance in establishing the moral stance of the scriptural texts toward suicide.

Consider, for instance, the passage in I Samuel that describes the deaths of Saul and his armor-bearer in battle against the Philistines:

The Philistines fought a battle against Israel, and the men of Israel were routed, leaving their dead on Mount Gilboa. The Philistines hotly pursued Saul and his sons and killed the three sons, Jonathan, Abinadab, and Malchishua. The battle went hard for Saul, for some archers came upon him and he was wounded in the belly by the archers. So he said to his armour-bearer, "Draw your sword and run me through, so that these uncircumcised brutes may not come and taunt me and make sport of me." But the armour-bearer refused, he dared not; whereupon Saul took his own sword and fell on it. When the armour-bearer saw that Saul was dead, he too fell on his sword and died with him. Thus they all died together on that day, Saul, his three sons, and his armour-bearer, as well as his men.

It is clear that Saul kills himself only after all hope of victory is lost, after his sons are dead and his army destroyed, and after it is certain that he will be captured, tortured, and will die either of torture or the wounds in his belly. Saul's act could be interpreted as one of cowardice. Yet it could equally well be maintained that Saul killed himself in order to avoid degradation at the hands of the enemy, since the treatment to which these "uncircumcised brutes" would subject him would not befit the Lord's anointed; to avoid this would be to defend the honor of Israel. In either case, however, it is clear that the biblical narrator makes no overt condemnation of Saul's act. Futhermore [sic], the populace of the surrounding area is said to have accorded both Saul, a suicide, and his sons, who were not suicides, identical anointment, burial, and fasting rites; this further suggests that no moral disapprobation is attached to suicide.

Other Old Testament suicides include Ahithophel, the wise counselor of Absalom, who hanged himself not so much because his pride was wounded when Absalom refused to follow his advice, but because he recognized that Absalom's cause was therefore lost; the usurper Zimri, who burned the royal citadel over him in what is apparently viewed by the redactor as a self-imposed judgment for the sins he had committed; Abimilech, whose suicide also appears to be viewed as a punishment for sins; and Samson, who in destroying the Philistines pulled the temple down upon himself. The only completed New Testament suicide is that of Judas, who hanged himself; the Matthean narrator implies that the motive is remorse over the betrayal of Jesus, and seems to see Judas' death as appropriate in the context. Again, there is nowhere, in either the Old or New Testament, an explicit discussion of the moral status of suicide. There are cases in which a biblical figure expresses despair or weariness of life, often from persecution or physical affliction—for example, Elijah, Job, Jonah, Sarah (the daughter of Raguel), and possibly

Jesus at Gethsemane—but although these figures all recover an earlier enthusiasm for life, there is no condemnation of any consideration of suicide they may have made. On the whole, however, suicide is a comparatively rare phenomenon in biblical texts. . . .

With the development of the Talmud in the first several centuries A.D., later rabbinic tradition begins to make explicit a prohibition of suicide, both in stories condemning suicide and by means of mourning and funeral restrictions. The Talmud, unlike earlier Hebrew sources, contains numerous stories of suicide and suicidal martyrdom, and in many of these disapproval of the act is clearly indicated by the narrator or author.

*Source*: Margaret Pabst Battin, *The Least Worst Death* (New York and Oxford, Oxford University Press, 1994), 207–208 (notes omitted).

* * *

In the first centuries of the Christian era, persecuted Christians became convinced that martyrdom would lead them to heaven. As a result, some sought death by gladiators' swords or the claws and teeth of wild beasts in Roman arenas. In 421–22, Augustine argued strongly against this practice in "Concerning the City of God Against the Pagans" and, by extension of the argument, against suicide.

## DOCUMENT 105: *The Least Worst Death*, Margaret Pabst Battin (1994)

The Christian use of the Sixth Commandment as the basis for the prohibition of suicide originates with St. Augustine; prior to the early fifth century A.D., the church had no unified position on the moral status of suicide, and was widely divided on whether various forms of self-killing, including deliberate martyrdom and religiously motivated suicide, were to be allowed. Like the Genesis passage [Genesis 9:5], the Sixth Commandment also presents severe interpretational problems; these involve both the meanings of the words employed, and the scope of the prohibition stated.

First, the semantic difficulties. The term usually translated "kill" actually means "wrongful killing"; the commandment is best translated "Thou shalt do no wrongful killing," or perhaps "Thou shalt do no murder." Nowhere in the Old Testament does the term "wrongful killing" appear in connection with suicide, and there is no philological reason to think that suicide is included under this term. The commandment thus does not serve as a general prohibition of self-killing, since self-killing may not always be wrongful killing. That suicide is *wrongful* killing would need to be established independently; only then could the Sixth Commandment be used to confirm the centrality of a suicide prohibition in the Christian scriptures.

Second, the scope problems. Augustine claims that "Thou shalt not kill" means not only that one should not kill others, but that one ought not kill oneself. But Augustine's conclusion is not immediately evident. For one thing, not only is "Thou shalt not kill" almost universally relaxed to permit the killing of plants and animals, it is usually also interpreted to allow the killing of human beings in self-defense, capital punishment, and war. However, one might argue, if under this commandment the killing of human beings is permitted in these situations, it is hard to see way [*sic*] it should not also be permitted in the case of suicide. Indeed, suicide would seem to have a stronger claim to morality, since suicide alone does not violate the wishes of the individual killed.

To meet such an objection, Augustine draws a distinction between "private killing" and killing that is carried out at the orders of a divine or divinely constituted authority. Private killing, or killing undertaken "on one's own authority," is never right; it is wrong whether one kills oneself or someone else, and it is wrong whether the victim is innocent or guilty of crime in any degree. Consequently, private killing of oneself—that is, self-initiated suicide—is wrong whether one kills oneself in order to declare one's innocence (like Lucretia), or to punish oneself for a crime (like Judas).

However, according to Augustine, not all killing is private. God may command a killing, and when this is the case, full obedience is required. The command may take either of two principal forms: it may be a direct command from God, such as the commandment to Abraham to sacrifice Isaac, or it may be required by a just law. In these two cases, the individual who performs the killing does not do it "on his own authority" and is not morally accountable for it; he is "an instrument, a sword in its user's hand." This accounts for the permissibility of both killing in war and in capital punishment, since both types of killing are performed by persons acting under law. Augustine appears not to permit killing in self-defense, though present-day Catholic moral theology does permit it for persons not capable of attaining the "higher way" of self-sacrifice.

*Source*: Margaret Pabst Battin, *The Least Worst Death* (New York and Oxford: Oxford University Press, 1994), 210–211. Most notes omitted.

* * *

The prohibition against suicide was maintained in the Christian and Jewish faiths. An interesting exception, however, was the following statement in *Utopia*, written by Sir Thomas More. Despite More's approval of assisted suicide, which was antithetical to Catholic doctrine, he was beatified in 1886 by Pope Leo XIII and canonized by Pope Pius XI in 1935 on the 400th anniversary of his murder by order of Henry VIII.

---

## DOCUMENT 106: *Utopia*, Sir Thomas More (1516)

The sick they see with great affection, and let nothing at all pass, concerning either physic or good diet, whereby they may be restored again to their health. Them that be sick of incurable diseases they comfort by sitting by them, with talking with them, and, to be short, with all manner of helps that may be. But if the disease be not only incurable, but also full of continual pain and anguish, then the priests and magistrates exhort the man, seeing he is not able to do any duty of life, and by overliving his own life is noisome and irksome to others and grievous to himself, that he will determine with himself no longer to cherish that pestilent and painful disease. And seeing that his life is to him but a torment, that he will not be unwilling to die, but rather take a good hope to him, and either dispatch himself out of that painful life, as out of a prison or rack of torment, or else suffer himself willingly to be rid out of it by others.

And in so doing they (the priests and magistrates) tell him he shall do wisely, seeing by his death he shall lose no happiness, but end his torture. And because in that act he shall follow the counsel of the priests, that is to say of the interpreters of God's will and pleasure, they show him that he shall do like a Godly and virtuous man. They that be thus convinced finish their lives willingly, either by fasting, or else they are released by an opiate in their sleep without any feeling of death. But they cause none such to die against his will, nor do they use less diligence in attending him, believing this to be an honorable death.

*Source*: Sir Thomas More, *Utopia* (Mineola, NY: Dover Publications, 1997), 58.

\* \* \*

Disapproval of suicide increased through the centuries, as evidenced by the ill-treatment of the corpses of those who had committed suicide and the punishment by hanging of those unfortunates whose attempt at suicide was unsuccessful. Judge Guido Calabresi gives a brief history of suicide in the nineteenth and early twentieth centuries.

## DOCUMENT 107: "A Bit of History," in the Concurring Opinion of Judge Guido Calabresi, *Quill v. Vacco*, U.S. Court of Appeals, Second Circuit (1996)

English authorities had long declared suicide to be murder. . . . And the leading American case echoed these English authorities. . . . [In 1816] Chief Justice Parker instructed the jury: "Self-destruction is doubtless a crime of awful turpitude; it is considered in the eye of the law of equal heinousness with the murder of one by another. In this offence, it is true the actual murderer escapes punishment; for the very commission of the crime, which the the [sic] law would otherwise punish with its utmost rigor, puts the offender beyond the reach of its infliction. And in this he is distinguished from other murderers. But his punishment is as severe as the nature of the case will admit; his body is buried in infamy, and in England his property is forfeited to the King." . . .

[In 1881], the New York Legislature revised the Penal Code. The new code provided that an intentional *attempt* to commit suicide was a felony with a maximum penalty of two years' imprisonment. . . . But while the Code declared suicide itself to be "a grave public wrong," it imposed no forfeiture because of "the impossibility of reaching the successful perpetrator." . . . The 1881 statute . . . punished assisting a successful suicide as manslaughter in the first degree. . . . The Code also punished assistance in attempted suicide as an unspecified felony. . . . In 1965, the Legislature took the next step and deleted the declaration that suicide was "a grave public wrong." It, however, left in place redrafted versions . . . of the 1881 Code, stating: "A person is guilty of manslaughter in the second degree when . . . [h]e intentionally causes or aids another person to commit suicide.

*Source*: Judge Guido Calabresi, "A Bit of History," in his concurring opinion in *Quill v. Vacco*, 80 F.3d 716 (2nd Cir. 1996), 732–734.

\* \* \*

## ASSISTED SUICIDE AND EUTHANASIA

### Heightened Interest of the Public in Assisted Suicide

Two books, *Jean's Way* and *Last Wish*, that recounted the assisted suicide of individuals who were dying of cancer portrayed a realistic attitude of dying patients and their families and the compassion shown by the patients' loved ones. Both captured the attention of much of the general public.

---

## DOCUMENT 108: *Jean's Way*, Derek Humphry with Ann Wickett (1978)

---

### 'IS THIS THE DAY?'

When I awoke the next morning, I turned my head on my pillow and saw Jean was gazing at me. I sensed that she had been lying there looking at me for some time, waiting for the end of my sleep, and I was filled with the premonition that something was the matter. However, I said nothing apart from the usual, 'Good morning, darling. How are you feeling?'

'My neck is very bad. I can't move it,' Jean replied.

I climbed out of bed and prepared her usual dosage of medicines and pain-killing drugs which she swallowed in a gulp. I opened the curtains, remarking on what a clear and bright spring day it was but there was no reaction from Jean who was quiet and reflective, absorbed in her thoughts.

'Shall I get breakfast now?' I asked.

'Yes, good,' she replied. 'Just tea and toast.'

I picked up the morning papers on my way to the kitchen and began to prepare the snack. I kept thinking to myself, what shall I do if she asks if she has reached the end? Am I absolutely certain that it is close to the end? This was the one time when I could not fail her: I would have to be honest and say 'Yes'. I realized that the end was here for I had been seriously considering taking her life myself. She could not go on suffering like this any longer, particularly with the risk of more bone fractures which would mean rushing her to the hospital to die there— something she did not want at any cost. I realized that, were she to go to the hospital on the following Tuesday for more radio-therapy treatment, she would never return home either (Dr Laing told me later that immediately after he saw Jean for the last time in Swindon, he wrote to Dr Gornall in Chippenham: 'I am not anxious to prolong this woman's life at this stage. Nevertheless, one must do one's utmost to control the symptoms.')

I recalled Jean's words spoken a few months previously: 'When I die, I want to be at home with you, Derek, and only you and me. Whatever you do, don't let me die in hospital.' My eyes filled with tears and burned so much I had to bathe them in cold water. Trying to appear normal, I carried the breakfast tray into the sick-room, tossing the *Guardian* in the usual manner on to Jean's bed. For once she ignored it, preferring to sip her tea and nibble at her toast, looking out the window at the rose bushes. We were each buried deeply in our own thoughts. I was so tense I could not bear looking at her and kept my gaze directed towards the golden privet bushes lining the drive.

'Derek?' Jean called softly.

'Yes, darling.'

'Is this the day?'

I panicked. My mouth dried up and I could not control the tears which rushed to my eyes. It was the most awful moment of my life. However, I had to answer, 'Yes, my darling, it is.'

There followed many minutes of silence as we both considered the decision we had taken. Had I done the right thing? Was it too soon? Should she go back to the hospital for more treatment? My tormented thoughts were checked in the midst of their chaotic rambling by Jean's calm, measured voice. 'How shall it be? You promised me you would get me something.'

'I have,' I answered. 'A doctor in London has mixed me a combination of drugs which are quite lethal. You have only to take them and that is the end.'

We became silent again and I asked myself if I should cross-examine her about the correctness of her part of the decision. However, I resisted this because it was so apparent that she was depending on me for judgement. To raise any doubts at this point would only muddle the certainty and clarity of our instincts and intelligence. We both knew intuitively that this was the right time. To waver would have been wrong.

Again she spoke first. 'I shall die at one o'clock. You must give me the overdose and then go into the garden and not return for an hour. We'll say our last good-bye here but I don't want you to actually see me die.' . . .

'There's one thing I want you to promise me,' she continued. 'You must go to Manchester after I'm dead and tell my father exactly how I died. I don't want him to think I died in pain or like a vegetable. He suffered enough when Mother died because no one would make any decisions. I want him to be sure to know that I died this way. Do you promise me?'

I agreed to do anything she asked, marvelling at how beautifully organized she was. . . .

I knew in my heart . . . that this way it was for the best, and the knowledge relieved some of my agony. In the circumstances, this was the most perfect end attainable to our marriage. Jean had stoically endured tremendous adversity with such dignity for the past two years that it was now her turn to take the initiative. However, something was bothering her when she asked, 'Aren't you breaking the law in helping me to take my own life? Won't you get into trouble? I couldn't bear that.'

I had anticipated this and assured her that I had thought it all out. 'I shall say nothing about it. At any rate, the doctors looking after you know that you are seriously ill. Dr Gornall thought you would be dead by last Christmas so how can they question your death now? Even if they suspect something unusual, which I doubt, I think they are too intelligent and sensitive to the situation to make needless trouble.'

She persisted with her questions. 'But it *is* against the law, isn't it?'

I told her that it was a breach of the law but that such offences were rarely prosecuted. 'I can handle it,' I assured her. 'We must not worry on this score. I've been able to think this over since last August and there is not the slightest doubt in my mind that if this is the way you wish to die, then it is my duty to help you.'

She was comforted by this and we resumed talking about our pleasant memories. Jean reminisced about the opening of the shop, furnishing the farmhouse, and helping Edgar and Vivienne [their son and his wife] make a success of their marriage. 'Viv has promised me that she will look after you,' she said. 'And I've told them all that they must accept whoever you choose. I've told them that it doesn't matter how soon you're married after I'm dead—I don't care if it's a month! Promise me that you will marry again.'

Through an abundance of tears which I could not control, I managed to nod an assent which meant that I would keep the promise.

'Stop crying,' she admonished me. 'Look at the time.'

It was just ten minutes before one o'clock.

I dried my tears and went out of the room to get the brew of sleeping pills and pain-killers which I had decided could be best mixed in a cup of coffee. The youngsters were all slumped in chairs in the breakfast room and I suggested, as I passed them, that they prepare themselves, adding, 'I think she's close to death.' I made two mugs of strong coffee with milk and into one I poured the potion. Putting them on a tray, I went back into the sick-room and placed Jean's on the table beside her bed.

'Is that it?' she asked.

I did not need to reply at all. I took her in my arms and kissed her.

'Good-bye, my love.'

'Good-bye, darling.'

She lifted the mug and gulped the contents down swiftly, leaned back on her pillow and closed her eyes. Within seconds she appeared to fall asleep and soon her breathing was slow and heavy. . . .

After fifteen minutes she vomited slightly and as I wiped her mouth the panic mounted in me as I thought that the pills were not going to work. Perhaps she had not kept down enough of the drug? On a chair beside the bed lay two pillows which had been used to prop her into a sitting position; I decided that with the first stirring of life I would smother her with them. It did not matter to me that I would be breaking the law: this was an act which two partners owed to each other, a private death pact. Anyhow, I did not intend that anyone should know.

Jean lay breathing heavily as I continued my desperate vigil. However, she did not need further help. At 1.50 P.M., 29 March 1975, as I sat watching, she died peacefully.

*Source*: Derek Humphry with Ann Wickett, *Jean's Way* (London and New York: Quartet Books, 1978), 107–113 (notes omitted).

## DOCUMENT 109: *Last Wish*, Betty Rollin (1985)

My mother slept for a while. When she woke up she said she felt better—not better enough to ingest anything, only better enough not to feel like throwing up again.

"Rose was here this morning," she said, too weak now to speak above a whisper. "She seemed so young to me, so lively. I looked at her and realized how far I've fallen." I pulled my chair closer to the bed and took her hand. "You know I love Rose, but the whole time she was here I kept wanting her to go so that I could sleep. It's the only relief I have now—sleep." Gently she took her hand out of mine and looked at me, her eyes wide and hard. "How am I going to get out of this?" she said. "Where's the door?"

Her eyes were too much for me. I looked down, but when I looked up they were still there. I think that's when I knew she was really asking me.

"I've had a wonderful life, but now it's over, or it should be. I'm not afraid to die but I am afraid of this illness, what it's doing to me. I'm not better. I'm worse. There's never any relief from it now. Nothing but nausea and this pain. The pain—it never stops. There won't be any more chemotherapy. There's no treatment anymore. Dr. Burns said when I reached this stage I'd go fast. But I'm not going; I can feel that. So what happens to me now? I know what happens. I'll die slowly." She paused, she coughed, but she kept her eyes on me. "I don't want that. I wouldn't mind if it killed me fast. Fast I wouldn't mind. Slow I mind." She stopped and at last she looked away. I laced my fingers and pressed my palms together. I thought that was the end of it, but she went on.

"Who does it benefit if I die slowly? If it benefits my children I'd be willing. If some good came to them, so I'd suffer a little. For my children I'd do that. Any mother would do that. But it's not going to do you any good. It's not going to do Ed any good. Just the opposite. Don't I see what I'm doing to you already? You haven't been this thin since you were in high school. There's no point in a slow death, none. I've never liked doing things with no point. I've got to end this."

She stopped. Now I was supposed to speak. My tongue was dry. "Mother," I said in a voice so low it was almost no voice at all, "what are you saying to me? I know it's been . . . I know you've had a really terrible twenty-four hours, forty hours. I know, I read the chart. But some days aren't so bad, isn't that right? Don't you—don't you want to be alive on the days that aren't so bad?"

"Every day is bad. Every day. I'm not saying it couldn't be worse. I know how some people suffer and still they cling to life. But to me this isn't life. Life is taking a walk, visiting my children, eating! Remember how I loved to eat? The *thought* of food makes me sick now." She closed her eyes. "Everything makes me sick now. This isn't life. If I had life I'd want it. I don't want this." She looked up at me the same way she had before, in the same hard-eyed way.

"Mother," I said, holding each word before letting it go, "is that really what you want—to die?"

"Of course I want to die," she said. "Next to the happiness of my children, I want to die more than anything in the world."

*Source*: Betty Rollin, *Last Wish*, Warner Books ed. (New York Linden Press/Simon & Schuster, 1985), 149–150.

* * *

## LEGALITY OF AND OPINIONS ABOUT ASSISTED SUICIDE

Although laws in the United States were changed during the twentieth century so that it was no longer illegal to commit suicide, assisting in a suicide and committing euthanasia remained crimes. By December 31, 1998, 37 states had statutes that explicitly criminalized assisting in a suicide, and 7 states and the District of Columbia criminalized assisted suicide through the common law. In five states, the legality of assisting suicide was not clear. One state, Oregon, permits physician-assisted suicide under specified circumstances (see Document 131).

The courts have varied in determining the criminal liability of a person whose participation in the suicide of another contributes to the death of that person. In some instances, defendants have been held liable for murder or for manslaughter. More recently, courts have avoided such harsh penalties and have even refused to impose criminal liability in the absence of a statute criminalizing assisted suicide.

The actions of a Michigan physician, Jack Kevorkian, further aroused interest in and provoked discussion of assisted suicide among the general public. In June 1990, Kevorkian used a "suicide machine" that he

had developed to enable Janet Adkins, a fifty-four-year-old woman suffering from early Alzheimer's disease, to end her life. This was the first
in a long line of Kevorkian-assisted suicides that reached 130 in March
1999.

Early attempts to convict Kevorkian on charges of assisting in a suicide were unsuccessful. For example, two months after Adkins's death,
a statewide injunction was issued against use of his machine. Four
months later, he was charged with first-degree murder, but the charges
were dismissed after a videotape provided evidence of Janet Adkins's
wishes. A few months later, despite a permanent injunction against use
of his machine, Kevorkian assisted two more individuals in suicide. At
that time, there was no state statute prohibiting assisting in a suicide,
but he was arrested three months later and indicted for two counts of
murder under the common law. These charges were dismissed in July
1992. The Michigan legislature passed a ban on assisted suicide effective in February 1993, but the act was later repealed. Between these
dates, Kevorkian assisted in eight more suicides.

The subsequent history of the legal decisions regarding Kevorkian's
actions is equally complex. Between 1993 and 1996, juries acquitted
him in three trials. The proceedings of jury deliberations are not recorded, but it is likely that the jurors considered that the patient's death
occurred because a physician was attempting to alleviate suffering.

In 1994, the Michigan Supreme Court upheld the constitutionality
of the assisted-suicide statute and also held that the U.S. Constitution
does not prohibit a state from criminalizing the act of assisting in a
suicide. The court also decided that assisting in a suicide did not fall
under Michigan's definition of murder, but was a felony under the
common law.

In September 1998, Kevorkian further challenged the law. He made
a videotape while injecting a fatal solution into Thomas Youk, a paralyzed man dying of amyotrophic lateral sclerosis (Lou Gehrig's disease). In November, the television show *60 Minutes* aired the tape and
an interview with Kevorkian. Since Kevorkian, rather than the patient,
carried out the injection, he could be charged with murder. Unlike the
earlier trials of Kevorkian and so-called "mercy killings" (Documents
33–35), the judge refused to permit testimony from the patient's family
and the jury convicted Kevorkian of second-degree murder. Kevorkian
plans to appeal the decision.

Kevorkian's actions, whether legal or not, have been widely criticized because of his brief acquaintance with the people whose suicides
he supervised and his limited experience in practicing medicine (he
was trained as a pathologist). Furthermore, a number of his "patients"
were not terminally ill. On the other hand, many people have ap-
plauded his actions because they brought an important topic to the

attention of the general public and hastened the possibility of legalizing assisted suicide. Some comments in the media follow.

---

## DOCUMENT 110: "Death's Dissident," *Economist* (November 13, 1993)

---

From his front window Jack Kevorkian, also known as "Dr Death", can see a red shop-sign screaming "Bright Ideas". Opposite, at the back, is the police station. In this frugal flat in a 1920s brick building on Main Street, Royal Oak, a trendified suburb of Detroit (the new Mongolian restaurant is packed at lunchtime), Merian Frederick, a 72-year-old with an acute wasting disease, last month became the 19th person whose suicide Dr Kevorkian has witnessed. In the same flat, Michael Berzold, the author of a new book, "Appointment with Doctor Death", once asked the retired pathologist what he thought happened after you die. Without hesitation, the doctor replied: "You rot."

Dr Kevorkian did not become a household name by being afraid, metaphorically as well as literally, to chill the blood. Since 1958 (in between his normal work as a pathologist and flirtations with film-making, painting and poetry) he has fought a dogged campaign to convert death row into a factory for organ transplants. As if that was not shocking enough, he turned his obsessive mind to physician-assisted suicide, inspired by a visit to Amsterdam, euthanasia capital of the world. He invented the "Mercitron", a machine that allows his patients to kill themselves painlessly at the flick of a switch. He advertised for customers. In June 1990, in Dr Kevorkian's old camper van, Janet Adkins used the Mercitron to escape from the sentence of Alzheimer's disease.

Why did this and subsequent suicides cause such a stir? Americans have come to accept as almost normal the daily bloodbath on their streets. They make no fuss about the life-and-death decisions doctors discreetly make all the time. Yet the idea of designer death makes them shuffle uneasily. Death is something to be postponed almost indefinitely, until it happens by some appalling accident or mistake. The idea of dying on purpose, with the help of the very profession traditionally relied upon to keep death away, confronts Americans with their last great taboo.

Dr Kevorkian has been called a "serial killer" in the Senate. He has been ridiculed on the talk shows ("Just try it once—that's all we ask", is one of David Letterman's "Top ten promotional slogans for the suicide machine"). The Michigan State Board of Medicine has suspended his medical licence. Michigan law was revised to outlaw physician-assisted suicide, helping to bring the Kevorkian drama to its latest climax.

Last week Dr Kevorkian refused to pay $20,000 bail for charges relating to the new law. He was dragged off to prison where, as he had long promised he would under such circumstances, he started a hunger strike. It ended three days later only after a lawyer who disapproves of the Kevorkian campaign and the publicity it was getting posted the bail for him. But since Dr Kevorkian may any day now face new charges connected to the Frederick suicide, the drama is far from over.

Limp body resisting arrest, hunger strike, one man defying the weight of the establishment—there is something strangely familiar about all this. Dr Kevorkian is fast becoming the sort of person who was supposed to disappear with the end of the Soviet Union. He is a home-grown, all-American dissident.

Like other dissidents, he has unshakable belief in the rightness of his cause. He is surrounded, as he sees it, by ignorance and hypocrisy. "I'm alone," he says, "a formidable mind in the Dark Ages." As for any Sakharov or Gandhi, publicity is oxygen. His lawyer and handler, Geoffrey Fieger, is a man with two drama degrees and a taste for the cameras. "We have no 800-number, no organisation," Mr Fieger booms, "all we have is the hearts and minds."

And like all dissidents, Dr Death disturbs. He disturbs even sympathisers, who worry about the possibilities of abuse, about the idea of a machine that demystifies death, about the complications all the publicity might cause for the mercy-killing that quietly goes on every day in hospitals. He unsettles a medical establishment that has traditionally assumed the purpose of medicine to be to maintain life at any cost. He alarms the churches—to the point where the Catholic archdiocese of Detroit this week placed a full-page "Statement on Euthanasia" as an advertisement in the local press. Dr Kevorkian argues that religion and medicine should be completely divorced; or, as his lawyer more colourfully puts it, "If the church is in charge, man, we might as well go back to the fucking Inquisition."

A growing debate about euthanasia was inevitable even without the help of Dr Kevorkian. Demographics would see to that. The cost of keeping death away from an ageing population has been rising. A huge share of Medicare money is spent in the last two weeks of patients' lives. This has helped to unleash the movement for health-care reform. Yet the deeper question—what exactly is the system trying to deliver?—has barely been asked.

The climate is changing. Patients have been recognized to have rights, including the right to refuse treatment. They are less inhibited about demanding to stay in control, as far as possible, whether through "living wills" or other means. Medical ethics are being thoroughly re-examined.

And now, thanks to a determined dissident, the death debate has begun. It is just a start; but death, remember, is a subject in which every

American has a personal interest. The battle over it may eventually make the little trouble over abortion look like a minor skirmish.

Source: "Death's Dissident," Economist, November 13, 1993, 34.

## DOCUMENT 111: "Rx for Death," Nancy Gibbs (May 1993)

The Mansur case [the most recent of Kevorkian's assisted suicides], like those that preceded it, captures the worst fears of opponents of doctor-assisted suicide. By operating outside the law, they say, doctors like Kevorkian go unregulated, unsupervised, abiding only by those safeguards they impose on themselves. They alone make judgments about the patient's state of mind; about what means, short of death, might relieve the suffering. They transform the image of the doctor from pure, empathic healer to something more ambiguous, even sinister, whose purpose at the patient's bedside is no longer clear.

But in the eyes even of some who disagree with his methods, Kevorkian has become the devil that doctors deserve. Arthur Caplan, director of the University of Minnesota's Center for Biomedical Ethics, puts it succinctly. "I'll give him this," he says. "He tells us exactly where the health-care system stinks." Even some doctors reluctantly agree. "A significant percent of the American public sees Kevorkian as a reasonable alternative to modern medicine," says professor George Annas of Boston University's School of Medicine. "He's a total indictment of the way we treat dying patients in hospitals and at home. We don't treat them well, and they know it."

Source: Nancy Gibbs, "Rx for Death," Time, May 31, 1993, 35–39.

\* \* \*

The following opinion piece was written by Kevorkian's lawyer.

## DOCUMENT 112: "Kevorkian's Crusade," Geoffrey Nels Fieger (1993)

Southfield, Mich.
The events that have put Dr. Jack Kevorkian in a solitary cell in a dreary county jail are a throwback to the medieval era, a result of the most frightening phenomenon of our time: resurgent religious fanaticism at a time when intolerance is alarmingly on the rise.

The same people who would deny women their constitutional freedom of choice about pregnancy are conspiring to imprison perhaps the most painfully honest and principled man I have ever met, a man who represents the idea at the core of what the Founding Fathers stood for: the right to determine your own destiny in the face of hopeless affliction. That's why Jack Kevorkian, son of survivors of the Armenian holocaust, refuses to eat or to post bond for his freedom.

He has done nothing wrong. Not one person—other than judges, legislators and prosecutors seeking to impose their will and convictions by fiat—has ever filed a complaint against Dr. Kevorkian. No one has ever accused him of violating any law except Michigan's ban on helping people commit suicide, which was designed by the religious lobby that controls the Legislature and was aimed solely at one person: Jack Kevorkian, M.D.

That's why he refuses food as long as he is being held prisoner. No, he is not trying to commit suicide himself, or achieve some weird martyrdom. Take it from me: I have known him now for more than three years, in the course of which he has become one of my best friends. He is a warm, fun-loving man who loves baseball, pretty girls, Bach and big band music. But he is incapable of being a hypocrite. He thinks we are slipping back into the Dark Ages. He knows more about that than most of us; many of his relatives were murdered in 1915. He simply doesn't care to live in a climate where the state can tell you, "Sorry, we have decided that you have to suffer."

That's what this is all about, by the way. People still say Dr. Kevorkian's case is about the right to die. It's not. We all are going to die. It's about the right not to suffer.

Twenty gravely ill, severely suffering people have come to Dr. Kevorkian and been helped to gain relief since 1990. Jack is a physician first and foremost, and he believes the duty of every physician is to relieve suffering and provide a soft landing out of this world, if necessary.

I'll let you in on a secret: Jack has far more patients than you'll ever know. That's because most of them never commit suicide. Knowing that he is there as a final option gives many of them the will to keep going. When he has agreed to help ease someone's journey out of this world, the response of every family member has always been simple gratitude.

Society has a choice now: Dr. Kevorkian's life or Michigan's assisted-suicide ban, which was declared unconstitutional by a Wayne County judge in May but reinstated until the backlogged and dilatory Michigan Court of Appeals can get around to considering it. If this immoral "law" and the fanatics behind it win, we had all better weep. Not so much for my client and my brave and brilliant friend, but for ourselves.

For we are all going into that good night, and too many of us are not going gently. We honor the doctors who gave us anesthesia. But we are allowing the slow death of a man who is equally determined to relieve suffering. We should all rage against the dying of the light.

*Source*: Geoffrey Nels Fieger, "Kevorkian's Crusade," *New York Times*, 12/3/93: A33.

* * *

### Attitudes of Physicians about Assisted Suicide and Euthanasia

The Oath of Hippocrates, until recently recited by graduating medical students, is a well-known statement that enjoins physicians from assisting in suicide. Interestingly, this prohibition was not in accord with the practice of most contemporary Greek physicians (Margaret Pabst Battin, *The Least Worst Death* [New York: Oxford University Press, 1994], 16).

---

## DOCUMENT 113: Oath of Hippocrates, in *Source Book of Medical History*, Logan Clendening (1960)

---

I swear by Apollo Physician, by Asclepius, by Health, by Panacea and by all the gods and goddesses, making them my witnesses, that I will carry out, according to my ability and judgement, this oath and this indenture. To hold my teacher in this art equal to my own parents; to make him partner in my livelihood; when he is in need of money to share mine with him; to consider his family as my own brothers, and to teach them this art, if they want to learn it, without fee or indenture; to impart precept, oral instruction, and all other instruction to my own sons, the sons of my teacher, and to indentured pupils who have taken the physician's oath, but to nobody else. I will use treatment to help the sick according to my ability and judgment, but never with a view to injury and wrong-doing. Neither will I administer a poison to anybody when asked to do so, nor will I suggest such a course. Similarly I will not give a woman a pessary to cause abortion. But I will keep pure and holy both my life and my art. I will not use the knife, not even, verily, on sufferers from stone, but I will give place to such as are craftsmen therein. Into whatsoever houses I enter, I will enter to help the sick, and I will abstain from all intentional wrong-doing and harm, especially from abusing the bodies of man or woman, bond or free. And whatsoever I shall see or hear in the course of my profession, as well as outside my profession in my intercourse with men, if it be what should not be published abroad, I will never divulge, holding such things to be holy secrets. Now if I carry out this oath, and break it not, may I gain for ever reputation among all men for my life and for my art; but if I transgress it and forswear myself, may the opposite befall me.

*Source*: Logan Clendening, *Source Book of Medical History* (New York: Dover Publications, 1960), 14–15.

In 1975, an influential article by philosopher James Rachels was published in the *New England Journal of Medicine*. Rachels questioned the difference between allowing a terminally ill patient to die and actively causing the patient's death. The journal published thirteen letters in response to this article, virtually all of them highly critical of Rachels's viewpoint.

## DOCUMENT 114: "Active and Passive Euthanasia," James Rachels (1975)

**Abstract**   The traditional distinction between active and passive euthanasia requires critical analysis. The conventional doctrine is that there is such an important moral difference between the two that, although the latter is sometimes permissible, the former is always forbidden. This doctrine may be challenged for several reasons. First of all, active euthanasia is in many cases more humane than passive euthanasia. Secondly, the conventional doctrine leads to decisions concerning life and death on irrelevant grounds. Thirdly, the doctrine rests on a distinction between killing and letting die that itself has no moral importance. Fourthly, the most common arguments in favor of the doctrine are invalid. I therefore suggest that the American Medical Association policy statement that endorses this doctrine is unsound.

The distinction between active and passive euthanasia is thought to be crucial for medical ethics. The idea is that it is permissible, at least in some cases, to withhold treatment and allow a patient to die, but it is never permissible to take any direct action designed to kill the patient. This doctrine seems to be accepted by most doctors, and it is endorsed in a statement adopted by the House of Delegates of the American Medical Association on December 4, 1973:

The intentional termination of the life of one human being by another—mercy killing—is contrary to that for which the medical profession stands and is contrary to the policy of the American Medical Association.
The cessation of the employment of extraordinary means to prolong the life of

the body when there is irrefutable evidence that biological death is imminent is the decision of the patient and/or his immediate family. The advice and judgment of the physicians should be freely available to the patient and/or his immediate family.

However, a strong case can be made against this doctrine. In what follows I will set out some of the relevant arguments, and urge doctors to reconsider their views on this matter.

To begin with a familiar type of situation, a patient who is dying of incurable cancer of the throat is in terrible pain, which can no longer be satisfactorily alleviated. He is certain to die within a few days, even if present treatment is continued, but he does not want to go on living for those days since the pain is unbearable. So he asks the doctor for an end to it, and his family joins in the request.

Suppose the doctor agrees to withhold treatment, as the conventional doctrine says he may. The justification for his doing so is that the patient is in terrible agony, and since he is going to die anyway, it would be wrong to prolong his suffering needlessly. But now notice this. If one simply withholds treatment, it may take the patient longer to die, and so he may suffer more than he would if more direct action were taken and a lethal injection given. This fact provides strong reason for thinking that, once the initial decision not to prolong his agony has been made, active euthanasia is actually preferable to passive euthanasia, rather than the reverse. To say otherwise is to endorse the option that leads to more suffering rather than less, and is contrary to the humanitarian impulse that prompts the decision not to prolong his life in the first place.

Part of my point is that the process of being "allowed to die" can be relatively slow and painful, whereas being given a lethal injection is relatively quick and painless. Let me give a different sort of example. In the United States about one in 600 babies is born with Down's syndrome. Most of these babies are otherwise healthy—that is, with only the usual pediatric care, they will proceed to an otherwise normal infancy. Some, however, are born with congenital defects such as intestinal obstructions that require operations if they are to live. Sometimes, the parents and the doctor will decide not to operate, and let the infant die. Anthony Shaw describes what happens then:

... When surgery is denied [the doctor] must try to keep the infant from suffering while natural forces sap the baby's life away. As a surgeon whose natural inclination is to use the scalpel to fight off death, standing by and watching a salvageable baby die is the most emotionally exhausting experience I know. It is easy at a conference, in a theoretical discussion, to decide that such infants should be allowed to die. It is altogether different to stand by in the nursery and watch as dehydration and infection wither a tiny being over hours and days. This is a terrible ordeal for me and the hospital staff—much more so than for the parents who never set foot in the nursery.*

I can understand why some people are opposed to all euthanasia, and insist that such infants must be allowed to live. I think I can also understand why other people favor destroying these babies quickly and painlessly. But why should anyone favor letting "dehydration and infection wither a tiny being over hours and days?" The doctrine that says that a baby may be allowed to dehydrate and wither, but may not be given an injection that would end its life without suffering, seems so patently cruel as to require no further refutation. The strong language is not intended to offend, but only to put the point in the clearest possible way.

My second argument is that the conventional doctrine leads to decisions concerning life and death made on irrelevant grounds.

Consider again the case of the infants with Down's syndrome who need operations for congenital defects unrelated to the syndrome to live. Sometimes, there is no operation, and the baby dies, but when there is no such defect, the baby lives on. Now, an operation such as that to remove an intestinal obstruction is not prohibitively difficult. The reason why such operations are not performed in these cases is, clearly, that the child has Down's syndrome and the parents and doctor judge that because of that fact it is better for the child to die.

But notice that this situation is absurd, no matter what view one takes of the lives and potentials of such babies. If the life of such an infant is worth preserving, what does it matter if it needs a simple operation? Or, if one thinks it better that such a baby should not live on, what difference does it make that it happens to have an unobstructed intestinal tract? In either case, the matter of life and death is being decided on irrelevant grounds. It is the Down's syndrome, and not the intestines, that is the issue. The matter should be decided, if at all, on that basis, and not be allowed to depend on the essentially irrelevant question of whether the intestinal tract is blocked.

What makes this situation possible, of course, is the idea that when there is an intestinal blockage, one can "let the baby die," but when there is no such defect there is nothing that can be done, for one must not "kill" it. The fact that this idea leads to such results as deciding life or death on irrelevant grounds is another good reason why the doctrine should be rejected.

One reason why so many people think that there is an important moral difference between active and passive euthanasia is that they think killing someone is morally worse than letting someone die. But is it? Is

*Shaw A: "Doctor, Do We Have a Choice?" The New York Times Magazine, January 30, 1972, p 54

killing, in itself, worse than letting die? To investigate this issue, two cases may be considered that are exactly alike except that one involves killing whereas the other involves letting someone die. Then, it can be asked whether this difference makes any difference to the moral assessments. It is important that the cases be exactly alike, except for this one difference, since otherwise one cannot be confident that it is this difference and not some other that accounts for any variation in the assessments of the two cases. So, let us consider this pair of cases:

In the first, Smith stands to gain a large inheritance if anything should happen to his six-year-old cousin. One evening while the child is taking his bath, Smith sneaks into the bathroom and drowns the child, and then arranges things so that it will look like an accident.

In the second, Jones also stands to gain if anything should happen to his six-year-old cousin. Like Smith, Jones sneaks in planning to drown the child in his bath. However, just as he enters the bathroom Jones sees the child slip and hit his head, and fall face down in the water. Jones is delighted; he stands by, ready to push the child's head back under if it is necessary, but it is not necessary. With only a little thrashing about, the child drowns all by himself, "accidentally," as Jones watches and does nothing.

Now Smith killed the child, whereas Jones "merely" let the child die. That is the only difference between them. Did either man behave better, from a moral point of view? If the difference between killing and letting die were in itself a morally important matter, one should say that Jones's behavior was less reprehensible than Smith's. But does one really want to say that? I think not. In the first place, both men acted from the same motive, personal gain, and both had exactly the same end in view when they acted. It may be inferred from Smith's conduct that he is a bad man, although that judgment may be withdrawn or modified if certain further facts are learned about him—for example, that he is mentally deranged. But would not the very same thing be inferred about Jones from his conduct? And would not the same further considerations also be relevant to any modification of this judgment? Moreover, suppose Jones pleaded, in his own defense. "After all, I didn't do anything except just stand there and watch the child drown. I didn't kill him; I only let him die." Again, if letting die were in itself less bad than killing, this defense should have at least some weight. But it does not. Such a "defense" can only be regarded as a grotesque perversion of moral reasoning. Morally speaking, it is no defense at all.

Now, it may be pointed out, quite properly, that the cases of euthanasia with which doctors are concerned are not like this at all. They do not involve personal gain or the destruction of normal healthy children. Doctors are concerned only with cases in which the patient's life is of no further use to him, or in which the patient's life has become or will soon become a terrible burden. However, the point is the same in these cases: the bare difference between killing and letting die does not, in itself, make a moral difference. If a doctor lets a patient die, for humane reasons, he is in the same moral position as if he had given the patient a lethal injection for humane reasons. If his decision was wrong—if, for example, the patient's illness was in fact curable—the decision would be equally regrettable no matter which method was used to carry it out. And if the doctor's decision was the right one, the method used is not in itself important.

The AMA policy statement isolates the crucial issue very well; the crucial issue is "the intentional termination of the life of one human being by another." But after identifying this issue, and forbidding "mercy killing," the statement goes on to deny that the cessation of treatment is the intentional termination of a life. This is where the mistake comes in, for what is the cessation of treatment, in these circumstances, if it is not "the intentional termination of the life of one human being by another?" Of course it is exactly that, and if it were not, there would be no point to it.

Many people will find this judgment hard to accept. One reason, I think, is that it is very easy to conflate the question of whether killing is, in itself, worse than letting die, with the very different question of whether most actual cases of killing are more reprehensible than most actual cases of letting die. Most actual cases of killing are clearly terrible (think, for example, of all the murders reported in the newspapers), and one hears of such cases everyday. On the other hand, one hardly ever hears of a case of letting die, except for the actions of doctors who are motivated by humanitarian reasons. So one learns to think of killing in a much worse light than of letting die. But this does not mean that there is something about killing that makes it in itself worse than letting die, for it is not the bare difference between killing and letting die that makes the difference in these cases. Rather, the other factors—the murderer's motive of personal gain, for example, contrasted with the doctor's humanitarian motivation—account for different reactions to the different cases.

I have argued that killing is not in itself any worse than letting die; if my contention is right, it follows that active euthanasia is not any worse than passive euthanasia. What arguments can be given on the other side? The most common, I believe, is the following:

"The important difference between active and passive euthanasia is that, in passive euthanasia, the doctor does not do anything to bring about the patient's death. The doctor does nothing, and the patient dies of whatever ills already afflict him. In active euthanasia, however, the doctor does something to bring about the patient's death: he kills him.

The doctor who gives the patient with cancer a lethal injection has himself caused his patient's death; whereas if he merely ceases treatment, the cancer is the cause of the death.''

A number of points need to be made here. The first is that it is not exactly correct to say that in passive euthanasia the doctor does nothing, for he does do one thing that is very important: he lets the patient die. "Letting someone die" is certainly different, in some respects, from other types of action—mainly in that it is a kind of action that one may perform by way of not performing certain other actions. For example, one may let a patient die by way of not giving medication, just as one may insult someone by way of not shaking his hand. But for any purpose of moral assessment, it is a type of action nonetheless. The decision to let a patient die is subject to moral appraisal in the same way that a decision to kill him would be subject to moral appraisal: it may be assessed as wise or unwise, compassionate or sadistic, right or wrong. If a doctor deliberately let a patient die who was suffering from a routinely curable illness, the doctor would certainly be to blame for what he had done, just as he would be to blame if he had needlessly killed the patient. Charges against him would then be appropriate. If so, it would be no defense at all for him to insist that he didn't "do anything." He would have done something very serious indeed, for he let his patient die.

Fixing the cause of death may be very important from a legal point of view, for it may determine whether criminal charges are brought against the doctor. But I do not think that this notion can be used to show a moral difference between active and passive euthanasia. The reason why it is considered bad to be the cause of someone's death is that death is regarded as a great evil—and so it is. However, if it has been decided that euthanasia—even passive euthanasia—is desirable in a given case, it has also been decided that in this instance death is no greater an evil than the patient's continued existence. And if this is true, the usual reason for not wanting to be the cause of someone's death simply does not apply.

Finally, doctors may think that all of this is only of academic interest— the sort of thing that philosophers may worry about but that has no practical bearing on their own work. After all, doctors must be concerned about the legal consequences of what they do, and active euthanasia is clearly forbidden by the law. But even so, doctors should also be concerned with the fact that the law is forcing upon them a moral doctrine that may well be indefensible, and has a considerable effect on their practices. Of course, most doctors are not now in the position of being coerced in this matter, for they do not regard themselves as merely going along with what the law requires. Rather, in statements such as the AMA policy statement that I have quoted, they are endorsing this doctrine as a central point of medical ethics. In that statement, active euthanasia is condemned not merely as illegal but as "contrary to that for which the medical profession stands," whereas passive euthanasia is approved. However, the preceding considerations suggest that there is really no moral difference between the two, considered in themselves (there may be important moral differences in some cases in their *consequences*, but, as I pointed out, these differences may make active euthanasia, and not passive euthanasia, the morally preferable option). So, whereas doctors may have to discriminate between active and passive euthanasia to satisfy the law, they should not do any more than that. In particular, they should not give the distinction any added authority and weight by writing it into official statements of medical ethics.

*Source*: James Rachels, "Active and Passive Euthanasia," *The New England Journal of Medicine* 292 (January 9, 1975): 78–80. Copyright © 1975 Massachusetts Medical Society. All rights reserved.

* * *

Thirteen years later, another influential medical journal published the following anonymous article in its weekly column of opinion pieces. This piece provoked more than 150 letters. Some of the letters criticized the action described in the article, especially because the author seemed to act impulsively, without the patient's explicit agreement and with little knowledge of the patient's wishes or even her medical condition. Other letters criticized the journal for publishing the article. However, the piece fulfilled the goal of the journal's editors by opening discussion of a highly controversial subject.

## DOCUMENT 115: "It's Over, Debbie," Name Withheld by Request (1988)

The call came in the middle of the night. As a gynecology resident rotating through a large, private hospital, I had come to detest telephone calls, because invariably I would be up for several hours and would not feel good the next day. However, duty called, so I answered the phone. A nurse informed me that a patient was having difficulty getting rest, could I please see her. She was on 3 North. That was the gynecologic-oncology unit, not my usual duty station. As I trudged along, bumping sleepily against walls and corners and not believing I was up again, I tried to imagine what I might find at the end of my walk. Maybe an elderly woman with an anxiety reaction, or perhaps something particularly horrible.

I grabbed the chart from the nurses station on my way to the patient's room, and the nurse gave me some hurried details: a 20-year-old girl named Debbie was dying of ovarian cancer. She was having unrelenting vomiting apparently as the result of an alcohol drip administered for sedation. Hmmm, I thought. Very sad. As I approached the room I could hear loud, labored breathing. I entered and saw an emaciated, dark-haired woman who appeared much older than 20. She was receiving nasal oxygen, had an IV, and was sitting in bed suffering from what was obviously severe air hunger. The chart noted her weight at 80 pounds. A second woman, also dark-haired but of middle age, stood at her right, holding her hand. Both looked up as I entered. The room seemed filled with the patient's desperate effort to survive. Her eyes were hollow, and she had suprasternal and intercostal retractions with her rapid inspirations. She had not eaten or slept in two days. She had not responded to chemotherapy and was being given supportive care only. It was a gallows scene, a cruel mockery of her youth and unfulfilled potential. Her only words to me were, "Let's get this over with."

I retreated with my thoughts to the nurses station. The patient was tired and needed rest. I could not give her health, but I could give her rest. I asked the nurse to draw 20 mg of morphine sulfate into a syringe. Enough, I thought, to do the job. I took the syringe into the room and told the two women I was going to give Debbie something that would let her rest and to say good-bye. Debbie looked at the syringe, then laid her head on the pillow with her eyes open, watching what was left of the world. I injected the morphine intravenously and watched to see if my calculations on its effects would be correct. Within seconds her breathing slowed to a normal rate, her eyes closed, and her features softened as she seemed restful at last. The older woman stroked the hair of the now-sleeping patient. I waited for the inevitable next effect of depressing the respiratory drive. With clocklike certainty, within four minutes the breathing rates slowed even more, then became irregular, then ceased. The dark-haired woman stood erect and seemed relieved.

It's over, Debbie.

*Source*: Name Withheld by Request, "It's Over, Debbie," *Journal of the American Medical Association* 259 (1988): 272.

* * *

In a 1989 article discussing care of dying patients, ten of twelve prestigious physicians made the following radical statement; the other two dissociated themselves from it.

## DOCUMENT 116: "The Physician's Responsibility toward Hopelessly Ill Patients: A Second Look," Sidney H. Wanzer et al. (1989)

. . . it is not immoral for a physician to assist in the rational suicide of a terminally ill person. However, we recognize that such an act represents a departure from the principle of continually adjusted care that we have presented. As such, it should be considered a separate alternative and not an extension of the flexible approach to care that we have recommended. Clearly, the subject of assisted suicide deserves wide and open discussion.

*Source*: Sidney H. Wanzer, Daniel D. Federman, S. James Adelstein, Christine K. Cassel, Edwin H. Cassem, Ronald E. Cranford, Edward W. Hook, Bernard Lo, Charles G. Moertel, Peter Safar, Alan Stone, and Jan van Eys, "The Physician's Responsibility toward Hopelessly Ill Patients: A Second Look," *New England Journal of Medicine* 320 (1989): 844–849.

\* \* \*

More recently, a physician flouted the law and sympathetically described the circumstances under which he assisted in the suicide of his patient Diane.

## DOCUMENT 117: "Death and Dignity: A Case of Individualized Decision Making," Timothy E. Quill (1991)

DIANE was feeling tired and had a rash. A common scenario, though there was something subliminally worrisome that prompted me to check her blood count. Her hematocrit was 22, and the white-cell count was 4.3 with some metamyelocytes and unusual white cells. I wanted it to be viral, trying to deny what was staring me in the face. Perhaps in a repeated count it would disappear. I called Diane and told her it might be more serious than I had initially thought—that the test needed to be repeated and that if she felt worse, we might have to move quickly. When she pressed for the possibilities, I reluctantly opened the door to leukemia. Hearing the word seemed to make it exist. "Oh, shit!" she said. "Don't tell me that." Oh, shit! I thought, I wish I didn't have to.

Diane was no ordinary person (although no one I have ever come to know has been really ordinary). She was raised in an alcoholic family and had felt alone for much of her life. She had vaginal cancer as a young woman. Through much of her adult life, she had struggled with depression and her own alcoholism. I had come to know, respect, and admire her over the previous eight years as she confronted these problems and gradually overcame them. She was an incredibly clear, at times brutally honest, thinker and communicator. As she took control of her life, she developed a strong sense of independence and confidence. In the previous 3 ½ years, her hard work had paid off. She was completely abstinent from alcohol, she had established much deeper connections with her husband, college-age son, and several friends, and her business and her artistic work were blossoming. She felt she was really living fully for the first time.

Not surprisingly, the repeated blood count was abnormal, and detailed examination of the peripheral-blood smear showed myelocytes. I advised her to come into the hospital, explaining that we needed to do a bone marrow biopsy and make some decisions relatively rapidly. She came to the hospital knowing what we would find. She was terrified, angry, and sad. Although we knew the odds, we both clung to the thread of possibility that it might be something else.

The bone marrow confirmed the worst: acute myelomonocytic leukemia. In the face of this tragedy, we looked for signs of hope. This is an area of medicine in which technological intervention has been successful, with cures 25 percent of the time—long-term cures. As I probed the costs of these cures, I heard about induction chemotherapy (three weeks in the hospital, prolonged neutropenia, probable infectious complications, and hair loss; 75 percent of patients respond, 25 percent do not). For the survivors, this is followed by consolidation chemotherapy (with similar side effects; another 25 percent die, for a net survival of 50 percent). Those still alive, to have a reasonable chance of long-term survival, then need bone marrow transplantation (hospitalization for two months and whole-body irradiation, with complete killing of the bone marrow, infectious complications, and the possibility for graft-versus-host disease— with a survival of approximately 50 percent, or 25 percent of the original group). Though hematologists may argue over the exact percentages, they don't argue about the outcome of no treatment—certain death in days, weeks, or at most a few months.

Believing that delay was dangerous, our oncologist broke the news to Diane and began making plans to insert a Hickman catheter and begin induction chemotherapy that afternoon. When I saw her shortly thereafter, she was enraged at his presumption that she would want treatment, and devastated by the finality of the diagnosis. All she wanted to do was go home and be with her family. She had no further questions about treatment and in fact had decided that she wanted none. Together we lamented her tragedy and the unfairness of life. Before she left, I felt the need to be sure that she and her husband understood that there was some risk in delay, that the problem was not going to go away, and that we needed to keep considering the options over the next several days. We agreed to meet in two days.

She returned in two days with her husband and son. They had talked extensively about the problem and the options. She remained very clear about her wish not to undergo chemotherapy and to live whatever time she had left outside the hospital. As we explored her thinking further, it became clear that she was convinced she would die during the period of treatment and would suffer unspeakably in the process (from hospitalization, from lack of control over her body, from the side effects of chemotherapy, and from pain and anguish). Although I could offer support and my best effort to minimize her suffering if she chose treatment, there was no way I could say any of this would not occur. In fact, the last four patients with acute leukemia at our hospital had died very painful deaths in the hospital during various stages of treatment (a fact I did not share with her). Her family wished she would choose treatment but sadly accepted her decision. She articulated very clearly that it was she who would be experiencing all the side effects of treatment and that odds of 25 percent were not good enough for her to undergo so toxic a course of therapy, given her expectations of chemotherapy and hospitalization and the absence of a closely matched bone marrow donor. I had her repeat her understanding of the treatment, the odds, and what to expect if there were no treatment. I clarified a few misunderstandings, but she had a remarkable grasp of the options and implications.

I have been a longtime advocate of active, informed patient choice of treatment or nontreatment, and of a patient's right to die with as much control and dignity as possible. Yet there was something about her giving up a 25 percent chance of long-term survival in favor of almost certain death that disturbed me. I had seen Diane fight and use her considerable inner resources to overcome alcoholism and depression, and I half expected her to change her mind over the next week. Since the window of time in which effective treatment can be initiated is rather narrow, we met several times that week. We obtained a second hematology consultation and talked at length about the meaning and implications of treatment and nontreatment. She talked to a psychologist she had seen in the past. I gradually understood the decision from her perspective and became convinced that it was the right decision for her. We arranged for home hospice care (although at that time Diane felt reasonably well, was active, and looked healthy), left the door open for her to change her mind, and tried to anticipate how to keep her comfortable in the time she had left.

Just as I was adjusting to her decision, she opened up another area that would stretch me profoundly. It was extraordinarily important to Diane to maintain control of herself and her own dignity during the time remaining to her. When this was no longer possible, she clearly wanted to die. As a former director of a hospice program, I know how to use pain medicines to keep patients comfortable and lessen suffering. I explained the philosophy of comfort care, which I strongly believe in. Although Diane understood and appreciated this, she had known of people lingering in what was called relative comfort, and she wanted no part of it. When the time came, she wanted to take her life in the least painful way possible. Knowing of her desire for independence and her decision to stay in control, I thought this request made perfect sense. I acknowledged and explored this wish but also thought that it was out of the realm of currently accepted medical practice and that it was more than I could offer or promise. In our discussion, it became clear that preoccupation with her fear of a lingering death would interfere with Diane's getting the most out of the time she had left until she found a safe way to ensure her death. I feared the effects of a violent death on her family, the consequences of an ineffective suicide that would leave her lingering in precisely the state she dreaded so much, and the possibility that a family member would be forced to assist her, with all the legal and personal repercussions that would follow. She discussed this at length with her family. They believed that they should respect her choice. With this in mind, I told Diane that information was available from the Hemlock Society that might be helpful to her.

A week later she phoned me with a request for barbiturates for sleep. Since I knew that this was an essential ingredient in a Hemlock Society suicide, I asked her to come to the office to talk things over. She was more than willing to protect me by participating in a superficial conversation about her insomnia, but it was important to me to know how she planned to use the drugs and to be sure that she was not in despair or overwhelmed in a way that might color her judgment. In our discussion, it was apparent that she was having trouble sleeping, but it was also evident that the security of having enough barbiturates available to commit suicide when and if the time came would leave her secure enough to live fully and concentrate on the present. It was clear that she was not despondent and that in fact she was making deep, personal connections with her family and close friends. I made sure that she knew how to use the barbiturates for sleep, and also that she knew the amount needed to commit suicide. We agreed to meet regularly, and she promised to meet with me before taking her life, to ensure that all other avenues had been exhausted. I wrote the prescription with an uneasy feeling about the boundaries I was exploring—spiritual, legal, professional, and personal. Yet I also felt strongly that I was setting her free to get the most out of the time she had left, and to maintain dignity and control on her own terms until her death.

The next several months were very intense and important for Diane. Her son stayed home from college, and they were able to be with one another and say much that had not been said earlier. Her husband did his work at home so that he and Diane could spend more time together. She spent time with her closest friends. I had her come into the hospital for a conference with our residents, at which she illustrated in a most profound and personal way the importance of informed decision making, the right to refuse treatment, and the extraordinarily personal effects of illness and interaction with the medical system. There were emotional and physical hardships as well. She had periods of intense sadness and anger. Several times she became very weak, but she received transfusions as an outpatient and responded with marked improvement of symptoms. She had two serious infections that responded surprisingly well to empirical courses of oral antibiotics. After three tumultuous months, there were two weeks of relative calm and well-being, and fantasies of a miracle began to surface.

Unfortunately, we had no miracle. Bone pain, weakness, fatigue, and fevers began to dominate her life. Although the hospice workers, family members, and I tried our best to minimize the suffering and promote comfort, it was clear that the end was approaching. Diane's immediate future held what she feared the most—increasing discomfort, dependence, and hard choices between pain and sedation. She called up her closest friends and asked them to come over to say goodbye, telling them that she would be leaving soon. As we had agreed, she let me know as well. When we met, it was clear that she knew what she was doing, that she was sad and frightened to be leaving, but that she would be even more terrified to stay and suffer. In our tearful goodbye, she promised a reunion in the future at her favorite spot on the edge of Lake Geneva, with dragons swimming in the sunset.

Two days later her husband called to say that Diane had died. She had said her final goodbyes to her husband and son that morning, and asked them to leave her alone for an hour. After an hour, which must have seemed an eternity, they found her on the couch, lying very still and covered by her favorite shawl. There was no sign of struggle. She seemed to be at peace. They called me for advice about how to proceed. When I arrived at their house, Diane indeed seemed peaceful. Her husband and son were quiet. We talked about what a remarkable person she had been. They seemed to have no doubts about the course she had chosen or about their cooperation, although the unfairness of her illness and the finality of her death were overwhelming to us all.

I called the medical examiner to inform him that a hospice patient had died. When asked about the cause of death, I said, "acute leukemia." He said that was fine and that we should call a funeral director. Although acute leukemia was the truth, it was not the whole story. Yet any mention of suicide would have given rise to a police investigation and probably brought the arrival of an ambulance crew for resuscitation. Diane would have become a "coroner's case," and the decision to perform an autopsy would have been made at the discretion of the medical examiner. The family or I could have been subject to criminal prosecution, and I to professional review, for our roles in support of Diane's choices. Although I truly believe that the family and I gave her the best care possible, allowing her to define her limits and directions as much as possible, I am not sure the law, society, or the medical profession would agree. So I said "acute leukemia" to protect all of us, to protect Diane from an invasion into her past and her body, and to continue to shield society from the knowledge of the degree of suffering that people often undergo in the process of dying. Suffering can be lessened to some extent, but in no way eliminated or made benign, by the careful intervention of a competent, caring physician, given current social constraints.

Diane taught me about the range of help I can provide if I know people well and if I allow them to say what they really want. She taught me about life, death, and honesty and about taking charge and facing tragedy squarely when it strikes. She taught me that I can take small risks for people that I really know and care about. Although I did not assist in her suicide directly, I helped indirectly to make it possible, successful, and relatively painless. Although I know we have measures to help control pain and lessen suffering, to think that people do not suffer in the process of dying is an illusion. Prolonged dying can occasionally be peaceful, but more often the role of the physician and family is limited to lessening but not eliminating severe suffering.

I wonder how many families and physicians secretly help patients over the edge into death in the face of such severe suffering. I wonder how many severely ill or dying patients secretly take their lives, dying alone in despair. I wonder whether the image of Diane's final aloneness will persist in the minds of her family, or if they will remember more the intense, meaningful months they had together before she died. I wonder whether Diane struggled in that last hour, and whether the Hemlock Society's way of death by suicide is the most benign. I wonder why Diane, who gave so much to so many of us, had to be alone for the last hour of her life. I wonder whether I will see Diane again, on the shore of Lake Geneva at sunset, with dragons swimming on the horizon.

* * *

In another publication, Quill described the reasons for his action as well as its aftermath.

---

## DOCUMENT 118: *Death and Dignity: Making Choices and Taking Charge*, Timothy E. Quill (1993)

---

My intention in publishing the article . . . was to challenge the medical profession to take a more personal, in-depth look at end-of-life suffering. Previously published cases involving physician-assisted deaths were either anonymous or so extreme that they could be relatively easily dismissed by the medical profession. Consideration of the issue by medical ethicists tended to be abstract and intellectual, minimizing the anguish faced by many dying patients and their families. From my work as a hospice consultant and as a personal physician, I knew that untreatable suffering prior to death is unfortunately not rare. I also knew from confidential discussions that other physicians have secretly assisted patients of their own to die under similar circumstances. Being a physician in the established academic mainstream of medicine, I believed that my presentation of this real experience would be difficult for the profession to dismiss. Given the compelling nature of Diane's request, I felt that the article illustrated as much about careful, patient-centered decision making as it did about the physician's potential role in compassionately assisting death.

After the article was published, I received an unwanted education as to how our legal system both works and doesn't work, and how it is influenced by political forces. Although I intended to challenge the profession of medicine, I underestimated the extent to which the general public and the legal system would become interested and involved. Diane's identity was eventually discovered. Her family and I were harassed by the media and enmeshed in the criminal justice system. Diane's body, which she had generously donated to science, was located and subjected to an unwanted, meaningless autopsy to confirm the presence of a lethal amount of medication. The criminal charges considered against me ranged from tampering with public records to manslaughter, and endless newspaper articles recited the potential outcome (though remote) of fifteen years in jail. The case was finally presented to a grand jury, which determined that my actions did not warrant prosecution. The New York State Health Department also reviewed the case; it subsequently found no evidence of professional misconduct and recommended that the New York State Task Force on Life and the Law review the overall subject.

Although I have several misgivings about how the legal investigation unfolded and was to some extent driven by the media, the only regret I have about the care which I gave to Diane herself is that she was alone at her death. The case was dismissed by the grand jury in part because of this tragic fact. Diane had requested to be by herself at the end, but I believe she did so to protect her family and me from potential prosecution should her act be discovered. Diane was a brave person who faced death squarely, but it violates every principle of humane care of the dying if she felt she had to be alone at the end because of our laws. As a physician, I make a solemn promise to my dying patients that I will not abandon them no matter where their illness may take them. Ironically, had I been with Diane at her death, the outcome of the grand jury hearing might have been different.

In the aftermath of my article, I have received over two thousand remarkable letters, many of which contained moving personal stories. People I had known as friends or as patients for years now told me of their experiences, as well as their hopes and fears about their own death. Many who had anguished over the death of a beloved friend or family member now felt that they could share with me what had previously been kept secret. Indignity at the end of life has touched so many, and the stories are so plentiful and profound, that I now believe the problem to be deeper and more common than I originally anticipated. I also believe that if change is to occur, it will be driven by the stories and passions of these witnesses. Firsthand experience with such tragedy makes one more fearful of a difficult death, and also wary of a profession that does not openly acknowledge or respond to its possibility.

*Source*: Timothy E. Quill, *Death and Dignity: Making Choices and Taking Charge* (New York and London: W. W. Norton, 1993), 20–22.

* * *

A number of surveys of physicians' attitudes toward physician-assisted suicide have been carried out recently. In a study carried out in Michigan, 40 percent of physicians supported legalization of assisted suicide, 37 percent preferred no government regulation, 17 percent favored prohibition, and 5 percent were uncertain (Jerald G. Bachman, Kirsten H. Akser, David J. Doukas et al., "Attitudes of Michigan Physicians and the Public toward Legalizing Physician-assisted Suicide and

Voluntary Euthanasia," *The New England Journal of Medicine* 334 [1996]: 303). Doctors who were religiously committed were much less likely to support legalization or to consider personal involvement with assisted suicide. Another study asked about euthanasia as well as assisted suicide.

---

## DOCUMENT 119: "Physician-assisted Suicide and Euthanasia in Washington State," Anthony L. Back et al. (1996)

**Results.**—In the past year, 12% of responding physicians received one or more explicit requests for physician-assisted suicide, and 4% received one or more requests for euthanasia. . . . The diagnoses most often associated with requests were cancer, neurological disease, and the acquired immunodeficiency syndrome (AIDS). The patient concerns most often perceived by physicians were worries about loss of control, being a burden, being dependent on others for personal care, and loss of dignity. Physicians provided assistance more often to patients with physical symptoms. Physicians infrequently sought advice from colleagues. Of 156 patients who requested physician-assisted suicide, 38 (24%) received prescriptions, and 21 of these died as a result. Of 58 patients who requested euthanasia, 14 (24%) received parenteral medication and died.

*Source*: Anthony L. Back, Jeffrey I. Wallace, Helene E. Starks, and Robert A. Pearlman, "Physician-assisted Suicide and Euthanasia in Washington State: Patient Requests and Physician Responses," *Journal of the American Medical Association* 275 (1996): 919–925. Excerpt from the Abstract.

*    *    *

A national study determined that under the present conditions, 11 percent of physicians would be willing to assist in a patient's suicide by prescribing medication, and 7 percent would administer a lethal injection if asked. If assisted suicide were legal, 36 percent of the respondents would be willing to comply. Since entering practice, 18.3 percent of the physicians had had a request for assisting in a suicide, and 16 percent of those who had received such a request (3.3 percent of the sample) had complied with it (Diane E. Meier, Carol-Ann Emmons, Sylvan Wallenstein et al., "A National Survey of Physician-assisted Suicide and Euthanasia in the United States," *New England Journal of Medicine* 338 [1998]: 1193–1201). The senior author of this national study presented her reasons for changing her mind about the desirability of legalizing physician-assisted suicide in the *New York Times*.

---

## DOCUMENT 120: "A Change of Heart on Assisted Suicide," Diane E. Meier (April 24, 1998)

---

A recent survey, which I co-wrote, found that doctors are often asked by their patients for help in dying, but seldom honor these requests.

Some years ago, I believed that doctor-assisted suicide should be legalized and that terminally ill people in great pain deserved more control over the circumstances of their death.

It is true that terminally ill patients sometimes find themselves in truly unbearable circumstances. But after caring for many patients myself, I now think that the risks of assisted suicide outweigh the benefits.

Proponents of doctor-assisted suicide say that strict regulations can reduce the chances of abuse and protect the most vulnerable from feeling coerced. But rules would be difficult, if not impossible, to enforce. For instance, Oregon, the only state to legalize assisted suicide, has guidelines that mandate the following:

• *A patient must be mentally alert.* It is the rare dying patient, particularly if elderly, who remains consistently capable of rational deliberation about medical alternatives. Intermittent confusion, anxiety and depression are the rule rather than the exception, inevitably clouding judgment.

• *A patient must be within six months of death.* Abundant evidence shows that accurately predicting when patients are going to die doesn't become possible until just days before death. The guidelines assume that such a prognosis is possible and deny the uncertainty inherent in such predictions.

• *A doctor must certify that the patient's decision is not coerced.* This is an impossible task, given the financial and other burdens that seriously ill patients pose to their families. Indeed, legalizing assisted suicide is coercive in and of itself. Society would no longer promote the value of each life, and instead sanction an expedient death rather than continued care and support.

The push to legalize doctor-assisted suicide could not come at a worse time. Spiraling health costs and our aging population have led to radical changes in how care is financed, with doctors and hospitals rewarded for doing less for their patients. Seriously ill people need help easing their pain, time to talk to their doctor, answers to their questions and reasonable attempts to prolong their life when death is not imminent.

If this kind of care were available to every patient, it would certainly reduce, if not eliminate, the desire for a hastened death. But legalizing assisted suicide would become a cheap and easy way to avoid the costly and time-intensive care needed by the terminally ill. It could be seen as an appealing alternative when resources are stretched and family members and doctors are exhausted. The terminally ill patient could feel subtle and not-so-subtle pressure to opt for suicide. Our society should not be reduced to offering patients a choice between inadequate care and suicide.

The proposed guidelines for assisted suicide are well-meaning, but unrealistic and largely irrelevant to the reality faced by the dying. While I have had patients whose desire to die was compelling and understandable, such patients are few. The distress of the last days, when it occurs, can be effectively treated with analgesics and sedatives. Although we have the knowledge and tools to reduce suffering near the end of life, we are debating instead whether it should be legal for doctors to hasten death.

*Source*: Diane E. Meier, "A Change of Heart on Assisted Suicide," *New York Times*, April 24, 1998, A27.

* * *

The American Medical Association, the organization to which a majority of physicians belong, is strongly opposed to physician-assisted suicide.

## DOCUMENT 121: Recommendations of the Council on Ethical and Judicial Affairs, American Medical Association (1993)

1. Physician assisted suicide is fundamentally inconsistent with the physician's professional role.

2. It is critical that the medical profession redouble its efforts to ensure that dying patients are provided optimal treatment for their pain and other discomfort. The use of more aggressive comfort care measures, including greater reliance on hospice care, can alleviate the physical and emotional suffering that dying patients experience. Evaluation and treatment by a health professional with expertise in the psychiatric aspects of terminal illness can often alleviate the suffering that leads a patient to desire assisted suicide.

3. Physicians must resist the natural tendency to withdraw physically and emotionally from their terminally ill patients. When the treatment goals for a patient in the end stages of a terminal illness shift from cu-

rative efforts to comfort care, the level of physician involvement in the patient's care should in no way decrease.

4. Requests for physician-assisted suicide should be a signal to the physician that the patient's needs are unmet and further evaluation to identify the elements contributing to the patient's suffering is necessary. Multidisciplinary intervention, including specialty consultation, pastoral care, family counseling and other modalities, should be sought as clinically indicated.

5. Further efforts to educate physicians about advanced pain management techniques, both at the undergraduate and graduate levels, are necessary to overcome any shortcomings in this area. Physicians should recognize that courts and regulatory bodies readily distinguish between use of narcotic drugs to relieve pain in dying patients and use in other situations.

*Source*: Council on Ethical and Judicial Affairs, American Medical Association, Recommendations, December 1993, published as Report 59 in *Code of Medical Ethics* 4 (1994): 274.

* * *

### Public Opinion about Physician-assisted Suicide and Euthanasia

A poll of 1,103 adults conducted by the *Washington Post* in March 1996 indicated that 51 percent of adults favored legalization of physician-assisted suicide and 40 percent were opposed. Individuals more likely to favor legal assisted suicide were better off financially and better educated. Those individuals most opposed were blacks, people with incomes less than $15,000, and individuals over seventy years of age.

Three polls conducted by the Gallup Organization asked, "When a person has a disease that cannot be cured, do you think doctors should be allowed by law to end the patient's life by some painless means if the patient and his family request it?" Affirmative answers were received from 53 percent of those asked in 1973, whereas the numbers were 75 percent in 1990 and 69 percent in 1996. Other polls also showed that support for euthanasia increased (Document 122, Figure 1). Figure 2 in Document 122 shows the age distribution and religious affiliations of those who supported physician aid in ending the lives of patients with incurable diseases.

## DOCUMENT 122: "Should Physicians Aid Patients in Dying?" Robert J. Blendon, Ulrike S. Szalay, and Richard A. Knox (1992)

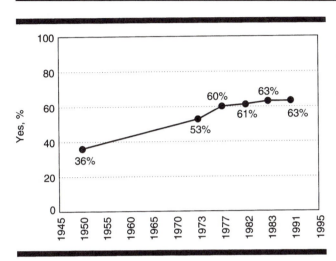

Figure 1. Should euthanasia be legalized? Question: When a person has a disease that cannot be cured, do you think doctors should be allowed by law to end the patient's life if the patient and his or her family request it?

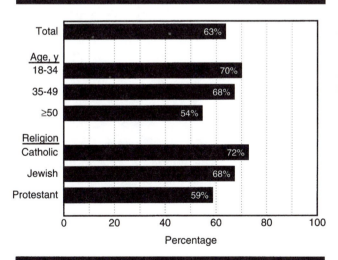

Figure 2. Support for legalizing physician aid in ending lives of patients with incurable diseases, by age and religion.

*Source*: Robert J. Blendon, Ulrike S. Szalay, and Richard A Knox, "Should Physicians Aid Their Patients in Dying?" *Journal of the American Medical Association* 267 (1992): 2658–2662.

\* \* \*

### Attitudes of Religious Groups about Assisted Suicide

Although polls indicate that a majority of individuals with religious affiliations favor physician-assisted suicide, many, though not all, organized Western religions disapprove of assisted suicide. For example, the Southern Baptists, who, with over 15 million members, form the largest Protestant denomination, passed the following resolution at their convention in June 1996.

## DOCUMENT 123: Resolution on Assisted Suicide of the Southern Baptist Convention (June 1996)

WHEREAS, Two U.S. Circuit Courts of Appeals have voted for the first time in American history to strike down laws prohibiting physician assisted suicide; and

WHEREAS, Michigan courts have consistently acquitted Dr. Jack Kevorkian of any criminal wrong-doing in assisting individuals to end their own lives by suicide; and

WHEREAS, A University of Pennsylvania survey recently found that 20 percent of nurses polled had performed euthanasia or assisted in the suicide of a patient; and

WHEREAS, Western medicine has heretofore followed both the Judeo-Christian tradition and the over 2500 year-old Hippocratic tradition forbidding physicians to assist in the death of their patients; and

WHEREAS, The Bible teaches that God created all human life in His own image and declares human life to be sacred from conception until natural death (Genesis 1:29:6ff); and

WHEREAS, The Bible likewise teaches that murder, including self-murder, is immoral (Exodus 20:13); and

WHEREAS, American society seems to be embracing of the "culture of death"; Now, therefore,

BE IT RESOLVED, That we the messengers of the Southern Baptist Convention, meeting in New Orleans, Louisiana, June 11–13, 1996, affirm the biblical and Hippocratic prohibitions against assisted suicide; and

BE IT FURTHER RESOLVED, That we commend and encourage medical science in its efforts to improve pain management techniques, thus removing one major impetus toward assisted dying; and

BE IT FURTHER RESOLVED, That we call upon physicians, nurses, hospice workers, individual Christians and local churches to make emotional, psychological, and spiritual care of suffering patients a priority, thereby relieving the sense of isolation and abandonment some dying patients feel; and

BE IT FURTHER RESOLVED, That we vigorously denounce assisted suicide as an appropriate means of treating suffering; and

BE IT FINALLY RESOLVED, That we call upon federal, state, and local governments to prosecute under the law physicians or others who practice assisted suicide.

*Source*: Resolution on assisted suicide adopted by the Southern Baptist Convention, New Orleans, Louisiana, June 11–13, 1996.

\* \* \*

### Recommendation of the New York State Task Force on Life and the Law

The New York State Task Force on Life and the Law is a body appointed in 1985 by Governor Mario M. Cuomo to develop recommendations for public policy in New York State in the form of proposed legislation, regulations, public education, and other measures arising from recent medical advances. Their most recent recommendations related to the legalization of assisted suicide.

## DOCUMENT 124: Executive Summary of "When Death Is Sought," New York State Task Force on Life and the Law (May 1994)

Over the past two decades, the right to decide about medical treatment, including the right to refuse life-sustaining measures, has become a fundamental tenet of American law. The Task Force has sought to make this right a reality for the citizens of New York State, recommending legislation on do-not-resuscitate orders, health care proxies, and, most recently, surrogate decision making for patients without capacity. The Task Force's legislative proposals reflect a deep respect for individual autonomy as well as concern for the welfare of individuals nearing the end of life.

Recent proposals to legalize assisted suicide and euthanasia in some states would transform the right to decide about medical treatment into a far broader right to control the timing and manner of death. After lengthy deliberations, the Task Force unanimously concluded that the dangers of such a dramatic change in public policy would far outweigh any possible benefits. In light of the pervasive failure of our health care system to treat pain and diagnose and treat depression, legalizing assisted suicide and euthanasia would be profoundly dangerous for many individuals who are ill and vulnerable. The risks would be most severe for those who are elderly, poor, socially disadvantaged, or without access to good medical care.

In the course of their research, many Task Force members were particularly struck by the degree to which requests for suicide assistance by terminally ill patients are correlated with clinical depression or unmanaged pain, both of which can ordinarily be treated effectively with current medical techniques. As a society, we can do far more to benefit these patients by improving pain relief and palliative care than by changing the law to make it easier to commit suicide or to obtain a lethal injection.

*Source*: New York State Task Force on Life and the Law "When Death Is Sought: Assisted Suicide and Euthanasia in the Medical Context," May 1994. Executive Summary.

---

## DOCUMENT 125: Statement of the National Legislative Council of the American Association of Retired Persons (AARP) (1997)

After careful consideration, our National Legislative Council recommends to the Board of Directors of the AARP that it not take a position on physician-assisted suicide. The Council concluded that this intensely personal issue is one about which each individual should make his or her own decision.

*Source: Modern Maturity*, November–December 1997, 92.

* * *

### Attitudes of the Disabled toward Assisted Suicide

Although a Harris poll in 1995 showed that 66 percent of people with disabilities supported the right to assisted suicide, a number of disabled individuals in several organizations strongly oppose the legalization of assisted suicide, expressing serious concern that disabled individuals might be pressured into choosing suicide. Over 200 of these disabled persons demonstrated in front of the Supreme Court building when the Court was hearing the important New York and Washington cases about legalizing assisted suicide in January 1997. A debate between two disabled individuals with opposing viewpoints was published in 1997.

---

## DOCUMENT 126: "Death Do Us Part," Paul Longmore and Andrew Batavia (1997)

---

The confrontation was polite—even respectful—but it was undeniably a clash of adversaries.

Paul Longmore, an associate professor at San Francisco State University, is one of the disability community's most outspoken opponents of legalized assisted suicide. Andrew Batavia of Miami Beach, Fla., is a well-known attorney and health and disability policy expert who favors legalization.

Longmore had polio and uses a ventilator; Batavia is a C2–3 quadriplegic from a spinal cord injury. Both frame the assisted suicide issue in terms of disability rights; both are highly articulate spokesmen.

In a February 3, 1997, conference call, Longmore and Batavia debated physician-assisted suicide for NEW MOBILITY readers. The occasion was their first meeting, and was both improbable and inevitable. Their views are worlds apart, yet the vital importance of the issue demands that adversaries talk.

The discussion began with a question: Can a request by a disabled person for a physician's assistance in dying be seen as a rational and uncoerced choice?

**Paul Longmore:** Historically, when people with disabilities have wanted a physician's help in ending their lives, courts have automatically assumed that first, they were acting in response to their disability alone and second, it was a reasonable thing to want to die. Whereas, for somebody who is not disabled, the automatic response is to try to help the person and solve the problems. This happens to people with disabilities even when it's made clear that there are all sorts of societal factors that have brought the person to this point.

**Andrew Batavia**: I understand that people with disabilities have always been devalued and we need to rectify that. Certainly, we need to educate the public and the medical community. But I feel that the individual should be able to make the decision. In the context of the Supreme Court case being considered now, we're talking about the right of competent, terminally ill individuals to end their lives. These people are suffering, they're in the last few months of their lives, and there's no reason that the state should interfere. Their decisions have to be respected as rational.

## FOR WHOM? BY WHOM?

**AB**: When it comes to terminally ill individuals, I strongly support their right to physician assistance in dying. The state's interest in denying this right is very, very small and the individual's interest in ending suffering is very great. I have a greater concern once you get beyond the terminal condition, for the reasons Paul states, but ultimately I would support the right of states to give all individuals—including people with disabilities—that right.

**PL**: The right to end their lives, or the right to end their lives with a physician's help? Physician assistance is the key difference here.

**AB**: I would certainly support their right to end their lives. But once you start bringing in the apparatus of the medical community, I have some reservations about coercion. I do think state law could have protections built into it. If, for example, non-terminal people with disabilities were required to make the decision to die several times over an extended period of time to several different individuals, I would support that. But in terms of constitutionalizing the right—and thereby preventing states from denying it—I would limit it to competent, terminally ill individuals.

**PL**: The safeguards being proposed seem awfully flimsy and inadequate to me. I appreciate the fact that you want to limit assisted suicide to competent, terminally ill people, but so do many other proponents of legalization. The first problem is that there are many people in the right-to-die movement—including the Hemlock Society—who have made it very clear that they want to extend assisted suicide to people with disabilities. Second, there are already court cases in which judges have ruled that if a person with a disability makes this request, it's not suicide. It's refusal of medical treatment. . . .

**AB**: They wanted to terminate the use of their respirators—which is suicide for all practical purposes. And they should have the right to do that.

**PL**: But I find it ironic that, on the one hand, proponents of legalization are arguing that doctors can't be trusted because they too often want to compel people to live. The experience of people with disabilities is directly opposite to that. And then they want doctors to both determine eligibility and carry it out—the same doctors who are currently under tremendous pressure from the managed care revolution to ration health care to people who are regarded as costly. . . .

## SOCIETAL OPPRESSION

**PL**: Part of the disagreement we have is our analysis of the general situation and condition of people with disabilities. I think that we live in a society that is deeply prejudiced against us, and that we are an oppressed minority.

**AB**: I have major problems with this notion of societal oppression and how that somehow precludes an individual from making a rational choice. The fact is that there are a multitude of ways in which our society doesn't fully meet the needs of people with disabilities, but I find it extremely dangerous to say that, for that reason, disabled people shouldn't be able to make fundamental choices about their lives. If a state tells me I can't end my life if I'm terminally ill, the state is oppressing me.

**PL**: It's one thing to make fundamental choices; it's another thing to have the society that's oppressing us set up mechanisms to facilitate our suicides. Any society that would guarantee assistance in committing suicide by an oppressed person is simply indicating just how oppressive and hypocritical it is.

**AB**: There are some fascists out there, but overall, I don't think that's accurate at all. I believe that we'll end up with a better health care system and a more responsible society if people are given their rights to autonomy over their lives.

**PL**: I'm not worried about the fascists, I'm worried about a health care system that is profit-driven and is trying to ration health care. And I think it's naive to think that a health care system that is becoming *more* profit-driven and *more* unjust is somehow going to become more fair and equitable because the people the system is trying to deny care to are granted the right to end their lives more quickly.

**AB**: People with terminal illnesses and people with disabilities, once they have this right, are going to shout out loud that this system stinks! And I think the press will pick up on that and ultimately there will be strong political pressures to improve the system.

**PL**: We've been shouting for a long time, and we've been ignored.

**AB**: The disability rights movement is not about complaining about oppression. It's about empowering individuals to do what they want to do. You're right that our society is far from perfect, you're right that we need to improve programs and policies; but if you cry about oppression all the time, any respect that we've won over the years is going to dissipate. It's a damn shame. I believe that the protest in front of the Supreme Court set the disability rights movement back 10 years, it was so pathetic. People were screaming, "Please don't kill me, please don't kill me."

**PL**: No, they weren't saying, "Please don't kill me." They were saying, "We're going to fight against people who are so bigoted they think that we're better off dead."

**AB**: I was there on those steps, and I can assure you the message was not empowering. I refuse to consider myself oppressed and I do believe that I can make autonomous choices. And if I were terminally ill, I would be deeply offended if the state were to tell me that I could not, with the assistance of my physician, end my life. Don't take away my rights by virtue of your notion of oppression.

### PERSONAL DECISIONS

**AB**: When I was paralyzed 23 years ago, it gave me a lot of peace of mind knowing that if things got bad enough, if I didn't want to keep on living, then I could make that decision. Let me ask you Paul. If you were terminally ill, wouldn't you want to be able to make this choice for yourself?

**PL**: I'm not sure what I'd do if I were terminally ill. I know that my experience as a person with a disability would make me very concerned that doctors and others would want to hurry me into death as quickly as possible. And it might be very hard for me to get appropriate health care and pain management and palliative care and psychological support services and insurance to cover all that.

**AB**: That's not my experience as a person with a disability, and it doesn't address my question. Ultimately, wouldn't you want to be able to make the choice?

**PL**: What I want is for the state to guarantee me adequate health care in all its forms. What kind of a society would give me the right to die as the *first* right it guarantees, when it hasn't been willing to guarantee these other rights? Could I really trust a society like that to fairly and justly administer a right to physician-assisted suicide? I don't think so.

*Source*: Paul Longmore and Andrew Batavia, "Death Do Us Part," *New Mobility*, April 1997, 48–51.

\* \* \*

## Arguments Against Legalizing Assisted Suicide

Some opponents of legalizing physician-assisted suicide and euthanasia believe that intentionally causing the death of someone, even
one who is dying, is morally unacceptable. Others believe that assisting
suicide is counter to the medical ethos of healing. Opponents are also
concerned about the feasibility of regulating assisted suicide. There is
concern that legalizing physician-assisted suicide would start the nation down a slippery slope that could weaken the criteria for permitting
assisted suicide, allow societal pressures to lead individuals with irreversible illness to choose assisted suicide, and even lead to involuntary
euthanasia. The following document deals with some of these concerns.

---

## DOCUMENT 127: "Self-Extinction: The Morality of the Helping Hand," Daniel Callahan (1997)

. . . Our common moral intuition that suicide is ordinarily an act of
desperation, that it usually bespeaks some degree of treatable depression,
and that it ought not to be encouraged, strikes me as entirely valid. It is
a way to defend ourselves, and help others defend us, from the despair
that life can bring our way; and it is generally recognized that we need
to help each other cope with it, not succumb to it. To give a physician,
moreover, the power to kill another, even with the permission of that
person, or to assist someone to kill himself is to place too much power
in the physician's hands, that of a right to take life as a means of eliminating despair. . . .

Quite apart from that argument, however, do I not here confuse and
conflate euthanasia and PAS [physician-assisted suicide]? After all, in
PAS the physician does not kill at all. It is the patient who is the direct
cause and agent of death. The distinction between euthanasia and PAS
is not morally significant. A physician who provides a patient with a
deadly drug and instructions about its use to bring about death bears as
much responsibility for the death as the patient himself. The doctor is
knowingly a part, and a necessary part, of the causal chain leading to
the death of the patient. In most jurisdictions, the law holds equally
responsible those who are "accessory" to capital crimes: if I give one
person the gun with which I know he intends to kill another person,
then stand by while he does so, the law will hold me as responsible for
the death as the person who pulled the trigger. The same reasoning
applies here: doctors who kill directly by injection or give others the pills

to kill themselves are fully blameworthy (or praiseworthy if one accepts such actions as ethically acceptable) for what occurs.

I contend, then, that it is wrong to give one person an absolute power over the life of another, whether this power is gained by force or by voluntary means, and whether it is achieved directly or by accessory means. Consenting adult killing, where the parties are in voluntary agreement, is a moral wrong, not mitigated by its voluntary nature nor excusable because of its possibly beneficial consequences. I concede one exception to a general rule against giving people the legal power to kill each other or help each other to die: when that is the only way of saving or protecting the lives of others.

*Source*: Daniel Callahan, "Self-Extinction: The Morality of the Helping Hand," Chapter 3, in Robert F. Weir, ed., *Physician-assisted Suicide* (Bloomington: Indiana University Press, 1997), 71.

* * *

Among the objections to legalizing physician-assisted suicide, there is concern that legalization would increase the financial incentive to limit care, and that vulnerable groups such as elderly individuals, people with disabilities, and those from different racial and ethnic groups might be particularly subject to pressure to request physician-assisted suicide. A serious concern is that poor people who may receive inadequate management of their pain and other symptoms might have a greater incentive to wish to end their lives than would patients with better palliative care.

Among the hazards of permitting assisted suicide is the possibility that the patient is not mortally ill and can recover. Another danger is that the patient may change his or her mind when it is too late. These concerns can be addressed by requiring agreement of two physicians about the patient's clinical condition and repeated requests for death by the patient over a period of days or even weeks.

Probably the commonest and most important hazard of legalizing assisted suicide is the possibility that the patient is suffering from a clinical depression in the face of his or her illness and anticipated death. Since depression is potentially treatable, a physician contemplating assisting in suicide must be very much aware of this possibility. The relationship of this symptom to the wish for death is shown in the following study.

## DOCUMENT 128: "Desire for Death in the Terminally Ill," Harvey Max Chochinov et al. (1995)

Objective: Euthanasia and physician-assisted suicide have become prominent medical and social issues. This study investigated the prevalence of the desire for death in terminally ill patients, the stability of this desire over time, and its association with psychiatric disorders. Method: Two hundred terminally ill inpatients were given semistructured interviews that assessed their desire for death and evaluated them for major and minor depressive episodes according to the Research Diagnostic Criteria. Each patient also completed a short form of the Beck Depression Inventory and provided ratings of pain and social support. When possible, patients who expressed a desire for death received a follow-up interview after a 2-week interval. Results: Although occasional wishes that death would come soon were common (reported by 44.5% of the patients), only 17 (8.5%) of these individuals acknowledged a serious and pervasive desire to die. The desire for death was correlated with ratings of pain and low family support but most significantly with measures of depression. The prevalence of diagnosed depressive syndromes was 58.8% among patients with a desire to die and 7.7% among patients without such a desire. Follow-up interviews were conducted with six patients; in four cases, the desire to die had decreased during the 2-week interval. Conclusions: The desire for death in terminally ill patients is closely associated with clinical depression—a potentially treatable condition—and can also decrease over time. Informed debate about euthanasia should recognize the importance of psychiatric considerations, as well as the inherent transience of many patients' expressed desire to die.

*Source*: Harvey Max Chochinov, Keith G. Wilson, Murray Enns, Neil Mowchun, Sheila Lander, Martin Levitt, and Jennifer J. Clinch, "Desire for Death in the Terminally Ill," *American Journal of Psychiatry* 152 (1995): 1185–1191. Abstract.

* * *

### Means of Terminating Life

As we have indicated, a hopelessly ill patient's life may be legally terminated by withdrawing life-sustaining treatment such as artificial ventilation or artificial nutrition and hydration, or by administering sedation for pain to the point of death. While many consider that these options can be readily distinguished from suicide or euthanasia, there are other points of view.

---

## DOCUMENT 129: "Palliative Options of Last Resort," Timothy E. Quill, Bernard Lo, and Dan W. Brock (1997)

---

Palliative care is generally agreed to be the standard of care for the dying, but there remain some patients for whom intolerable suffering persists. In the face of ethical and legal controversy about the acceptability of physician-assisted suicide and voluntary active euthanasia, voluntarily stopping eating and drinking and terminal sedation have been proposed as ethically superior responses of last resort that do not require changes in professional standards or the law. The clinical and ethical differences and similarities between these 4 practices are critically compared in light of the doctrine of double effect, the active/passive distinction, patient voluntariness, proportionality between risks and benefits, and the physician's potential conflict of duties. Terminal sedation and voluntarily stopping eating and drinking would allow clinicians to remain responsive to a wide range of patient suffering, but they are ethically and clinically more complex and closer to physician-assisted suicide and voluntary active euthanasia than is ordinarily acknowledged. Safeguards are presented for any medical action that may hasten death, including determining that palliative care is ineffective, obtaining informed consent, ensuring diagnostic and prognostic clarity, obtaining an independent second opinion, and implementing reporting and monitoring processes. Explicit public policy about which of these practices are permissible would reassure the many patients who fear a bad death in their future and allow for a predictable response for the few whose suffering becomes intolerable in spite of optimal palliative care.

*Source*: Timothy E. Quill, Bernard Lo, and Dan W. Brock, "Palliative Options of Last Resort: A Comparison of Voluntarily Stopping Eating and Drinking, Terminal Sedation, Physician-assisted Suicide, and Voluntary Active Euthanasia," *Journal of the American Medical Association* 278 (1997): 2099–2104. Abstract.

\* \* \*

### Will Legalizing Physician-assisted Suicide Save Money?

---

## DOCUMENT 130: "What Are the Potential Cost Savings from Legalizing Physician-assisted Suicide?" Ezekiel J. Emanuel and Margaret P. Battin (1998)

---

Drawing on data from the Netherlands on the use of euthanasia and physician-assisted suicide and on available U.S. data on costs at the end of life, this analysis explores the degree to which the legalization of physician-assisted suicide might reduce health care costs. The most reasonable estimate is a savings of $627 million, less than 0.07 percent of total health care expenditures. What is true on a national scale is also likely to be reflected in the potential savings for individual managed-care plans. Physician-assisted suicide is not likely to save substantial amounts of money in absolute or relative terms, either for particular institutions or for the nation as a whole.

*Source*: Ezekiel J. Emanuel and Margaret P. Battin, "What Are the Potential Cost Savings from Legalizing Physician-assisted Suicide?" *New England Journal of Medicine* 339 (1998): 167–171. Conclusions.

* * *

## ATTEMPTS TO LEGALIZE PHYSICIAN-ASSISTED SUICIDE

### State Referendums

Many individuals hoped to legalize assisted suicide and euthanasia through statewide referendums. Referendums for legalization of both assisted suicide and euthanasia failed in the state of Washington in 1991, California in 1992, and Michigan in 1998. In 1994, a referendum in Oregon legalizing assisted suicide passed with 52 percent of the vote.

The Oregon Death with Dignity Act, known as Measure 16, was immediately challenged in court, which delayed implementation of the act. After all legal challenges were exhausted, the legislature returned the issue to the voters in November 1997. The ballot before the voters was whether Measure 16 should be repealed. Despite strong and well-financed lobbying for its passage, the referendum failed by 60 percent to 40 percent. Oregon became the first state to permit physician-assisted suicide under limited circumstances.

The Oregon Death with Dignity Act contains numerous safeguards. The Task Force to Improve the Care of Terminally Ill Oregonians, which is neutral on the subject of physician-assisted suicide, issued a guidebook that helps health care providers to explore various aspects of end-of-life care, including how to conform with the guidelines for assisting in patient suicide. Hospitals are beginning to draw up guidelines, and on March 24, 1998, the first patient committed assisted suicide under the conditions outlined in the law.

Initially the administrator of the Drug Enforcement Administration of the Justice Department warned that an Oregon physician who prescribed lethal doses of a medication might be violating federal narcotics law and would risk losing his or her license to prescribe drugs. The Justice Department subsequently overruled that decision. The federal government enacted the Assisted Suicide Funding Restriction Act of 1997, which banned the use of federal funds to pay for assisted suicide, euthanasia, or mercy killing. However, in Oregon, expenses related to assisted suicide will be covered by appropriate state reimbursement.

## DOCUMENT 131: The Oregon Death with Dignity Act (1998)

### Section I
### General Provisions

1.01 Definitions

The following words and phrases, whenever used in this Act, shall have the following meanings:

(1) "Adult" means an individual who is 18 years of age or older.

(2) "Attending physician" means the physician who has primary responsibility for the care of the patient and treatment of the patient's disease.

(3) "Consulting physician" means the physician who is qualified by specialty or experience to make a professional diagnosis and prognosis regarding the patient's disease.

(4) "Counseling" means a consultation between a state licensed psychiatrist or psychologist and a patient for the purpose of determining whether the patient is suffering from a psychiatric or psychological disorder, or depression causing impaired judgment.

(5) "Health care provider" means a person licensed, certified, or otherwise authorized or permitted by the law of this State to administer health care in the ordinary course of business or practice of a profession, and includes a health care facility.

(6) "Incapable" means that in the opinion of a court or in the opinion of the patient's attending physician or consulting physician, a patient lacks the ability to make and communicate health care decisions to health care providers, includ-

ing communication through persons familiar with the patient's manner of communicating if those persons are available. "Capable" means not incapable.

(7) "Informed decision" means a decision by a qualified patient, to request and obtain a prescription to end his or her life in a humane and dignified manner, that is based on an appreciation of the relevant facts and after being fully informed by the attending physician of:

(a) his or her medical diagnosis;

(b) his or her prognosis;

(c) the potential risks associated with taking the medication to be prescribed;

(d) the probable result of taking the medication to be prescribed;

(e) the feasible alternatives, including, but not limited to, comfort care, hospice care and pain control.

(8) "Medically confirmed" means the medical opinion of the attending physician has been confirmed by a consulting physician who has examined the patient and the patient's relevant medical records.

(9) "Patient" means a person who is under the care of a physician.

(10) "Physician" means a doctor of medicine or osteopathy licensed to practice medicine by the Board of Medical Examiners for the State of Oregon.

(11) "Qualified patient" means a capable adult who is a resident of Oregon and has satisfied the requirements of this Act in order to obtain a prescription for medication to end his or her life in a humane and dignified manner.

(12) "Terminal disease" means an incurable and irreversible disease that has been medically confirmed and will, within reasonable medical judgment, produce death within six (6) months.

## Section 2
## Written Request for Medication to End One's Life in a Humane and Dignified Manner

2.01 Who may initiate a written request for medication

An adult who is capable, is a resident of Oregon, and has been determined by the attending physician and consulting physician to be suffering from a terminal disease, and who has voluntarily expressed his or her wish to die, may make a written request for medication for the purpose of ending his or her life in a humane and dignified manner in accordance with this Act.

2.01 Form of the written request

(1) A valid request for medication under this Act shall be in substantially the form described in Section 6 of this Act, signed and dated by the patient and witnessed by at least two individuals who, in the presence of the patient, attest that to the best of their knowledge and belief the patient is capable, acting voluntarily, and is not being coerced to sign the request. (2) One of the witnesses shall be a person who is not: (a) A

relative of the patient by blood, marriage or adoption; (b) A person who at the time the request is signed would be entitled to any portion of the estate of the qualified patient upon death under any will or by operation of law; or (c) An owner, operator or employee of a health care facility where the qualified patient is receiving medical treatment or is a resident. (3) The patient's attending physician at the time the request is signed shall not be a witness. (4) If the patient is a patient in a long term care facility at the time the written request is made, one of the witnesses shall be an individual designated by the facility and having the qualifications specified by the Department of Human Resources by rule.

## Section 3
## Safeguards

3.01 Attending physician responsibilities

The attending physician shall: (1) Make the initial determination of whether a patient has a terminal disease, is capable, and has made the request voluntarily; (2) Inform the patient of; (a) his or her medical diagnosis; (b) his or her prognosis; (c) the potential risks associated with taking the medication to be prescribed; (d) the probable result of taking the medication to be prescribed; (e) the feasible alternatives, including, but not limited to, comfort care, hospice care and pain control; (3) Refer the patient to a consulting physician for medical confirmation of the diagnosis, and for determination that the patient is capable and acting voluntarily; (4) Refer the patient for counseling if appropriate pursuant to Section 3.03; (5) Request that the patient notify next of kin; (6) Inform the patient that he or she has an opportunity to rescind the request at any time and in any manner, and offer the patient an opportunity to rescind at the end of the 15 day waiting period pursuant to Section 3.06; (7) Verify, immediately prior to writing the prescription for medication under this Act, that the patient is making an informed decision; (8) Fulfill the medical record documentation requirements of Section 3.09; (9) Ensure that all appropriate steps are carried out in accordance with this Act prior to writing a prescription for medication to enable a qualified patient to end his or her life in a humane and dignified manner.

3.02 Consulting physician confirmation

Before a patient is qualified under this Act, a consulting physician shall examine the patient and his or her relevant medical records and confirm, in writing, the attending physician's diagnosis that the patient is suffering from a terminal disease, and verify that the patient is capable, is acting voluntarily and has made an informed decision.

3.03 Counseling referral

If in the opinion of the attending physician or the consulting physician a patient may be suffering from a psychiatric or psychological disorder, or depression causing impaired judgment, either physician shall refer the patient for counseling. No medication to end a patient's life in a humane and dignified manner shall be prescribed until the person performing the counseling determines that the person is not suffering from a psychiatric or psychological disorder, or depression causing impaired judgment.

3.04 Informed decision

No person shall receive a prescription for medication to end his or her life in a humane and dignified manner unless he or she has made an informed decision as defined in Section 1.01(7). Immediately prior to writing a prescription for medication under this Act, the attending physician shall verify that the patient is making an informed decision.

3.05 Family notification

The attending physician shall ask the patient to notify next of kin of his or her request for medication pursuant to this Act. A patient who declines or is unable to notify next of kin shall not have his or her request denied for that reason.

3.06 Written and oral requests

In order to receive a prescription for medication to end his or her life in a humane and dignified manner, a qualified patient shall have made an oral request and a written request, and reiterate the oral request to his or her attending physician no less than fifteen (15) days after making the initial oral request. At the time the qualified patient makes his or her second oral request, the attending physician shall offer the patient an opportunity to rescind the request.

3.07 Right to rescind request

A patient may rescind his or her request at any time and in any manner without regard to his or her mental state. No prescription for medication under this Act may be written without the attending physician offering the qualified patient an opportunity to rescind the request.

3.08 Waiting periods

No less than fifteen (15) days shall elapse between the patient's initial and oral request and the writing of a prescription under this Act. No less than 48 hours shall elapse between the patient's written request and the writing of a prescription under this Act.

3.09 Medical record documentation requirements

The following shall be documented or filed in the patient's medical record: (1) All oral requests by a patient for medication to end his or her life in a humane and dignified manner; (2) All written requests by a patient for medication to end his or her life in a humane and dignified manner; (3) The attending physician's diagnosis and prognosis, determination that the patient is capable, acting voluntarily and has made an informed decision; (4) The consulting physician's diagnosis and prognosis, and verification that the patient is capable, acting voluntarily and has made an informed decision; (5) A report of the outcome and determinations made during counseling; (6) The attending physician's offer to the patient to rescind his or her request at the time of the patient's second oral request pursuant to Section 3.06; and (7) A note by the attending physician indicating that all requirements under this Act have been met and indicating the steps taken to carry out the request, including a notation of the medication prescribed.

3.10 Residency requirements

Only requests made by Oregon residents, under this Act, shall be granted.

3.11 Reporting requirements

(1) The Health Division shall annually review a sample of records maintained pursuant to this Act. (2) The Health Division shall make rules to facilitate the collection of information regarding compliance with this Act. The information collected shall not be a public record and may not be made available for inspection by the public. (3) The Health Division shall generate and make available to the public an annual statistical report of information collected under Section 3.11(2) of this Act.

3.12 Effect on construction of wills, contracts and statutes

(1) No provision in a contract, will or other agreement, whether written or oral, to the extent the provision would affect whether a person may make or rescind a request for medication to end his or her life in a humane and dignified manner, shall be valid. (2) No obligation owing under any currently existing contract shall be conditioned or affected by the making or rescinding of a request, by a person, for medication to end his or her life in a humane and dignified manner.

3.13 Insurance or annuity policies

The sale, procurement, or issuance of any life, health, or accident insurance or annuity policy or the rate charged for any policy shall not be conditioned upon or affected by the making or rescinding of a request, by a person, for medication to end his or her life in a humane and dignified manner. Neither shall a qualified patient's act of ingesting medication to end his or her life in a humane and dignified manner have an effect upon a life, health, or accident insurance or annuity policy.

3.14 Construction of Act

Nothing in this Act shall be construed to authorize a physician or any other person to end a patient's life by lethal injection, mercy killing or active euthanasia. Actions taken in accordance with this Act shall not, for any purpose, constitute suicide, assisted suicide, mercy killing or homicide, under the law.

Section 4
Immunities and Liabilities

4.01 Immunities

Except as provided in Section 4.02:

(1) No person shall be subject to civil or criminal liability or professional disciplinary action for participating in good faith compliance with this Act. This includes being present when a qualified patient takes the prescribed medication to end his or her life in a humane and dignified manner.

(2) No professional organization or association, or health care provider, may subject a person to censure, discipline, suspension, loss of license, loss of privileges, loss of membership or other penalty for participating or refusing to participate in good faith compliance with this Act.

(3) No request by a patient for or provision by an attending physician of medication in good faith compliance with the provisions of this Act shall constitute neglect for any purpose of law or provide the sole basis for the appointment of a guardian or conservator.

(4) No health care provider shall be under any duty, whether by contract, by statute or by any other legal requirement to participate in the provision to a qualified patient of medication to end his or her life in a humane and dignified manner. If a health care provider is unable or unwilling to carry out a patient's wishes, that health care provider shall transfer, upon request, a copy of the patient's relevant medical records to the new health care provider.

4.02 Liabilities

(1) A person who without authorization of the patient willfully alters or forges a request for medication or conceals or destroys a rescission of that request with the intent or effect of causing the patient's death shall be guilty of a Class A felony.

(2) A person who coerces or exerts undue influence on a patient to request medication for the purpose of ending the patient's life, or to destroy a rescission of such a request, shall be guilty of a Class A felony.

(3) Nothing in this Act limits further liability for civil damages result-

ing from other negligent conduct or intentional misconduct by any persons.

(4) The penalties in this Act do not preclude criminal penalties applicable under other law for conduct which is inconsistent with the provisions of this Act.

Section 5
Severability

5.01 Severability

Any section of this Act being held invalid as to any person or circumstance shall not affect the application of any other section of this Act which can be given full effect without the invalid section or application.

Section 6
Form of the Request

6.01 Form of the request

A request for a medication as authorized by this Act shall be in substantially the following form:

REQUEST FOR MEDICATION TO END MY LIFE IN A HUMANE AND DIGNIFIED MANNER

I, (name), am an adult of sound mind.

I am suffering from (illness), which my attending physician has determined is a terminal disease and which has been medically confirmed by a consulting physician.

I have been fully informed of my diagnosis, prognosis, the nature of medication to be prescribed and potential associated risks, the expected result, and the feasible alternatives, including comfort care, hospice care and pain control.

I request that my attending physician prescribe medication that will end my life in a humane and dignified manner.

INITIAL ONE:

_____ I have informed my family of my decision and taken their opinions into consideration.

_____ I have decided not to inform my family of my decision.

_____ I have no family to inform of my decision.

_____ I understand that I have the right to rescind this request at any time.

_____ I understand the full import of this request and I expect to die when I take the medication to be prescribed.

_____ I make this request voluntarily and without reservation and I accept full moral responsibility for my actions.

Signed: _____
Dated: _____

DECLARATION OF WITNESSES

We declare that the person signing this request: (a) Is personally known to us or has provided proof of identity; (b) Signed this request in our presence; (c) Appears to be of sound mind and not under duress, fraud or undue influence; (d) Is not a patient for whom either of us is attending physician.

Witness 1/_____
Date _____
Witness 2/_____
Date _____

*Note*: One witness shall not be a relative (by blood, marriage or adoption) of the person signing this request, shall not be entitled to any portion of the person's estate upon death and shall not own, operate or be employed at a health care facility where the person is a patient or resident. If the patient is an inpatient at a health care facility, one of the witnesses shall be an individual designated by the facility.

*Source*: Or. Rev. Stat. Sections 127.990. et seq. (Supp. 1998).

\* \* \*

## COURT DECISIONS

In two states, New York and Washington, groups of physicians and dying patients brought suits against the state, claiming that prohibitions against physician-assisted suicide violated the equal-protection and due-process clauses of the 14th Amendment of the U.S. Constitution. These suits did not attempt to legalize euthanasia.

## DOCUMENT 132: Fourteenth Amendment of the U.S. Constitution

1. All persons born or naturalized in the United States, and subject to the jurisdiction thereof, are citizens of the United States and of the State wherein they reside. No State shall make or enforce any law which shall abridge the privileges of immunities of citizens of the United States; nor shall any State deprive any person of life, liberty, or property, without due process of law; nor deny to any person within its jurisdiction the equal protection of the laws.

*Source*: U.S. Constitution, Fourteenth Amendment, Section 1.

* * *

### Federal Court Decisions

**New York State**. The plaintiffs—three mentally competent, terminally ill adults and three physicians who regularly treat terminally ill patients—challenged the section of the New York Penal Law that states that a person is guilty of manslaughter in the second degree when "he intentionally . . . aids another person to commit suicide." They also questioned the constitutionality of the penal-code section that provides that "a person is guilty of promoting a suicide attempt when he intentionally . . . aids another person to attempt suicide." The U.S. District Court in the Southern District of New York rejected the challenges to the statutes. The plaintiffs appeled to the U.S. Court of Appeals for the Second Circuit, which held in part that New York law banning assisted suicide was unconstitutional based on an equal-protection analysis. The court was unwilling to identify assisted suicide as a fundamental right protected by the due-process clause. The decision was appealed to the U.S. Supreme Court.

---

## DOCUMENT 133: *Quill v. Vacco*, U.S. Court of Appeals, Second Circuit (April 2, 1996)

---

### BACKGROUND

The action giving rise to this appeal was commenced by a complaint filed on July 20, 1994. The plaintiffs named in that complaint were the three physicians who are the appellants here and three individuals then in the final stages of terminal illness: Jane Doe (who chose to conceal her actual identity), George A. Kingsley and William A. Barth. . . . According to the complaint, Jane Doe was a 76-year-old retired physical education instructor who was dying of thyroid cancer; Mr. Kingsley was a 48-year-old publishing executive suffering from AIDS; and Mr. Barth was a 28-year-old former fashion editor under treatment for AIDS. Each of these plaintiffs alleged that she or he had been advised and understood that she or he was in the terminal stage of a terminal illness and that there was no chance of recovery. Each sought to hasten death "in a certain and humane manner" and for that purpose sought "necessary medical assistance in the form of medications prescribed by [her or his] physician to be self-administered."

The physician plaintiffs alleged that they encountered, in the course of their medical practices, "mentally competent, terminally ill patients who request assistance in the voluntary self-termination of life." Many of these patients apparently "experience chronic, intractable pain and/or intolerable suffering" and seek to hasten their deaths for those reasons. Mr. Barth was one of the patients who sought the assistance of Dr. Grossman. Each of the physician plaintiffs has alleged that "[u]nder certain circumstances it would be consistent with the standards of [his] medical practice" to assist in hastening death by prescribing drugs for patients to self-administer for that purpose. The physicians alleged that they were unable to exercise their best professional judgment to prescribe the requested drugs, and the other plaintiffs alleged that they were unable to receive the requested drugs, because of the prohibitions contained in sections 125.15(3) and 120.30 of the New York Penal Law, all plaintiffs being residents of New York. . . .

Count I of the complaint included an allegation that "[t]he Fourteenth Amendment guarantees the liberty of mentally competent, terminally ill adults with no chance of recovery to make decisions about the end of their lives." It also included an allegation that

[t]he Fourteenth Amendment guarantees the liberty of physicians to practice medicine consistent with their best professional judgment, including using their skills and powers to facilitate the exercise of the decision of competent, terminally ill adults to hasten inevitable death by prescribing suitable medications for the patient to self-administer for that purpose.

Count II of the complaint included an allegation that

[t]he relevant portions of . . . the New York Penal Law deny the patient-plaintiffs and the patients of the physician-plaintiffs the equal protection of the law by denying them the right to choose to hasten inevitable death, while terminally ill persons whose treatment includes life support are able to exercise this choice with necessary medical assistance by directing termination of such treatment.

In their prayer for relief the plaintiffs requested judgment declaring the New York statutes complained of constitutionally invalid and therefore in violation of 42 U.S.C. § 1983 "as applied to physicians who assist mentally competent, terminally ill adults who choose to hasten inevitable death." Plaintiffs also sought an order permanently enjoining defendants from enforcing the statutes and an award of attorney's fees.

By order to show cause filed on September 16, 1994, the plaintiffs moved for a preliminary injunction to enjoin then–Attorney General Koppell "and all persons acting in concert and participation with him from enforcing New York Penal Law sections 125.15(3) and 120.30 against physicians who prescribe medications which mentally competent, terminally ill patients may use to hasten their impending deaths." A declaration by each of the plaintiffs was submitted in support of the application, although Jane Doe had died prior to the filing of the order to show cause. Plaintiffs Kingsley and Barth were then in the advanced stages of AIDS and therefore sought an immediate determination by the district court. . . .

. . . In their supplemental declarations, Doctors Klagsbrun and Grossman reiterated their desire "to prescribe drugs, if and when medically and psychiatrically appropriate, for such patients to self-administer at the time and place of their choice for the purpose of hastening their impending deaths."

In his supplemental declaration, Dr. Quill declared:

The removal of a life support system that directly results in the patient's death requires the direct involvement by the doctor, as well as other medical personnel. When such patients are mentally competent, they are consciously choosing death as preferable to life under the circumstances that they are forced to live. Their doctors do a careful clinical assessment, including a full exploration of the patient's prognosis, mental competence to make such decisions, and the treatment alternatives to stopping treatment. It is legally and ethically permitted for physicians to actively assist patients to die who are dependent on life-sustaining treatments. . . . Unfortunately, some dying patients who are in agony that can no longer be relieved, yet are not dependent on life-sustaining treatment, have no such options under current legal restrictions. It seems unfair, discriminatory, and inhumane to deprive some dying patients of such vital choices because of arbitrary elements of their condition which determine whether they are on life-sustaining treatment that can be stopped.

. . .

## DISCUSSION

I. Justiciability

As they did in the district court, the state defendants contend on appeal that this action does not present a justiciable case or controversy. We reject this contention.

. . . Dr. Quill has had a criminal proceeding instituted against him in the past, and the state nowhere disclaims an intent to repeat a prosecution in the event of further assisted suicides. The other two physician plaintiffs also face the threat of criminal prosecution. Like the physicians in *Doe*, they "should not be required to await and undergo a criminal prosecution as the sole means of seeking relief." Finally, under *Doe*, the physicians may raise the rights of their terminally-ill patients. . . .

Although District Attorney Morgenthau argues in his brief on appeal that appellants have not shown that they are in any jeopardy of prosecution in New York County, a recent indictment by a New York County grand jury demonstrates the contrary. . . .

In rejecting the due process–fundamental rights argument of the plaintiffs, we are mindful of the admonition of the Supreme Court:

Nor are we inclined to take a more expansive view of our authority to discover new fundamental rights imbedded in the Due Process Clause: The Court is most vulnerable and comes nearest to illegitimacy when it deals with judge-made constitutional law having little or no cognizable roots in the language or design of the Constitution.

[cit.] The right to assisted suicide finds no cognizable basis in the Constitution's language or design, even in the very limited cases of those competent persons who, in the final stages of terminal illness, seek the right to hasten death. We therefore decline the plaintiffs' invitation to identify a new fundamental right, in the absence of a clear direction from the Court whose precedents we are bound to follow. The limited room for expansion of substantive due process rights and the reasons therefor have been clearly stated: "As a general matter, the Court has always been reluctant to expand the concept of substantive due process because guideposts for responsible decisionmaking in this unchartered area are scarce and open-ended."[cit.] Our position in the judicial hierarchy constrains us to be even more reluctant than the Court to undertake an expansive approach in this unchartered area.

*Source: Quill v. Vacco*, 80 F. 3d 716 (2nd Cir. 1996). Citations omitted.

\* \* \*

**Washington State**. The plaintiffs were three mentally competent, terminally ill adults, five physicians who regularly treat terminally ill patients, and Compassion in Dying, a Washington State–based organization that provides information and assistance to terminally ill, competent adults considering suicide. They challenged the section of the Washington statute that makes aiding in a suicide a crime. They contended that the law prevents physicians from prescribing life-ending medication to terminally ill, competent adult patients who wish to hasten their death, thus preventing the exercise of a constitutionally protected liberty interest under the due-process clause of the Fourteenth Amendment. They also contended that the statute violated the equal-protection clause since it treats terminally ill patients who require life support and are able to refuse or withdraw it differently from those terminally ill patients who do not require life support but wish to hasten death by seeking medical assistance in the form of a lethal dose of medication.

The U.S. district court declared the law unconstitutional under both the due-process and equal-protection clauses. However, a three-judge panel of the U.S. Court of Appeals for the Ninth Circuit reversed the ruling of the district court, finding that there is no due-process liberty interest in physician-assisted suicide. The panel also strongly disagreed with the lower court's findings of similarities between refusal of treatment and physician-assisted suicide.

The plaintiffs appealed, and the Ninth Circuit Court of Appeals decided to rehear the case en banc (i.e., in front of all eleven judges). In an 8–3 decision in favor of the plaintiffs, the court held that the statute violated the due-process clause of the Fourteenth Amendment, citing a recent abortion rights case (*Planned Parenthood v. Casey*) as well as the *Cruzan* decision (see Part V, Documents 91–93). The court did not comment on the equal-protection analysis discussed in the district-court ruling. We quote the conclusion of Judge Reinhardt for the majority as well as two paragraphs from the dissenting opinion of Judge Beezer.

---

**DOCUMENT 134:** *Compassion in Dying v. State of Washington,* **U.S. Court of Appeals, Ninth Circuit (March 6, 1996)**

---

### [Judge Reinhardt] Conclusion

We hold that a liberty interest exists in the choice of how and when one dies, and that the provision of the Washington statute banning assisted suicide, as applied to competent, terminally ill adults who wish to hasten their deaths by obtaining medication prescribed by their doctors, violates the Due Process Clause. We recognize that this decision is a most difficult and controversial one, and that it leaves unresolved a large number of equally troublesome issues that will require resolution in the years ahead. We also recognize that other able and dedicated jurists, construing the Constitution as they believe it must be construed, may disagree not only with the result we reach but with our method of constitutional analysis. Given the nature of the judicial process and the complexity of the task of determining the rights and interests comprehended by the Constitution, good faith disagreements within the judiciary should not surprise or disturb anyone who follows the development of the law. For these reasons, we express our hope that whatever debate may accompany the future exploration of the issues we have touched on today will be conducted in an objective, rational, and constructive manner that will increase, not diminish, respect for the Constitution.

There is one final point we must emphasize. Some argue strongly that decisions regarding matters affecting life or death should not be made by the courts. Essentially, we agree with that proposition. In this case, by permitting the *individual* to exercise the right to *choose* we are following the constitutional mandate to take such decisions out of the hands of the government, both state and federal, and to put them where they rightly belong, in the hands of the people. We are allowing individuals to make the decisions that so profoundly affect their very existence— and precluding the state from intruding excessively into that critical realm. The Constitution and the courts stand as a bulwark between individual freedom and arbitrary and intrusive governmental power. Under our constitutional system, neither the state nor the majority of the people in a state can impose its will upon the individual in a matter so highly "central to personal dignity and autonomy," *Casey....* Those who believe strongly that death must come without physician assistance are free to follow that creed, be they doctors or patients. They are not free, however, to force their views, their religious convictions, or their philosophies on all the other members of a democratic society, and to compel those whose values differ with theirs to die painful, protracted, and agonizing deaths.

### [Judge Beezer]

... Plaintiffs ask us to blur the line between withdrawal of life-sustaining treatment and physician-assisted suicide. At the same time, some proponents of physician-assisted suicide would maintain a conceptual distinction between physician-assisted suicide and euthanasia. Associating physician-assisted suicide with a relatively accepted procedure and dissociating it from an unpalatable one are rhetorically powerful devices, but run counter to U.S. Supreme Court precedent [see Documents 91–93], Washington State statutory law, medical ethics guidelines of the American Medical Association and the American College of Physicians, and legal reasoning [notes omitted].

The proper place to draw the line is between withdrawing life-sustaining treatment (which is based on the right to be free from unwanted intrusion) and physician-assisted suicide and euthanasia (which implicate the assistance of others in controlling the timing and manner of death). The former is constitutionally protected (under *Cruzan*); the latter is not.

*Source: Compassion in Dying v. State of Washington, U.S. Court of Appeals, 79 F. 3d 790 (9th Cir. 1996) (en banc). Notes omitted.*

\* \* \*

### Decisions of the U.S. Supreme Court

Both the New York *Vacco v. Quill* and the Washington *Compassion in Dying v. State of Washington* cases were argued together before the U.S. Supreme Court on January 8, 1997. Some of the questions posed by the justices were an indication of their thinking. For example: "Everything you have said, it seems to me, could go on in a legislative chamber." "Why shouldn't we conclude that as an institution, we are not in a position to make the judgment you want us to make?" "This case raises the basic question of who decides. Is this ever a proper question for courts to decide?" (quotes cited in the *New York Times*, January 9, 1997, page 1). On June 26, 1997, the Supreme Court reversed the decisions of both the Second Circuit Court (New York) and the Ninth Circuit Court (Washington).

---

## DOCUMENT 135: Opinion of Chief Justice William Rehnquist, *Vacco v. Quill*, U.S. Supreme Court (June 26, 1997)

The Equal Protection Clause commands that no State shall "deny to any person within its jurisdiction the equal protection of the laws." . . .

On their faces, neither New York's ban on assisting suicide nor its statutes permitting patients to refuse medical treatment treat anyone differently than anyone else or draw any distinctions between persons. *Everyone*, regardless of physical condition, is entitled, if competent, to refuse unwanted lifesaving medical treatment; *no one* is permitted to assist a suicide. Generally speaking, laws that apply evenhandedly to all "unquestionably comply" with the Equal Protection Clause. [cit.]

The Court of Appeals, however, concluded that some terminally ill people—those who are on life-support systems—are treated differently than those who are not, in that the former may "hasten death" by ending treatment, but the latter may not "hasten death" through physician-assisted suicide. [cit.] This conclusion depends on the submission that ending or refusing lifesaving medical treatment "is nothing more nor less than assisted suicide." [cit.] Unlike the Court of Appeals, we think the distinction between assisting suicide and withdrawing life-sustaining treatment, a distinction widely recognized and endorsed in the medical profession [note] and in our legal traditions, is both important and logical; it is certainly rational. . . .

This Court has also recognized, at least implicitly, the distinction between letting a patient die and making that patient die. In *Cruzan v. Director, Mo. Dept. of Health*, [cit.], [see Document 92], we concluded that "[t]he principle that a competent person has a constitutionally protected liberty interest in refusing unwanted medical treatment may be inferred from our prior decisions," and we assumed the existence of such a right for purposes of that case. [cit.] But our assumption of a right to refuse treatment was grounded not, as the Court of Appeals supposed, on the proposition that patients have a general and abstract "right to hasten death," [cit.], but on well established, traditional rights to bodily integrity and freedom from unwanted touching. . . . *Cruzan* therefore provides no support for the notion that refusing life-sustaining medical treatment is "nothing more nor less than suicide."

For all these reasons, we disagree with respondents' claim that the distinction between refusing lifesaving medical treatment and assisted suicide is "arbitrary" and "irrational."

*Source: Vacco v. Quill,* U.S. Supreme Court, 117 S. Ct. 2293 (1997).

---

## DOCUMENT 136: Opinion of Chief Justice William Rehnquist, *Washington v. Glucksberg,* U.S. Supreme Court (June 26, 1997)

. . . The Washington statute at issue in this case prohibits "aid[ing] another person to attempt suicide," [cit.], and, thus, the question before us is whether the "liberty" specially protected by the Due Process Clause includes a right to commit suicide which itself includes a right to assistance in doing so [note].

We now inquire whether this asserted right has any place in our Nation's traditions. Here, as discussed above, . . . we are confronted with a consistent and almost universal tradition that has long rejected the asserted right, and continues explicitly to reject it today, even for terminally ill, mentally competent adults. To hold for respondents, we would have to reverse centuries of legal doctrine and practice, and strike down the considered policy choice of almost every State. . . .

Respondents contend, however, that the liberty interest they assert *is* consistent with this Court's substantive-due-process line of cases, if not with this Nation's history and practice. Pointing to *Casey* and *Cruzan,* respondents read our jurisprudence in this area as reflecting a general tradition of "self-sovereignty," . . . and as teaching that the "liberty" protected by the Due Process Clause includes "basic and intimate exercises of personal autonomy." . . .

. . . That many of the rights and liberties protected by the Due Process Clause are sound in personal autonomy does not warrant the sweeping conclusion that any and all important, intimate, and personal decisions are so protected, [cit.]. . . .

Throughout the Nation, Americans are engaged in an earnest and profound debate about the morality, legality, and practicality of physician-assisted suicide. Our holding permits this debate to continue, as it should in a democratic society. The decision of the en banc Court of Appeals is reversed, and the case is remanded for further proceedings consistent with this opinion.

*Source: Washington v. Glucksberg, U.S. Supreme Court, 117 S. Ct. 2258 (1997).*

\* \* \*

## PALLIATIVE CARE

As Burt eloquently explains, the U.S. Supreme Court, unexpectedly opened the door to improvement of palliative care.

---

## DOCUMENT 137: "The Supreme Court Speaks: Not Assisted Suicide but a Constitutional Right to Palliative Care," Robert A. Burt (1997)

---

The Supreme Court has unanimously ruled that there is no constitutional right to physician-assisted suicide.[1,2] Unexpectedly, however, the Court did much more than simply uphold the New York and Washington statutes prohibiting assisted suicide. A Court majority effectively required all states to ensure that their laws do not obstruct the provision of adequate palliative care, especially for the alleviation of pain and other physical symptoms of people facing death.

The plaintiffs in these cases demanded a "right to die" with physician assistance, not a right to adequate palliative care. The defendant states—Washington and New York—countered that they were free to prohibit assisted suicide, but they did not acknowledge the existence of state laws and institutional arrangements that contribute to the inadequacy of current palliative care. The Supreme Court majority surprisingly and dramatically changed the focus of this dispute.

Initial accounts of the Supreme Court's decision did not appear to grasp the implications of the Court majority's ruling. This incomprehension is understandable, because no single opinion announces the majority's ruling. At first glance, it appears that Chief Justice William Rehnquist spoke for the Court majority; his opinions in the two cases were identified as the "opinion of the Court," and four other justices—

Sandra Day O'Connor, Antonin Scalia, Anthony Kennedy, and Clarence Thomas—concurred in them.

Rehnquist's opinions did not endorse a constitutional right to adequate palliative care but simply rejected the conclusions of the Ninth and Second Circuit Courts of Appeals. The Ninth Circuit Court had ruled that the Washington statute violated a "fundamental liberty interest" in obtaining physician-assisted suicide; the Second Circuit Court had ruled that the New York statute was irrational in permitting physicians to withhold or discontinue life-prolonging treatment while prohibiting assisted suicide. The Supreme Court's recognition of the distinction between "passive" acquiescence and "active" assistance in dying will have a substantial beneficial effect on medical practice. In the wake of the Second Circuit Court's ruling, some physicians in New York had found new reasons to overrule patient's refusals of life-prolonging treatment and even more reasons to fear the legal consequences of adequately managing symptoms through the use of opioids that are believed to carry a foreseeable risk of hastened death. On this issue, however, the Supreme Court was indeed unanimous: existing state laws are constitutionally valid in recognizing a distinction between prohibiting conduct on the part of physicians that intentionally hastens death and permitting conduct that may foreseeably hasten death but is intended for other important purposes, such as the relief of pain or other symptoms. By authoritatively pronouncing that terminal sedation intended for symptomatic relief is not assisted suicide, the Court has licensed an aggressive practice of palliative care.[3]

This beneficial impact on the quality of palliative care might be considered a "foreseeable but unintended consequence" of Chief Justice Rehnquist's opinion. His intention was simply to dismiss the plaintiffs' claims for any constitutional "right to die." Nonetheless, footnotes at the end of each of Rehnquist's opinions speak to some tension with this simple dismissive goal. In the final footnote of the Washington case, Rehnquist referred to Justice John Paul Stevens's view in his separate concurring opinion that "a more particularized challenge" to the state law might succeed, and Rehnquist observed, "Our opinion does not absolutely foreclose such a claim . . . [but it] would have to be quite different from the ones advanced [in this case]."[4] Similarly, Rehnquist's final footnote in the New York case cited Stevens's observation that the Court's ruling "does not foreclose the possibility that some applications of the New York statute may impose an intolerable intrusion on the patient's freedom" and then continued, "This is true, but . . . different and considerably stronger arguments than those advanced [here would be required]."[5]

These footnotes are not exactly welcoming invitations from the chief justice for renewed challenges to the state laws; he gave no hint of the possible content of any "quite different" or "considerably stronger" arguments that might lead the Court to a changed result. These footnotes have every marker of a reluctant concession by the chief justice—a concession necessary to attract a fifth vote for his opinions so that they might be identified as the "opinions of the Court."

The mystery of these footnotes is explained by Justice O'Connor's brief concurring opinion, which follows immediately at the conclusion of Rehnquist's. O'Connor stated that she joined Rehnquist's opinions—thus providing the necessary fifth vote along with Justices Scalia, Kennedy, and Thomas—but she did so on the basis of a quite specific understanding. In the second paragraph of her opinion, she observed,

The parties and amici agree that in these States a patient who is suffering from a terminal illness and who is experiencing great pain has no legal barriers to obtaining medication, from qualified physicians, to alleviate that suffering, even to the point of causing unconsciousness and hastening death. . . . In this light, . . . I agree that the State's interests in protecting those who are not truly competent or facing imminent death, or those whose decisions to hasten death would not truly be voluntary, are sufficiently weighty to justify a prohibition against physician-assisted suicide.[6]

In her fourth and final paragraph, she reiterated, "There is no dispute that dying patients in Washington and New York can obtain palliative care, even when doing so would hasten their deaths."[6] The clear implication of Justice O'Connor's repeated observation is that if a future case were presented to the Court in which there was a "dispute" about the existence of state legal barriers to adequate palliative care, then this would be the "quite different" and "considerably stronger" argument that could lead her to a different result.

Justice Stephen Breyer emphasized and amplified this understanding in his separate concurring opinion. He stated that a strong argument could be made for the existence of a constitutional "right to die with dignity," which "at its core" would involve "personal control over the manner of death, professional medical assistance, and the avoidance of unnecessary and severe physical suffering."[7] But, he observed,

as Justice O'Connor points out, the laws before us do not *force* a dying person to undergo that kind of pain. Rather, the laws of New York and of Washington do not prohibit doctors from providing patients with drugs sufficient to control pain despite the risk that those drugs themselves will kill. . . . Were the legal circumstances different—for example, were state law to prevent the provision of palliative care, including the administration of drugs as needed to avoid pain at the end of life—then the law's impact upon serious and otherwise unavoidable physical pain (accompanying death) would be more directly at issue. And as

Justice O'Connor suggests, the Court might have to revisit its conclusions in these cases.[8]

As if to underscore the dispositive importance of Justice O'Connor's statement regarding possible state restrictions on adequate palliative care, Justice Breyer joined her concurring opinion but refused to join Chief Justice Rehnquist's opinions for the Court; and Breyer pointedly began his concurrence by noting, "I believe that Justice O'Connor's views, which I share, have greater legal significance than the Court's opinion suggests."[9] To the same effect, Justice Ruth Bader Ginsburg filed a brief statement concurring in the Court's judgment but not in its opinions, "for the reasons stated by Justice O'Connor."[9]

Justices Stevens and David Souter also filed separate concurring opinions, refusing to overturn existing state prohibitions of assisted suicide but nonetheless envisioning the possibility of future judicial consideration of the constitutional claims and expressing considerable sympathy for those claims. Stevens and Souter were less explicit than Justices O'Connor, Breyer, and Ginsburg in identifying the existence of state obstructions or failures in the provision of adequate palliative care as a ground for future judicial intervention. Each identified it, however, as a concern that in itself could require judicial attention.[10,11]

Accordingly, three Justices (O'Connor, Ginsburg, and Breyer) specifically concluded that judicial intervention would become necessary, as Justice Breyer put it, "were state law to prevent the provision of palliative care, including the administration of drugs as needed to avoid pain at the end of life."[12] An additional two justices (Souter and Stevens) mentioned this issue as one among other problems afflicting terminally ill people that, if not adequately addressed by state legislatures, would require future judicial intervention. This tallying is the basis for concluding that a Court majority has found that states must not impose barriers on the availability of palliative care for terminally ill patients. This ruling would have the same status as the right to an abortion established by *Roe* v. *Wade*[13]—that is, an individual right that cannot be overridden by state actions prohibiting or "unreasonably burdening" access to a physician's assistance.

Current state laws and policies restricting the availability of opioids for the management of pain are the most likely targets for judicial invalidation by this criterion. The Institute of Medicine Committee on Care at the End of Life issued a report just three weeks before the Supreme Court's decision, urging "reform [of] drug prescription laws, burdensome regulations, and state medical board policies and practices that impede effective use of opioids to relieve pain and suffering."[14]

Judicial scrutiny of these state laws could take two forms. First, the general inhibitory effect of state drug laws is vulnerable to challenge.

Restrictive prescription laws, the imposition of rigid limitations on dosages, and administrative burdens such as the requirement of triplicate forms create substantial impediments to adequate palliation of pain for patients, especially in home care settings.[15] States justify this restrictive regulatory regime on the ground that it is necessary to prevent the diversion of opioids to illegal purposes such as street sales or use by addicts. The Institute of Medicine committee found, however, that there was "no evidence . . . that the prescription of opioids in the care of dying patients contributes in any meaningful way to drug diversion problems."[16] Moreover, even if some empirical basis can be established for believing that the restrictive prescription laws actually reduce illegitimate narcotics uses, this finding would justify current state laws only if it was legitimate for states to give higher priority to the "war on drugs" than to providing adequate palliative care for dying patients. The generalized goal of narcotics control could not, however, take precedence over an individual's constitutional right to adequate palliative care.

A second form of judicial scrutiny follows from the existence of a constitutional right. Current drug laws impose substantial inhibitions on individual physicians who are subjected to formal medical-board discipline, or are informally threatened with discipline, for prescribing high doses of opioids for terminally ill patients. As the Institute of Medicine committee found, "the frequency of punitive action against physicians for apparently legitimate prescribing practice is unknown, but the committee heard many anecdotes about threatening statements by medical disciplinary boards."[17,18] Armed with their patients' constitutional right to adequate palliative care, physicians could protect themselves in judicial forums against state regulatory boards ignorant or dismissive of the evidence that high-dosage prescriptions of opioids for treating pain and other distressing symptoms are safe, effective, and appropriate.[19]

Laws restricting the appropriate availability of drugs are, moreover, not the only aspect of state actions that obstruct adequate palliative care. As the Institute of Medicine report found, there are other obstructions, such as "mechanisms for financing care [that] impede good end-of-life care and . . . frustrate coordinated systems of excellent care,"[20] that require legislative attention. If state legislatures refused to address such obstructive elements of their laws, or gave them only perfunctory attention, they would be guilty (in Justice Souter's words) of "legislative foot-dragging,"[21] of failing to recognize "the high degree of importance, requiring a commensurate justification" with reference to the "claims raised by the patients and physicians"[22] in challenging the assisted-suicide prohibitions. Such states would (in Justice Breyer's words) "infringe directly upon . . . the core of the interest in dying with dignity," which involves "medical assistance, and the avoidance of unnecessary and severe physical suffering."[23]

A Supreme Court majority has thus provided an unexpected but strong and very welcome directive requiring states to remove the barriers that their laws and policies impose on the availability of palliative care.

ROBERT A. BURT, J.D.
Yale Law School
New Haven, CT 06520

## REFERENCES

1. Washington v. Glucksberg, 117 S.Ct. 2258 (1997).

2. Vacco v. Quill, 117 S.Ct. 2293 (1997).

3. Cherny NI, Portenoy RK. Sedation in the management of refractory symptoms: guidelines for evaluation and treatment. J Palliat Care 1994; 10(2):31–8.

4. Washington v. Glucksberg, 117 S.Ct. at 2275 n.24.

5. Vacco v. Quill 117 S.Ct. at 2302 n.13.

6. Id. at 2303.

7. Id. at 2311.

8. Id. at 2311–12.

9. Id. at 2310.

10. Washington v. Glucksberg, 117 S.Ct. at 2290 (Souter).

11. Id. at 2308 (Stevens).

12. 117 S.Ct. at 2312.

13. 410 U.S. 113 (1973).

14. Recommendation 3 (d). In: Institute of Medicine, Committee on Care at the End of Life. Approaching death: improving care at the end of life. Washington, D.C.: National Academy Press, 1997:10–7.

15. Pisano DJ. Controlled substances and pain management: regulatory oversight, formularies, and cost decisions. J Law Med Ethics 1996;24:310–6.

16. Institute of Medicine, Committee on Care at the End of Life. Approaching death: improving care at the end of life. Washington, D.C.: National Academy Press, 1997:7–3.

17. Idem] Approaching death: improving care at the end of life. Washington, D.C.: National Academy Press, 1997:7–7.

18. Johnson SH. Disciplinary actions and pain relief: analysis of the Pain Relief Act. J Law Med Ethics 1996;24:319–27.

19. Portenoy RK. Opioid therapy for chronic nonmalignant pain: clinicians' perspective. J Law Med Ethics 1996;24:296–309.

20. Recommendation 3 (c). In: Institute of Medicine, Committee on Care at the End of Life. Approaching death: improving care at the end of life. Washington, D.C.: National Academy Press, 1997:10–7.

21. Washington v. Glucksberg, 117 S.Ct. at 2293.

22. Vacco v. Quill, 117 S.Ct. at 2302.

23. Washington v. Glucksberg, 117 S.Ct. at 2311–12

* * *

Physicians are increasingly protected by law when they prescribe adequate pain medication. In 1996, the American Medical Association's Division of State Legislation approved a model bill which protects physicians from disciplinary action in instances of appropriate pain management. As of December 1998, thirty-two states had laws, regulations, or guidelines that address pain management and the use of controlled substances for severe pain (Choice In Dying, Washington, DC).

Another improvement in end-of-life care is the increasing use of the unified approach called "hospice care." It is based on the work of Dame Cicely Saunders,—a British nurse, medical social worker, and physician,—who cared for dying patients in 1958 at St. Joseph's Hospice in London.

## DOCUMENT 138: "Hospice Medicine," Zail S. Berry and Joanne Lynn (1993)

Hospice is a mode of care designed to support the physical, psychosocial, and spiritual needs of people at the end of life, with the goal of allowing the dying process to unfold with a minimum of discomfort and the maintenance of dignity and quality of life. Care is provided by family and friends at home or in a homelike setting within a hospital, nursing home, or special hospice care facility. The hospice team, including nurses, social workers, chaplains, and volunteers, as well as physicians, seeks to address the needs of family members in addition to those of the patient.

Hospice care is appropriate when traditional medical care, so often focused on length of life, is no longer the best way to serve the patient's interests. This may be when medical therapies no longer offer benefit to the patient or when the benefits offered are outweighed by accompanying burdens.

*Source*: Zail S. Berry and Joanne Lynn, "Hospice Medicine," *Journal of the American Medical Association* 270 (1993): 221.

### FURTHER READING

Battin, Margaret Pabst. *The Least Worst Death: Essays in Bioethics on the End of Life.* New York: Oxford University Press, 1994.
Battin, Margaret P., Rosamond Rhodes, and Anita Silvers, eds. *Physician Assisted Suicide: Expanding the Debate.* New York and London: Routledge, 1998.

Brody, Baruch A., ed. *Suicide and Euthanasia: Historical and Contemporary Themes.* Boston: Kluwer Academic Publishers, 1989.

Dworkin, Gerald, R. G. Frey and Sissela Bok. *Euthanasia and Physician-assisted Suicide.* New York: Cambridge University Press, 1998.

Humphry, Derek. *Final Exit: The Practicalities of Self-Deliverance and Assisted Suicide for the Dying.* Rev. ed. New York: Dell Publishing, 1997.

Quill, Timothy E. *A Midwife through the Dying Process: Stories of Healing and Hard Choices at the End of Life.* Baltimore: Johns Hopkins University Press, 1996.

Roberts, Carolyn S., and Martha Gorman, *Euthanasia: A Reference Handbook.* Santa Barbara, CA: ABC-CLIO, 1996.

Saunders, Cicely. *Care of the Dying.* London: Macmillan, 1959.

Steinberg, Maurice D., and Stuart J. Youngner, eds. *End-of-Life Decisions: A Psychosocial Perspective.* Washington, D.C.: American Psychiatric Press, 1998.

Weir, Robert F., ed. *Physician-assisted Suicide.* Bloomington IN: Indiana University Press, 1997.

# Index

**About the Editor**

MARJORIE B. ZUCKER is Program Associate, Choice In Dying.